THE ISRAEL MUSEUM

This publication has been made possible by the generosity of
Renée and Robert Belfer

THE ISRAEL MUSEUM
JERUSALEM

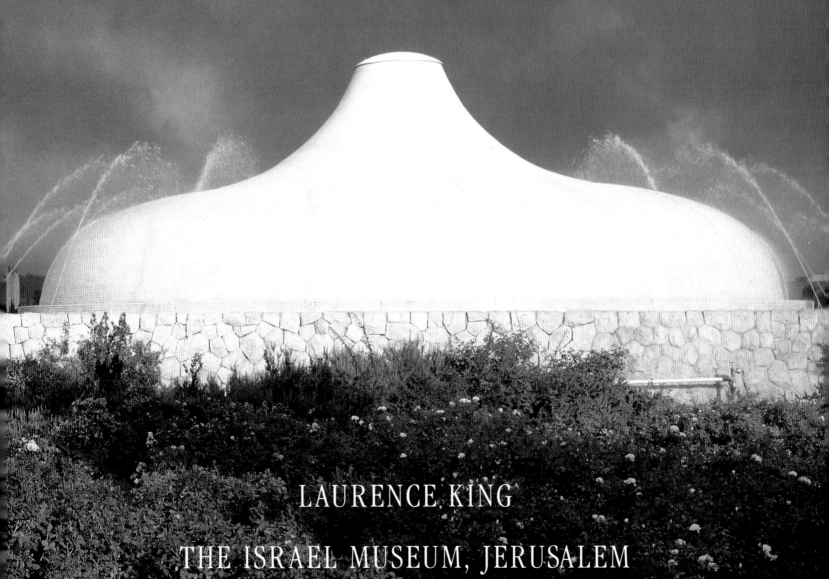

LAURENCE KING

THE ISRAEL MUSEUM, JERUSALEM

NOTE: In the catalogue section all objects from the collections of the Israel Antiquities Authority are credited to IAA. All other objects are from the collections of the Israel Museum.

Editor/Project Coordinator: Irène Lewitt

Editorial Assistants: Vivianne Barsky, Stacey Brooks, Judith Goldstein, David Ilan, Rebecca Haviv, Shulamith Navon, Aviva Schwarzfeld

Caption texts by:
Ruth Apter-Gabriel (pp 175, 177, 179); Alia Ben-Ami (p 129); Vivianne Barsky (p 200); Catherine Benkaim (pp 92,93); Daphna Ben-Tor (pp 102-105); Noam Ben-Yossef (pp 138, 139); Rebecca Bitterman (pp 159, 220-223); Na'ama Brosh (pp 90, 91); Magen Broshi (pp 81-87); Michal Dayagi-Mendels (pp 64-71); Iris Fishof (pp 27, 114-119 left, 120, 121 right, 125, 126 right, 127); Fabio Frachtenberg (pp 48-53); Haim Gitler (pp 40, 88, 89); Rivka Gonen (pp 130, 134 right, 143); Yael Israeli (pp 72, 75 left, 78–80); Suzanne Landau (pp 194–199, 201); Daphna Lapidot (pp 187 left, 188); David Mevorah (pp 75 right, 77); Osnat Misch-Brandl (pp 54-63); Ester Muchawsky-Schnapper (pp 121 left, 132, 135, 147, 177 top); Tallay Ornan (pp 98-101); Meira Perry-Lehmann (pp 170-174, 176, 178); Nissan Perez (pp 180-185); Daisy Raccah-Djivre (pp 119 right, 124, 126 left); Stephanie Rachum (pp 194-207); Silvia Rozenberg (pp 76, 94-97); Timna Seligman (pp 224-229); Ora Shwartz Be'eri (pp 136, 140, 141); Ora Slapak (p 131); Shlomit Steinberg (pp 186, 187 right, 190 left, 191); Izzika Gaon and Elaine Varady (pp 216-219); Rivka Weiss-Blok (pp 162-169); Yigal Zalmona (pp 190 right, 192, 193).

Published 1995 by Laurence King Publishing

Copyright © 1995 Israel Museum, Jerusalem

A catalogue record for this book is available from the British Library.

ISBN (h/back) 1 85669 063 6
ISBN (p/back) 1 85669 068 7

Designed by Richard Foenander
Printed in Hong Kong

For a complete catalogue, please write to:
Laurence King Publishing
71 Great Russell Street
London WC1B 3BN

Contents

Preface

It was with great awe that I witnessed, on 11 May 1965, the opening of the Israel Museum. As a young art student supporting my studies by working on the building of the Museum, I stood at the side with several other construction workers and maintenance people watching the many VIPs I had known only from the newspapers — famous artists, government dignitaries, and elegant-looking contributors from abroad. I shall never forget that beautiful day filled with flags, ceremonies and speeches, a day pervaded with a feeling of happy celebration, the glory of culture, the pride of achievement and confidence in a better future. More than anything else, it probably had to do with the privilege of witnessing an historic moment — the establishment of a national museum in our new homeland.

Today, thirty years later, after gradually rising in the hierarchy and having directed the Museum for a considerable time, I can safely state that this same spirit, this sense of pride and achievement, desire for excellence, and idealism are still what motivate the staff, the Board, and our many friends and supporters throughout the world. It is this true sense of belonging and identifying that has helped the Museum expand and improve in such a staggering way. I never cease being asked by visitors, especially those from abroad, 'You did all this in only 30 years?'

Is it possible to convey all of this in a book? No, it is not. A museum is a museum and a book is merely a vehicle which can convey, through texts and photographs, a sense of the premises and the scope of a museum's collections. Our ever-increasing collections belie the fear of the Museum's founding fathers that there would not be sufficient artifacts to exhibit, a concern that has been replaced by a selectiveness to include only artifacts of great interest and artworks of outstanding international museum quality in the exhibition halls. There is, however, much more that makes a museum outstanding than its collections. In a sense, a museum is a 'Gesamtkunstwerk,' itself a work of art in its totality. The collections are the beginning; afterwards it is the spirit, the atmosphere, the dedication, the creativity, the scholarship and professionalism that count, and these qualities are impossible to convey through a book. Here a book can only serve as a teaser. A museum must be visited in order to get that very special feeling.

The torch of this spirit was, of course, lit by Teddy Kollek, who, together with a number of other visionaries, conceived of and realized the establishment of the Israel Museum. During the 30 years of its existence, Teddy has served as Chairman of the Board, juggling his awesome duties as Mayor of Jerusalem for an almost identical period of time in order always to 'be there' for the Museum. Rightly so, he was honored with the special title of 'Father of the Museum.' However, this same love, concern and dedication can be found at all echelons within the Museum, and all together have contributed to making the Museum what it is today.

Special tribute should be paid to all those individuals in Israel and abroad who have generously contributed their time and resources for the betterment of the Museum. We owe a tremendous debt of gratitude to our local board of governors, our international Friends' organizations and their chairmen and presidents, as well as all our many donors whose gifts of art and money have enriched the Museum and brought it to the forefront of world renown.

The realization of this book is the result of the joint efforts of many people, but special thanks are due to Renée and Robert Belfer of New York for generously providing the funds to bring this publication to light, and to the American Friends of the Israel Museum and especially its chairman, Alexis Gregory, who helped us develop the concept. Our gratitude is extended to the publisher and to all those who helped us prepare the book for publication: authors, photographers and editorial assistants, and especially Dr Catherine Benkaim for volunteering to edit the captions. Very special appreciation is reserved for Irène Lewitt, a typical example of a staff member whose long career was marked by a love of and devotion to the Museum, and who agreed to return from retirement in order to devote her days and nights as managing editor in order to have this book ready for the occasion of the Museum's 30th anniversary.

An institution is only as good as its staff, and I would like to use this opportunity to pay tribute to the employees and volunteers of the Israel Museum whose dedication and professionalism reflect the level of achievement that can be witnessed in the Museum today.

I cannot end this preface without offering a word of apology to our many supporters whose names are missing from the following pages. One of the most difficult aspects we faced in compiling this book was having to omit the names of all our generous donors in order to keep within the limitations of space. Indeed, it would require a book of its own to credit the many people who have contributed, in one way or another, to the Museum over the years. We know that without the help of our many friends throughout the world, there would not be a museum of which to write. To each and every one of you, our heartfelt thanks.

Martin Weyl
Director

The Creation of the Israel Museum

Martin Weyl

On 30 May 1960, Prime Minister David Ben Gurion delivered a speech in the Knesset [Israel's Parliament] during a debate concerning the budget allocation for 'the National Museum of Israel.' 'As befits an ancient people, dedicated to the values of the spirit throughout its tortured history and now reviving its independence in its ancient land, Israel, in its twelfth year of statehood, is about to establish a National Museum. It will rise in Jerusalem, city of King David, amidst the timeless Judaean hills. . . . Despite the daily preoccupations with defence and security, economic and social development, and housing the newcomers, it has been resolved to spend part of our resources, energy and talent in what is destined to become the most impressive cultural center in the country.'

The timing and content of this speech were carefully orchestrated by Teddy Kollek, then director of the Prime Minister's Office. He was the driving force behind a small group of people who shared his vision of creating a national museum in the new homeland. Ben Gurion's speech was crucial, because the group needed all possible help in realizing this dream.

Decades earlier, other activists had striven towards a similar goal. The most outstanding among these early visionaries was a Lithuanian Jew born to an orthodox family. Zalman Dov Baruch (Boris) Schatz (1866–1932) began to study art while still attending a *yeshiva*, later he continued his art studies in Warsaw and Paris. In 1895 Schatz, already a renowned sculptor, helped to establish the Academy of Art in Bulgaria. In 1903, in the wake of the traumatic Kishinev pogroms, Schatz turned to Jewish subject matter with the purpose of arousing the national sentiments of his Jewish public. Inspired by the utopian philosophers of the early nineteenth century, he believed in the power of art for nationalist and propaganda purposes, and dreamt of forming a group of enlightened Jews who, committed to science, art and labor, would settle in Eretz Israel. The hub of their activity was to be an academy of arts and crafts, based on the Bulgarian model.

Fired by this prophetic vision, Schatz travelled to Vienna to propose his plan to Theodor Herzl, father of modern Zionism, who pledged his support for the school which Schatz named 'Bezalel' 'after the first Hebrew craftsman who built the Tabernacle in the desert.' Schatz's idea was brought before the seventh Zionist Congress in Basel in 1905. The discussions at the Congress bore witness to a great variety of opinions concerning the issue of Jewish culture. The adherents to political Zionism were not particularly concerned with the issue of national culture, and even less so with the question of art. In the end it was simple pragmatism that brought about the establishment of the proposed arts and crafts school for Eretz Israel.

Upon Herzl's death, Schatz went to Berlin and presented his program to the heads of the Zionist movement there, and subsequently the Bezalel Society was registered as an official German society on 8 October 1906. While Schatz had envisioned a museum as an essential component of his academy, his Berlin supporters fostered a more practical approach: a school of crafts to stimulate home industries (and bring financial compensation), which would also interest the Jewish intelligentsia. Pilgrimage and tourism would enable Eretz Israel to become a center for handicrafts, not just run-of-the-mill olive-wood artifacts and dried flower production, but also for synagogue and church ornamentation. The Berlin advisory board included artists such as Max Liebermann, Bodenstein, Hermann Struck, and Ephraim Moses Lilien. Among early supporters were major collectors such as James Simon and Dr Paul Nathan.

Schatz arrived in Eretz Israel early in 1906 together with the artist Lilien, and in February the Bezalel School of Arts and Crafts began functioning in Jerusalem with a handful of Jewish art students from various countries. In retrospect, the establishment of Bezalel was an enormous success story on whose foundations a more sophisticated 'artworld' would eventually develop. Schatz's enthusiasm and stamina soon attracted large numbers of students, new departments were opened, teachers arrived from all over the world, and exhibitors from Odessa to South America displayed the products of the school. It is hard to imagine that one man could stimulate such burgeoning creativity in a small, neglected, backwater city of the Ottoman Empire that was Jerusalem at that time.

While still in Bulgaria, Schatz had secured support for his plan to attach a museum to the Bezalel school. The search for a new national style now made it essential to collect local flora and fauna, archaeology, folk art and the like to serve as basic models for the creators of the new designs. Schatz was also inspired by existing Jewish museums in Paris, Vienna, Frankfurt and Hamburg, and started collecting Jewish ceremonial art, as well as paintings and sculptures by famous Jewish artists. However, the emphasis at first was on botany and zoology, and, in fact, Bezalel started out as a museum of natural history. Little by little, the collection began to expand and take shape and by 1908 the Museum had several exhibition halls. Through his travels, Schatz continued to collect gifts for the Museum, accepting only Jewish creations. Bringing Jewish art work from the Diaspora to Eretz Israel was for him an act of pure Zionism. He also had a particular interest in archaeology, and for a while the Museum was called 'the Jewish Palestine Archaeological Museum.'

The outbreak of World War I effectively called a halt to the activities of Bezalel — even the cisterns of the school were emptied in order to hide the art treasures of the Museum. Immediately after the war, Schatz adapted his museological ideas to the new reality, while continuing his efforts to enlarge the Museum's collections. He now proposed to the Zionist commission that a large building be erected for 'the National Museum of Jerusalem.' In spring 1925 invitations were sent out for what was proudly formulated as 'the opening of the first National Jewish Museum in Eretz Israel and in the entire world,' comprising fourteen halls, ranging from antiquities from the Second Temple period to modern Jewish art and items of historical significance.

The new museum was officially opened on 2 June 1925, as the Bezalel National Museum. Its first chief curator was Mordechai Narkiss, a former Bezalel student, whose idea it was to establish the new museum as a separate entity from the school. These were, however, times of extreme economic hardship, and the Museum suffered badly, despite Narkiss's desperate efforts to sustain it. Following Schatz's death in 1932, Narkiss succeeded him as director of the Museum. The two men had shared many traits, including a total dedication to their life's work as well as boundless energy.

Bezalel School and Museum, Jerusalem, *c.* 1910s.

But while Schatz was first and foremost a flamboyant utopian sculptor, Narkiss was more of an introverted scholar.

The year in which Narkiss became director witnessed the arrival of a stream of German immigrants fleeing from Nazi Germany. They provided new sources of intellect, energy and interest on which Narkiss knew how to capitalize. He built up an important library, enlarged the collections, and embarked on a dynamic program of exhibitions drawn from the widest possible fields, writing all the catalogues himself (at the time of his death in 1957 he had compiled 116 catalogues!). He also made frequent trips to Europe, during which he was able to secure many treasures for the Museum. Masterpieces now in the Israel Museum, such as the famous Birds' Head *Haggadah*, the Rothschild manuscript, and several others are the result of his activities. His success was not unqualified, however. For while Narkiss had truly universal interests, there were critics who felt that the Museum was not sufficiently 'contemporary.' Chagall, who visited Eretz Israel for the first time in 1932, also thought that the Museum was too 'Jewish.' Braving enormous financial and political difficulties, Narkiss, while often fulfilling the combined functions of curator, caretaker, cashier, registrar, fund-raiser, and scholar, gradually established a small staff to help manage the dramatically expanding collections and activities. During the years 1906–1932, the Museum had managed to amass some 8000 items. Unlike Schatz, Narkiss did not limit himself to collecting Jewish art, and under his leadership Bezalel began to function as a modern museum. By the time it was incorporated into the Israel Museum in 1965, its collections had increased tenfold, and consisted mainly of Judaica, drawings, prints, and posters.

The mass immigration from central Europe and Germany which continued throughout the 1930s exerted a major influence on the Museum's development. Art collectors were common among German Jews, and those who left early enough had often managed to take their treasures with them. Thus, a number of good and some outstanding collections arrived in Eretz Israel, several of which found their way to the Museum. Strange as it may seem, during World War II the Museum was not only able to continue functioning, but actually increased its number of exhibitions. These included displays of Far Eastern, Dutch, Impressionist, and Israeli art, one-man shows presenting works by Max Slevogt, Max Liebermann, Edward Munch, and Hermann Struck, various group shows, and even an exhibit devoted to 'the creative woman in Eretz Israel.'

At the end of the war, the American Occupation Authorities in Germany began to assemble unclaimed works of art formerly owned by German Jews who had perished in the Holocaust. Under the auspices of

JRSO (Jewish Restitution Successor Organization), these works, mainly drawings and Jewish ceremonial art, were distributed among Jewish institutions, including the Bezalel Museum. One of the outstanding works to reach the Museum was a cityscape by Egon Schiele. In 1947 Mordechai Narkiss travelled to Europe, and returned with personal gifts from Picasso, Matisse, Chagall, Rouault and many other artists. Traveling again to Paris a year later, he established Les Amis du Bezalel; other Friends' organizations were to follow in Holland, England and eventually the United States.

Following the establishment of the State of Israel in 1948, Narkiss saw the Museum's role as pivotal to the cultural life of the new country and its capital, and indeed as 'the central institution for art of the Jewish people in Israel and the Diaspora.' He also started dreaming of a new and truly modern museum fit to house the expanding collections: a building of glass, steel and concrete atop a high hill. Long before the necessary funds had been secured, he commissioned the Austrian-born immigrant artist and architect Leopold Krakauer to draw up the plans for this unique building. The new museum was to encompass archaeology as well as art. The desire of Schatz and Narkiss to exhibit archaeology together with art reflected the (now disclaimed) Western European tradition of seeing archaeological objects as works of art. In 1953, Narkiss detailed a program for the new museum. It included studios for Jewish artists, workshops for guest artists, a children's department, a department for antiquities, sections for Jewish ceremonial art, graphic art and reproductions, and areas for the display of Oriental, European and African art. It also took into consideration the components needed to serve a living museum and its public, such as temporary exhibition galleries, a lecture hall, library, laboratories, a restaurant and even an office for the society of friends.

Entrance sign, in glazed tiles, for the Bezalel National Museum.

Sadly, Mordechai Narkiss did not live to see the eventual realization of his dream, but others took up the torch and continued his life's work. In retrospect, it is difficult to fathom how, during those tremendously difficult early years, people found the time and energy to translate the dream for a 'national' museum into reality. The push came simultaneously on several fronts, but in the end it was probably the pragmatic assiduity of leaders of the small Jerusalem community rather than ideology, government policy or the petitions of professionals that actually started the ball rolling towards the founding of the long-sought-after, comprehensive 'national museum.'

In the early 1950s, Teddy Kollek, in his capacity as minister in the Israeli Embassy in Washington, had occasion in the course of his duties to meet a number of collectors. When he learned that a well-known Jewish banker had just promised his important art collection to Harvard University, Teddy asked him why he had not considered Israel. The answer was simple: there was no museum fit to receive the paintings. Teddy received similar replies from other collectors, leading him to the conclusion that 'people relate to their paintings as children, they like to see them live in a nice environment and be well taken care of.' In short, it was necessary to build a museum to the highest international standards in order to compete with the rest of the world for works of art.

Teddy returned to Israel in 1953 to become director of the Prime Minister's Office, and immediately took up the cause for a national museum. He tried to interest Ben Gurion himself, as well as the Minister of Education, but the issue was not one of their priorities. He was, however, able to secure the support of Gershon Agron, then Mayor of Jerusalem, Yigal Yadin, the prestigious first Commander-in-Chief of the Israel Defense Forces and a distinguished archaeologist, and Avraham Biran, who had also returned to Israel from a diplomatic mission in the United States to head the Department of Antiquities.

The next development was a twist of fortune. In the Cold War propaganda competition between Soviet Russia and the United States, both countries sent huge quantities of literature to Israel. The United States Government urged publishers to deliver books to Israel within the framework of the Information Media Guarantee Program. The publishers were paid by the US Government, whereas the income from sales remained in Israel as 'counterpart funds.' In 1956, Bernard Katzen, an American Jew, was asked by his friend, the American Secretary of State John Foster Dulles, to go to Israel in order to see what was happening to these funds. Once in Israel, Katzen was infected by Teddy Kollek's enthusiasm. Upon his return to the United States, he recommended that 1.5 million Israeli pounds be allocated to the museum project. The Congressional bill initially failed, but was finally approved in 1957 after intense lobbying on the part of Katzen and the State Department. Simultaneously, progress had been made in Israel. The Americans stipulated matching funds, and Kollek had been able to secure a promise from the Israeli government of 80 dunams (19.76 acres) of land for the museum site.

The founding fathers now had to cope with the question of how to put the museum together and what to exhibit within it. The national galleries of Western Europe, to whom they looked as role models, had been in existence for generations and many had their origins in princely collections.

The great museums of the United States were based on collections and donations of merchant princes and prominent bankers. Unfortunately, King David and the other royal ancestors of the Jewish people had bequeathed only spiritual treasures.

Jerusalem, however, once again proved itself to be a city of miracles. The existence of the American counterpart funds was followed by the agreement of the Gottesman family in New York to finance a special building for the Dead Sea Scrolls, the most important archaeological find in the region to date, to be designed by the American architects Frederick Kiesler and Armand Bartos. At the same time, the children of Samuel Bronfman in Canada, honoring their father on the occasion of his 70th birthday, announced they would underwrite 'the national archaeological museum' which was ultimately incorporated into the Israel Museum campus as the Samuel Bronfman Biblical and Archaeological Museum. The museum founders were also able to convince a major collector of modern sculpture, the colorful, enigmatic and determined New York showman, Billy Rose, to donate his collection. His one condition was that the collection be displayed in a sculpture garden to be designed by the renowned American sculptor, Isamu Noguchi.

After much debate regarding the placement of the new museum, the present site on Neveh Sha'anan — the 'Hill of Tranquility' — was decided upon, primarily because of its relative accessibility. However, as soon as one problem was solved, a new one arose. There was pressure to name the new museum after a major donor (precedents for this existed at the Smithsonian Institution in Washington). At the same time the Minister of Education suggested making the new museum a government institution like most of the European national galleries. The latter proposal was fiercely rejected, as it was considered important that the new museum preserve its independence vis-à-vis all possible interest groups. With benefit of hindsight this decision has proved very wise in the light of members of Knesset raising questions regarding the display of archaeological artifacts that run counter to religious traditions, or contemporary Israeli art exhibitions that express political criticism. In all of these matters practicality again played the decisive role. Due to American tax laws governing aid to foreign entities, it was actually impossible for the museum to be a government institution. It was therefore agreed to omit the word 'National' from the museum's name, despite

Israel Museum atop the 'Hill of Tranquility' overlooking the Monastery of the Cross (1965).

its aspirations, and to call it simply The Israel Museum.

Narkiss's museum plan of 1953 was revised by the Bezalel curator Karl Katz and by Jerusalem artist Mordechai Ardon to take account of practical considerations, including a curtailed floor space. The program for the archaeological section was presented by Dr P. P. Kahane, who had been directing the small archaeological museum of the Israel Department of Antiquities for several years. His plan involved a permanent chronological display of the archaeology of Eretz Israel from prehistory through to the Turkish period, with additional sections for neighboring cultures. The intention to merge the small museum of archaeology, erected after 1948, with the Bezalel museum gave rise to some friction. In a crucial meeting in October 1957, it was formally decided to create separate entities for archaeology and the arts, to be bridged by technical services. The building would progress in stages as finances allowed, according to a modular structure outlined in a master plan. Inevitably the ancient question was raised as to what belongs to archaeology and what to art. The archaeologist Yigal Yadin claimed that all material culture up to the Islamic period should be part of the archaeology section, while the artist Mordechai Ardon called for numismatics and all archaeological artifacts of artistic value to be included in the art sections. The issue was ultimately referred to a future committee, but Yadin cautioned the members that one should not build too many buildings at the same time lest there not be sufficient material to exhibit in the museum galleries — a concern often expressed in the early years.

Workers installing the Maillol nude in the Billy Rose Art Garden (1965).

Despite these doubts and tensions, the museum concept was becoming an established fact. Plans and programs were further cemented when in March 1958 the Italian architect Franco Minissi was commissioned by UNESCO to advise on matters of architecture. He confirmed the suitability of the Hill of Tranquility site, arguing that its proximity to the Monastery of the Cross would serve as a bridge between the old part of the city and the new, and assuaged the fears of the board and staff of the two museums concerning their merger. He also helped to organize and judge the competition for the design of the museum complex that was held among ten architectural practices in April 1959.

However, the creation of the Billy Rose Art Garden remained an outstanding problem. The ultra-orthodox Rabbi Menachem Porush wrote to Billy Rose on 15 June 1960: 'It is very difficult for me to understand how you can still wish to bring horror with this sculpture to our city. I am sure you are aware that not only the Orthodox circles are protesting against this.' Many people tried to calm Rose, who was on the verge of withdrawing from the project. A letter from Abba Eban assured him that 'the authorities will go ahead,' and Teddy Kollek also reassured him, writing that 'the polemics are great fun.' When the issue was raised by Rabbi Porush in the Knesset on 30 May 1960, Ben Gurion countered that the second commandment was not directed against the making of graven images, but against their worship. Otherwise, he asked, how can the rabbis sit in this chamber with the picture of Herzl?

As early as 1962, discussions had begun with regard to the exhibition concept for the grand opening. The archaeologists wanted a local exhibition of archaeology, choosing the synagogue as their theme. The Bezalel curators, fearful of provincialism, urged an international art exhibition on the theme of the Bible, a suggestion countered by fears that it could generate criticism since most of the artists involved were not Jewish. Teddy Kollek, who apparently was concerned about the political implications, proposed that the Minister of Education resolve the dispute. In the end, the Bezalel curators prevailed and the opening exhibition was on the theme of the Bible.

View of the Israel Museum (1994).

What was still lacking was a legal framework or organizational structure. It was finally decided that the proper format would be for the museum to be a non-profit company with the Ministry of Education, the Hebrew University, the Municipality of Jerusalem, the Bezalel School, the Friends of the Bezalel Museum and the Jewish Agency as shareholders.

The winners of the architectural competition were the Israelis, Al Mansfeld and Dora Gad, who collaborated on the project as architect and interior designer respectively. The architects' aims were 'to achieve an individual concept and a new approach towards the design of a contemporary museum which would truly integrate itself into the Jerusalem landscape … to achieve unity in diversity, architectural integrity and harmony with the landscape.. and a genuine, though unconventional, monumentality without resorting to formality or pompousness.' The result was indeed a strikingly beautiful cluster of buildings for which Mansfeld and Gad received the highest national award, the Israel Prize. A string of pavilions, based on a module of 11 × 11 m, their roofs formed by a hyperbolic paraboloid shell supported on a central column (called 'mushrooms' by the staff), descend

from the top of the hill 'like an Arab village.' Glass walls enable visitors to look out over the surrounding landscape. The upper part of the complex was designed to house exhibition halls, while the lower area was intended for offices, laboratories, storerooms and services.

While the building was taking shape, a certain unease prevailed regarding the professional qualifications of the staff. Although the founding fathers had consulted the curators from time to time, the latter had had very little say in the final decision-making. Only two senior members, P. P. Kahane, director of the archaeology section, and Elisheva Cohen, the Bezalel museum's curator of prints and drawings, had been trained abroad. In addition, the need was felt for a prominent museum professional with international connections who could convince collectors and artists to donate works of art, secure loans, and above all be a guiding spirit to the curatorial team. The choice fell upon Willem Sandberg, the director of the Stedelijk Museum in Amsterdam then on the point of retirement. For the eccentric, adventurous Sandberg – one of the main heros of the Dutch resistance against the Germans and the 'enfant terrible' of the museum world in promoting contemporary art – this was a challenge to his liking. He stipulated his functions and, wary of stepping on the toes of the existing management, accepted the title of advisor. It was April 1964, just a year before the official opening, and a great deal of work still remained to be done.

The appointment of Sandberg both opened the museum to the outside world and amplified the curatorial voice. Throughout the planning stages, it had been Teddy Kollek's concern, being from a European background and having traveled extensively, that the museum should not be regionally limited nor provincial in outlook. His aim was to create an entity that would be on a par with the most important museums abroad. Two facets threatened this concept of universality: the prospect that the new institution would restrict its scope and become another Jewish museum; alternatively, that it would come to be seen mainly as a local museum housing Israeli art. Sandberg's position on these issues was crucial. Asked to advise on which part of the collections to transfer from the old Bezalel Museum, he made his attitude clear in strong and decisive terms. He found numerous items to be meaningful from an historic or sentimental standpoint, but of no artistic value. Not surprisingly, his decisions created some friction with the veteran board members.

Today it is hard to believe that the Israel Museum opened without a pavilion of Israeli art. At the time, it was felt that the Museum should establish itself internationally before focusing on the work of local artists. A few Israeli artists were included in the opening exhibition and Mordechai Ardon was asked to design the poster. But pressure increased, and the newly-appointed curator of modern art, Yona Fischer, was asked to organize an exhibition of Israeli artists to be shown at a nearby congress hall. It was more than a decade later that a pavilion for Israel Art was inaugurated within the Museum complex.

Mordechai Narkiss's museum concept had emphasized the need for a special section for children. Karl Katz had pursued this idea in the old Bezalel Museum where, on the roof, a wooden immigrant's shipping crate had been transformed into a classroom, launching the museum career of Ayala Gordon, the pioneering curator in this field. Bolstered by Sandberg's last-minute support for the idea, it was decided to allocate quite a considerable space for a youth wing in the new museum.

During the year before the opening, exhibition space was still being 'sold' to contributors. The large exhibition hall donated by Herman Spertus of Chicago was barely completed in time; the roof was cast just two weeks before the inauguration. As the opening date neared, Teddy Kollek, who by then was the Chairman of the Board, asked the Prime Minister for leave of absence in order to dedicate himself to the project and ensure its success. There were numerous last-minute demands, not least from the many VIPs who paid visits while the Museum was still being built!

Guests walking to entrance plaza for Israel Museum opening ceremonies, 11 May 1965.

Finally, on 11 May 1965, the new Museum was inaugurated amid great festivities. On the podium were the founding fathers, and dignitaries including the Speaker of the Knesset, Kadish Luz; Teddy Kollek; President Zalman Shazar; Prime Minister Levi Eshkol; Samuel Bronfman and the then Mayor of Jerusalem, Mordechai Ish Shalom. The Ida Crown Plaza was filled to capacity with guests who folded their programs into paper hats as protection against the glaring sun. It was, as Stella Fischbach of New York recalls, 'one of the most beautiful sights we had ever seen. People came from all over the world for the occasion, the weather was beautiful, the flags flew and when the Hatikva [national anthem] was played, everyone had a lump in his throat.' The vision had been fulfilled and the new campus with its manifold architectural innovations was of the international scope that Kollek had envisaged. However, while the museum founders could take pride in their achievement, the management and staff now faced the challenge of making the venture work.

As time progressed, the momentum of the enterprise was indeed reinforced. Despite serious financial difficulties, the Museum continued to expand. The modular structure of the building lent itself to the addition of new pavilions. The principal expansion was called for in the art section. One of the exciting early additions was the Rothschild eighteenth-century French salon. Additional period rooms were installed, the design department opened, and galleries of Far Eastern, Oceanic, African and Pre-Columbian sections were established.

Under the guidance of Sandberg and later of Sir Philip Hendy, formerly of the National Gallery, London, new professional criteria were established. Sandberg, a specialist in graphics, designed the Museum logo, and helped modernize the Museum's publications.

The Jewish Ethnography department established by curator Aviva Müller-Lancet also grew in scope, incorporating material originating in Jewish communities throughout the world. Outreach programs to new immigrants in Israel as well as to the overseas communities themselves enriched the collections. Here, too, new galleries were to be added over the years.

Summer concert in the Impressionist Gallery.

A few months after the Museum opened, Teddy Kollek was elected Mayor of Jerusalem, but continued serving as Chairman of the Board even after the 1967 Six Day War, during a period in which increasing numbers of visitors discovered the Museum. During this time and in the years that immediately followed, the newly reunified Jerusalem enjoyed unprecedented development and growth. Despite the superhuman demands on its mayor resulting from this activity, Teddy nevertheless continued his efforts on behalf of the newly-established Museum and within a short time an art library, auditorium, and new and enlarged youth wing building were added, the latter becoming one of the largest and most dynamic institutions of its kind in the world.

In the early 1970s, curatorial requirements led to a deviation from the old structural model. The new Impressionist painting gallery was designed to accommodate ideal lighting conditions for the paintings rather than to be seen as an architectural statement. This trend continued in the galleries added over the years to house period rooms, Old Master paintings, modern art, prints and drawings, photography, sculpture, and contemporary art.

It also gradually became clear that the Museum was serving a variety of publics. The average tourist might visit the Museum once or twice in a lifetime, and be mainly interested in the permanent exhibitions: the Dead Sea Scrolls, archaeology, Judaica and Jewish ethnography. The general Israeli public, on the other hand, also want to see major temporary exhibitions, while Jerusalemites expect diversity in what is for them their local museum. This challenge entails an active program of exhibitions, most originating from within the Museum, but with others imported. With the heightening of the Museum's international prestige, there are also increasing demands for loan exhibitions, and joint ventures are becoming common practice.

From the beginning, it was evident that the Museum would have to rely on its friends for support. The government subsidized only a portion of the maintenance costs. Self-generated income increased, but it was indeed the extraordinary generosity of its friends that made the Museum bloom. Inspired by the example of the American Friends of the Israel Museum, Friends' organizations were formed in Britain, France, Belgium, Switzerland, Canada, and more recently also in Germany, Italy, Holland, Mexico, South Africa, Australia, and Sweden.

Today, after thirty years of growth and success, new realities are emerging. The museum world as a whole is changing. The influence of the media is strongly felt, and the public expects better and more versatile services. Changes in the way people view art require museums to keep abreast of the times and continuously to re-examine their function and goals. In Israel, and particularly in Jerusalem, the situation has indeed changed dramatically in the past few decades. Archaeological excavations have brought to light a great amount of material that begs to be exhibited. The local art world, too, is buzzing with activity, and ideas for exhibitions in all fields exceed practical and budgetary limitations. If the founding fathers were concerned as to how to fill the burgeoning galleries, today's curators have to cope with lack of space. As I write these lines, the new political developments in the region are opening up the prospect of untold possibilities. Peace means open cultural as well as geographical borders, and this, it is hoped, will engender exchanges of exhibitions and the presence of more visitors. We welcome the prospect of such a development with open hearts and minds.

The age of thirty is a beautiful stage in life, a time of youth and vigor, while also one of incipient maturity. It means having mastered a vocation without having fallen into a routine. It means looking with optimism towards the future. What a wonderful age for a museum to be!

The Israel Museum at 30

Teddy Kollek

The Israel Museum at 30. My initial thoughts are those of Tevye and Golde in *Fiddler on the Roof:* 'When did she get to be a beauty? When did he grow to be so tall? I don't remember growing older. When did they?'

And while I cannot say that I do not entirely remember growing older (my memory, my eyesight, and my knees are not nearly as dependable as they once were), my colleagues and I did see the Museum as our child, from the glint in our eyes, through a long and rather difficult pregnancy, to the birth of something very special, to its infancy, childhood and adulthood (and we should not omit the complex teenage years …). On the Museum's 25th anniversary, just yesterday, I received one of the most important honors of my entire career: 'Father of the Museum.' I guess this title was not mere chance.

Through the years, I have told and retold the story of how — and why — the Museum came into being. I have recounted the early opposition to its creation at a time when our country faced countless problems: the nation's security was a constant concern; we had to worry about housing, education and health care for the mass influx of immigrants, actually refugees, both from the Holocaust in Europe and from oppression in Arab countries; we had to establish an economic base even while filling these pressing needs. The idea of a major national museum elicited cries of 'folly.'

I was, however, fully convinced that a museum was not a luxury but a necessity as well and if we waited until all our problems were solved, well, we would still be waiting. This taught me an important lesson in life and served me well in a vast array of decisions.

The Museum opened its doors in May 1965 and while it was evident that our task had just begun — there was no time for any laurel-resting — I had no inkling that just half a year later my life would take an entirely different course. There was probably no one more surprised than I to find myself Mayor of Jerusalem before the winter rains began.

As the city's Mayor for the succeeding 28 years, I learned to value the Museum in a far more macrocosmic way. I could see even more clearly the important function it had in the life of our city. For Jerusalemites, it is their local museum and it played a singular role in this context. The Museum had to serve on the one hand a population which had been reared from early childhood in museum galleries while instilling this tradition in the majority to whom it was foreign. The Museum's youth wing was the most effective conduit for this and one often saw our youngsters bringing parents and grandparents in hand to share this experience. Even in recent years, the Museum has played a vital role not only for veteran Jerusalemites but also for new immigrants, whether through the concert series providing opportunities for immigrant musicians or through the outreach program which our youth wing teachers began just days after the arrival of the Ethiopian children.

The Museum has also forged a link with the Arab residents of the city, through exhibitions, joint classes and camps for the youngsters, as well as the activities in the Paley Center. What was important was the cultural enrichment, often a mutual enrichment, and while it probably changed few political views, it did create an atmosphere of interaction and coexistence, even during the more difficult times.

For Israelis throughout the country, the Israel Museum serves as a national museum, as the repository of the finest works of art and archaeology. The annual visit to the Museum is on the excursion list of most schools and the major exhibitions, always reported on the nationwide news broadcast, bring Israelis from the smallest villages and farthest towns.

For tourists and pilgrims, the Museum is a must; indeed it is the most visited site after the Western Wall and the Yad Vashem Holocaust Memorial. These visitors can find the roots of local history, they can experience the archaeological and ethnographic heritage of the Jewish people, they can see the beginnings of Christianity and Islam, they can see the finest in art, they can wander through the unique Billy Rose Art Garden.

Prime Minister David Ben Gurion inspecting the Israel Museum under construction, early 1965, accompanied by Teddy Kollek (left) and Willem Sandberg.

The Art Garden is but one example of the good fortune of our visitors who can contemplate the finished product without the knowledge of the trials and tribulations which may have occurred behind the scenes. The serenity of the Garden (on all days except the Museum's annual kite-flying competition) belies the less-than-serene period of its creation. The Garden was designed by Isamu Noguchi, already an internationally known figure in the world of art, and the principal pieces of sculpture were a gift from the eminent impresario Billy Rose. To say the collaboration was volatile is a true understatement and the daily confrontations led to a familiar scenario:

every morning Billy Rose fired Noguchi, every afternoon, Noguchi quit. I could have had no better practice in developing the talents of a referee and these were to serve me well in my years as mayor.

From time to time, at gala evenings, in private meetings, in articles and publications, I have the opportunity to express the gratitude which we all feel towards those who have helped create and sustain the Museum. But it often seems that even a thesaurus of thank you's is not sufficient. The helping hand covers every facet of the Museum: galleries and acquisitions, exhibitions and catalogues, activities and events, programs for youngsters, for soldiers, for the elderly, renovations, computerization, even roof repairs (not to mention a major gift for our rest-rooms ...). The list is a long one. And this help is always given with warmth and love, with care and concern.

Our friends have been part of our Museum family since its inception, with many new friends added from year to year. We have Friends' organizations in twelve countries and it is often we who derive our inspiration from their devotion and generous support.

Throughout the years I kept my hideaway office at the Museum, which I often used at ungodly hours of the night when City Hall was closed (and most people were long asleep). No matter what the hour, I was never alone. In one office or another, the midnight oil was burning. And thus I would like to add a special thank you to a group whose dedication and hard work often go unsung: the Museum's staff, led for many years by Dr Martin Weyl whose leadership has been instrumental in the Museum's success story. It is the entire staff which makes it all possible: the curators and guards, the designers and secretaries, the librarians and accountants, the fund-raisers and the cleaning staff. One cannot forget our effective group of volunteers. They are not only the superb docents who are very much the link to the public but they also help out, dirty work and all, in every department.

There are still a few of us around who remember the celebrations of the Museum's first anniversary. Jerusalem in 1966 was still a divided city, a small backwater town where few visitors even spent the night. The Museum was just a few miles from the Israeli-Jordanian border which zig-zagged through the city with its mine fields, tank traps, anti-sniper walls and a no-man's land. The highest praise goes to our donors who, despite the fact that this fledgling Museum was located so close to a fighting frontier, still gave us important and much loved pieces of art.

As today we look with pride at how the Museum has developed over these three decades, we not only see how Jerusalem is flourishing but we feel great joy that the Museum's 30th anniversary takes place as historic steps are being taken towards peace with our neighbors. I guess much has happened in these 30 years.

Aspects of Collecting

Alexis Gregory

The reasons for the remarkably rapid growth of the Israel Museum in terms of its plant, collections and curatorial staff are highly appropriate topics for consideration on its 30th birthday. In its simplest terms, the museum has grown like Topsy thanks to the generosity of a large international community of Jewish collectors and dealers and is a vibrant institution because of the participation and interest of an unusually highly educated local constituency. While many museums can boast of six-figure attendances for blockbuster exhibitions, the Israel Museum is unique in its claim that over 10 per cent of the population in the country has attended events of particular interest.

Like ancient Gaul, the museum is divided into three curatorial departments, archaeology, Judaica, and a group of art collections that are quite astonishing in their breadth for an institution so young, located in a land so small. The archaeological collections are largely the gift of the land. Layer upon layer of Israel's rocks and soil are the repository of secrets of ancient history. The building of a house, the construction of a road, or the making of a park nearly always results in the appearance of the detritus of the past. In addition, highly-trained archaeologists are ever digging away in the blistering heat of the desert, while a conscientious population and an incorruptible civil service make certain that everything is registered and classified. As a result, much finds its way into the nation's museums and universities, and the most important discoveries inevitably end up in the vitrines of the Israel Museum. Tombaroli, or grave-robbers, are a distinctly non-Israeli phenomenon, and the archaeologist has often become a national hero. To the outside world, the late General Moshe Dayan, an amateur archaeologist and collector, handsome and virile, one eye patched, the other all-seeing, for many years was the John Wayne of a valiant new nation.

The Diaspora undoubtedly created a special interest in history for Jews spread around the entire world. After the destruction of the Second Temple, they studied the ancient civilizations of the Holy Land with passion, and wrote and taught extensively in centers of learning. The preservation of history and religion was the glue that bound Jews to the dream of their return, and the museum's large archaeological collection is the palpable evidence of an ancient glory that was preserved in hearts and minds through centuries of dislocation and suffering. To the less-involved visitor, the name of Caiaphas carved on a tomb, a bust of Hadrian or the shards of Bible peoples are confirmation that so much of Western civilization really had its roots in this tiny area of the world. It is altogether appropriate that the first visual encounter for a museum visitor is the shimmering white cone that shelters the Dead Sea Scrolls.

These archaeological collections are unique as is the important collection of Jewish ethnology, largely a gift of the local population. Brilliant dresses, colorful *ketubbot* or marriage certificates, enchanting spice boxes and multiform *mezuzoth* were mostly brought by immigrants and are of particular interest due to the influence they show of the many places in which Jews settled in both Europe and the Near East. In view of the destruction of so many communities, all this has become archaeology before its time and is of extraordinary value. Particularly important are the small synagogues, the latest from Cochin on India's Coromandel coast; in many cases, these were saved from neglect and decay due to the diminution of once large Jewish centers. The Museum's role as a place of refuge for unique religious property is of the utmost importance, particularly in this tormented century. Despite the tragic history of many of the exhibits, the ethnographic rooms exude color, gaiety, light and optimism, particularly on special gala evenings when musicians in traditional costume play lilting Oriental melodies on period instruments.

Needless to say, if archaeology is the gift of the land and ethnography one of the fruits of immigration, the rooms that house these collections were mostly contributed by generous donors from abroad. The art galleries and the collections they house were almost entirely given by Jews who chose to share their generosity between the Israel Museum and similar institutions in the countries where they lived and prospered. This gives the collections their particular character, just as a Jewish intelligentsia and new plutocracy put its stamp on and vastly enriched the cultural life of the great capitals of Europe as of the middle of the nineteenth century and until the rise of Hitler. Europe's Establishment, threatened by the gradual decline of the *ancien régime* and the rise of a new bourgeoisie, fought to maintain the status quo. Newcomers were considered upstarts and were unwelcome, as a rule, at the dinner parties, hunting week-ends and balls which made up society's annual round. Thus excluded, Jews funnelled their energies into supporting cultural life and the arts, and often used their fortunes to build major art collections. The same, naturally, held true at a slightly later period in the United States, after Jewish immigrants became successful there.

The amazing coming-of-age and coming together of these art collec-

The Rothschild Miscellany

Northern Italy, c. 1450-1480
Parchment, pen and ink, tempera and gold leaf; handwritten
473 leaves, 21 × 16 cm (8 ¼ × 6 ¼ in)
Gift of James A. de Rothschild, London

The Rothschild Miscellany is one of the most magnificent
Hebrew illuminated manuscripts in existence. Almost every
one of its very thin, refined parchment leaves is richly
decorated with colorful miniatures and marginal paintings in
tempera colors and in gold leaf.

The book assembles thirty-seven literary units, meticu-
lously copied both in the main body of the text and in the
margins of the page. The composition included biblical books,
a prayer book for the entire year, books on *halakha* (Jewish
Law), ethics and philosophy, *midrash* (a genre of rabbinic
literature) including historical legend, and even belles lettres,
mostly of a secular nature. It is obvious that the miscellany
was carefully planned with regard to the selection of works
and its layout.

The text contains no scribal colophon. The name of the
patron who commissioned this sumptuous codex, Moses ben
Yekutiel ha-Kohen, is incorporated within the prayer *mi
she'berach* (invocation of God's blessing on those called upon
to take part in the reading of the weekly portion of the
Torah). He may have been a wealthy Jewish banker of
Ashkenazi origin, who settled in northern Italy shortly before
commissioning this work.

tions justly inspires an attempt to explain the special contribution of Jews abroad to the artistic life of both Israel and the countries in which they settled, their passion for studying, buying, selling and collecting works of art, and, of course, the palpable effect of all this on the Israel Museum.

The Rothschilds, certainly the most famous Jewish collectors of all time, launched their epic rise thanks to dealing in coins. Handling ancient coins and peddling were thus the earliest form of art dealing. Jews were also active as goldsmiths, loaned against the jeweled *objets de vertu* that made up the Schatzkammern of middle-Europe's aristocracy, dealt in rare stamps and eventually branched out into porcelain, furniture and, finally, paintings and sculpture. Migratory by fate, cultivated, with an inclination to study history and philosophy, their commercial instincts honed by the limitations placed on their professional activity, Jews took to art dealing with a natural flair. Interestingly, even today in Poland— where the large Jewish population was tragically exterminated — there are still shops advertising 'Münze, Geldwechsel und Antiquitäten,' a throwback to the professions which were combined in a unique way by Europe's Jews in the late eighteenth century. Once the chosen people achieved emancipation in the nineteenth century, the Gilded Age abounded in titanic Jewish art dealers; the Duveen brothers, in particular Joe Duveen, without whom America's great museums would lack their renowned Old Master paintings, Georges Wildenstein, who revived the major and minor arts of eighteenth-century France and satisfied robber-barons' aspirations to emulate the defunct kings and princes of Europe's courts, Paul Rosenberg, who pushed his clients into the more adventurous paintings of the Impressionists and, as the modern age began, Daniel Kahnweiler, who forced his timorous followers to swallow the often disturbing medicine of Cubism.

Parallel to the activity of these now legendary dealers was the burgeoning of a brilliant group of Jewish art historians. Bernard Berenson classified the painting of the Italian Renaissance in his famous lists, Max Friedlander set up the groundwork for the study of Netherlandish painting, Erwin Panofsky brought iconography to a high art, and Ernst Gombrich taught generations of college students how to look at art. Later, John Rewald described the genesis of Impressionism while Claude Lévi-Strauss attempted to encapsulate it into a structuralist code. At one point, Clement Greenberg was even telling Abstract Expressionists how to paint. Considering this enormous ferment in dealing and art history, it is no wonder that so many great Jewish collections have been built up over the last hundred years and that many have enriched the world's great museums since the gilded age.

In that period Lord Duveen purposely kept his gilded age clients away from the then revolutionary painting of the Impressionists, justifiably fearing that they would prefer French light to Dutch darkness. The tide, however, was irresistible and American collectors—led by Mary Cassatt, the Havemeyers and Berthe Potter Palmer— launched a new wave in the New World. Prior to World War II there were many important Jewish Impressionist collectors in Europe led by dealers such as Curt Valentin and Otto Cassirer. Berlin's Zalman Schocken, whose department stores were designed by Eric Mendelsohn, left in time for Palestine, created his famed library in Jerusalem, started the newspaper *Ha'aretz* in Tel Aviv, and sent his paintings to safety in New York and Zurich. Jacob Goldschmidt, a skillful Berlin banker, reached New York with his fortune and collection intact, and its dispersal by his son Erwin in 1958 launched the Impresssionist boom. Others, less fortunate, had their treasures confiscated or sold them at distress prices to Swiss dealers and collectors on their way to a safe haven, vastly enriching that country's museums and often permitting refugees to start life anew. Many successful Jews in the United States started collecting Impressionist paintings in the 1940s, and as these rapidly increased in value, the trend became a landslide that vastly enriched their owners both spiritually and monetarily. Many of these paintings subsequently entered the collections of the Israel Museum.

The most unique contribution of Jewish dealers and collectors, however, has been in the area of modern and contemporary art. It would not be an exaggeration to say that they have always dominated the field, and for quite obvious reasons. First, the new is a challenge and its very questioning nature is of immense appeal. The Talmud is based on questions while the Bible attempts to give answers. While Christians are brought up on images, Jews are attached to the Word, so abstraction is much more acceptable and easily understood. And, finally, a personal involvement with artists is an intellectual challenge that greatly appeals to people who want to be in the cultural mainstream. It is quite appropriate that the 25th anniversary of the Museum was marked by the opening of the Twentieth-century Art building, and quite understandable that this department is one of the most active in the Museum.

Collectors and collections, buildings and galleries, curators, patrons, museum directors and all the other components of a great museum would serve little purpose in a land without a vibrant artistic life. The Museum's department of Israeli art is, in consequence, of utmost importance. The function of such a department is both to preserve the past and encourage the future, and there are extremely close ties between the Museum and the many Israeli artists working throughout the country and abroad. But it is the new work produced throughout the nation and exhibited under nearly ideal conditions that causes the most excitement and gives the Museum an additional and crucial dimension as an essential element in the life of its community.

Archaeology

Ya'akov Meshorer

Archaeology has long attracted scholars and laymen, as it holds a universal appeal for man's natural curiosity. Archaeology can sometimes be a mystery, in which unknown worlds are explored, launching voyages into forgotten civilizations. At other times archaeology is as simple as unearthing answers to unsolved historical riddles. For most nations, exploring the past is a source of national pride and prestige, symbolizing the historical continuity of a country, or even its timelessness. Hands-on work in archaeology combines the sheer joy of revealing unknown and sometimes unexpected remnants of our ancestors, with the pleasure stemming from the study of these finds, thereby exposing a more complete picture of human history. However, for the people of Israel, and for those for whom the Bible is meaningful, archaeology uncovers a special message.

Themes in the Archaeology of the Land of Israel

The archaeology of the Land of Israel has its own peculiar array of motifs, ideas and practitioners. Like the archaeology of any country, it is intimately linked to the land itself — its craggy hills, small fecund valleys and broad deserts, and the longitudinal divisions and ecological variety created by these land forms. Two major themes stretch throughout the history of the Holy Land. The first concerns Israel's position as a bridge between the great civilizations of Egypt and Mesopotamia. When either or both these lands were united and powerful, their armies and administrations usually wrought destruction and poverty upon a people already struggling against the limitations of nature. Yet at the same time, Israel was exposed to the cultures of these civilizations and the vibrant processes of cross-fertilization, syncretism and innovation.

The second prevailing theme is the fragmentary, segmented character of society in a landscape that encouraged regionalism and discouraged large-scale organization. Sometimes, however, under the right conditions, the peoples of this partitioned land would coalesce under charismatic leaders into larger and more assertive nation-states – the Israelite and Judahite monarchies of the Iron Age, or the kingdom of Herod the Great five hundred years later, for example.

The history and archaeology of the Land of Israel are wonderfully enhanced, and at times complicated, by the fact that three of the world's great religions – Judaism, Christianity and Islam – regard it as holy.. Archaeologists and curators in this part of the Museum must often deal with historical reality on the one hand, and faith on the other. But more than anything else, it is precisely the connection between faith and history that brings two million visitors a year to Israel, many of whom visit the Israel Museum. It is felt, therefore, to be incumbent upon the Museum to explore and explain the biblical texts in the exhibits. This is handled with caution, but it is dealt with. Many of the displays attempt to illuminate Scripture, and the Bible itself often provides important evidence for interpreting the archaeological finds.

However, the history, and prehistory, of the Holy Land began long before the Bible was written. This fact, and the fact that so many religions, cultures and peoples are represented in the Holy Land's archaeological heritage, extend the range of subjects exhibited in manifold ways.

The Samuel Bronfman Biblical and Archaeological Museum is unique and scientifically significant, in particular because the great majority of artifacts exhibited come from controlled excavations. Artifacts from such scientific excavations have a reliable context which helps to glean more information from them for scientists and laymen alike. These finds are usually on loan from the Israel Antiquities Authority (abbreviated to IAA in the captions). Often, a major find is put on display within a few months of its discovery.

The Samaritan high priest traces the Samaritan script, still used today, on a stone *mezuzah* from the 3rd–4th century CE.

Alongside the permanent display, temporary exhibitions of two kinds alternate in the galleries: thematic exhibitions, such as: 'Jewelry from the Ancient World,' 'Cosmetics in Ancient Times' or 'A Window to Islam,' and exhibitions that deal with specific sites or finds and emphasize new discoveries of significance: the finds from Jerusalem, Masada, or from underwater excavations. A recent example is the Chalcolithic gold from Nahal Qanah. In addition, exhibitions of an international character are also mounted. The most ambitious of these was 'Treasures of the Holy Land: Ancient Art from the Israel Museum' that traveled to major museums in North America. A new departure has been the import of archaeological exhibitions from other countries, such as the 'World's Earliest Gold from Varna, Bulgaria,' in 1994.

The Archaeology of Israel: an Outline

The collection is still exhibited chronologically, with certain types of objects (glass and coins, for example) displayed in separate pavilions incorporated in the main display. Some exemplary highlights from the Museum's archaeological holdings are presented and reproduced in this volume. By way of background and introduction, the main developments in Israel's history, from earliest prehistory to the Islamic period, are set out below.

Prehistory (from 1,500.000 years ago to the 5th millennium BCE, ending with the late Neolithic period)

The earliest traces of humankind in Israel were found at Ubeidiya (on the banks of the River Jordan south of the Sea of Galilee) and are dated to approximately 800,000 years before the present (BP), thus falling in the *Lower Paleolithic Period* (c. 2 million − 100,000 years BP). *Homo erectus* originated in East Africa and spread further afield during this period, traversing Israel as a principal corridor of migration. This hominid knew how to make fire, and fashioned tools of flint, bone and wood, hunting and scavenging in groups. Hand-axes and picks are the most recognizable tool forms. The finds from Ubeidiya, and from other Lower Paleolithic settlements found in the Jordan valley and along the coastal plain, greatly resemble finds from East Africa, Europe and Asia, demonstrating the migrational links referred to above. Remains of flora and fauna from these sites are on prominent display in the exhibition to give the visitor an idea of the environment in which *Homo erectus* lived. One highlight is the unique female figurine found at Birket Er-Ram in the Golan Heights, and dated to c. 300.000 years BP. Though its provenance was doubted by some, intensive new investigation has convinced experts that it is indeed the world's earliest art object so far discovered.

The *Middle Paleolithic Period* (100,000−40,000 BP) in Israel is distinguished by the appearance of *Homo sapiens,* both of the Neanderthal and the *Homo sapiens sapiens* families. The human skeletal remains found in the country at the Tabun, Kebara, and Skhul caves in Galilee and Kafza caves, near Nazareth, for example, are a crucial link in understanding this important stage in human evolution. Did modern people evolve from the Neanderthal or did both develop from a common ancestor? The verdict is not yet final, but finds in the prehistoric gallery present the evidence to be considered. This was a cooler, moister period in Israel — the northern hemisphere was in the grip of the last ice age. Most of the excavated sites are cave shelters and the finds include flora and fauna adapted to a cooler, moister climate. The flint utensils occur in several different assemblages, or 'tool kits,' which may represent either different functions or different contemporary populations with knapping traditions. Whatever the explanation, flint working shows increased sophistication and greater dexterity. Hunting and gathering were now the primary subsistence strategies (as opposed to scavenging). This period also reveals the earliest evidence for intentional burial and funerary rites.

Bone-heads, partly painted and smeared with asphalt. Nahal Hemar cave near the Dead Sea, 7th millennium BCE.

By the early *Upper Paleolithic Period* (40,000–18,500 years BP) Neanderthal man had disappeared (no-one is quite sure why) and *Homo sapiens sapiens* reigned supreme. This is reflected in an increasingly refined tool kit. Flint blades now took precedence over flakes, and tools generally became smaller. This may have been the period during which the bow and arrow were invented. Bone needles are also quite conspicuous; they were used in the joining of animal skins for various purposes. The depiction of a horse on a limestone plaque from Hayonim Cave in the Lower Galilee provides evidence of the creation of art and abstract thinking.

The *Epipaleolithic Period* (18,500–8,500 BCE) is distinguished by artifacts such as grinding stones and flint sickle blades, showing that certain kinds of plants — grains in particular — were being processed in new ways. In other words, this epoch represents the eve of what some called the 'agricultural revolution' — one that was to have a profound effect on humanity. This period is subdivided into successive cultures which sometimes overlapped geographically and temporally: the Kebaren, Kebaren Geometric, the Natufian, and others that represent regional groupings in the arid zones. The Natufian culture especially is well-known for its beautifully carved stone and bone animals and for its bone and shell jewelry. Quite a few burials have been recovered from this time and mortuary practices seem to indicate belief in an afterlife and the practice of ancestor worship. Indeed, from this time on, burial assemblages comprise a major source of archaeological information and artifacts.

The *Neolithic Period* from 8500 to 4500 BCE marks the onset of the agricultural revolution, with the domestication of wild grain and wild animals — sheep and goats in particular. It is also the time when people became sedentary, being freed from the need to follow herds and seasonal plants. Sedentarization seems directly responsible for the increased sophistication of building techniques and scale of construction — witness the tower and walls of Jericho. The invention of pottery in this period was also associated with permanent habitation. Art objects, mainly in connection with burial practices, have been uncovered at sites such as Jericho and Nahal Hemar. Exhibits include many ritual objects: masks, plastered skulls, figurines, textiles and jewelry — testifying to a rich spiritual life. The fertility figurine from Munhata is a choice example.

The Chalcolithic, Bronze and Iron Ages (4500–586 BCE)

The *Chalcolithic Period* (4500–3500 BCE) is intermediate between the Stone Age and the Bronze Age (*lithos* means stone in Greek and *chalcos* means copper, whose use preceded the bronze alloy produced from copper and tin). By this stage, agriculture and animal husbandry were well-established and formed society's economic backbone and ideological underpinning. Animals were now utilized not only for meat and skins, but for dairy products and textiles. Chalcolithic society may have been the first in which a form of class structure developed with a dialectic between rulers and ruled.

Ivory figurine of pregnant woman, Beer-Sheba, first half 4th millennium BCE.

Astounding wealth and artistic proficiency makes the Chalcolithic period one of the most impressive chapters in Holy Land archaeology. Highlights in this section include the Nahal Mishmar hoard — a group of hundreds of exquisite and technically marvelous copper scepters, mace heads and crowns uncovered in an inaccessible cave perched high above a wadi in the Judaean Desert. At Nahal Qanah in Samaria, large gold ingot rings were found amongst stalagtites, stalagmites and ossuaries in a large karstic cave. Male and female ivory figurines from Beer-Sheba, stone 'violin figurines' from Gilat, and other stone and pottery objects of a rich and mysterious symbolism are also exhibited. The world of funerary customs and beliefs is represented by decorated pottery ossuaries shaped like houses in which the bones of the dead were interred in family necropoli.

The *Early Canaanite (Bronze) Age* (3500–2300 BCE) marks the beginning of urbanization. The museum excavated the best preserved early city in the Holy Land — Tel Arad in the northern Negev desert. Over most of its expanse, the 5,000-year-old remains were never built upon, resulting in a fine state of preservation and relatively easy recovery. The Museum's Early

Bronze Age gallery exhibits a plan of this radial-planned city surrounded by bastioned walls with fortified gates, together with a scale model depicting the typical Arad-style house compound with all its installations. No less fascinating are the remains of different foodstuffs from the Arad houses — grains, olive pits, dates, legumes and other edibles — allowing us to reconstruct people's eating habits and nutrition. Planned cities such as Arad are now understood to indicate an hierarchical political system, perhaps organized into city-states or territories.

Imported vessels from Egypt and Sinai reveal that trade connections were widespread. Indeed, the archaeological finds indicate that, in the initial phase of the Early Bronze Age, the southern coast of Canaan was colonized by Egyptians, most probably a means of tapping into Canaan's olive oil and wine production — valued goods that could not be produced in Egypt due to its hot, arid climate. Among other items on display are inscribed *serekhs* (royal emblems) of the earliest known Egyptian kings, found at Arad, Tel Ereni and Nahal Besor. Other Early Bronze Age exhibits include the cultic stele from Arad and a large hoard of sophisticated copper weapons found by chance at Kfar Monash.

Most of these cities from the 3rd millennium BCE were destroyed or abandoned. Theories abound, but the truth is that we are still not sure what brought this collapse about — perhaps it was a result of political disintegration that ensued when the system became too complex and could no longer meet its social commitments. In several cases (Arad and Ai, for example) the old Early Bronze Age sites remained uninhabited until the Iron Age. In a fascinating turn of events, their ruins, according to some scholars, became associated with the Biblical tradition of the conquest of Canaan by Joshua.

The period between the Early Bronze Age and Middle Bronze Age is termed the *Intermediate Bronze Age* (2300–2000 BCE). This indicates that economic, social and political organization were different from what immediately preceded and followed. Society had fragmented into smaller, more mobile (often nomadic) groups when the large urban centers of the Early Bronze Age collapsed. Pastoralism (sheep and goat herding) took precedence over field agriculture, allowing people to exist in difficult ecological niches such as the deserts and the thickly covered hill country. It was safer and freer beyond the old frontiers. Beyond the borders of Canaan other lands were also in turmoil, brought on by sociopolitical collapse. Other peoples were also on the move; one such group, known both from the Bible and ancient documents, was the Amorites.

Model of 'Arad' house reconstructed from finds in the excavations in Arad, first half of 3rd millennium BCE.

Some aspects of material culture, particularly from the north of the country, indicate that groups of people did penetrate Canaan from Syria. The innovation of alloying copper with tin to make bronze perhaps came from this direction. Most of the artifacts exhibited — predominantly pottery, copper weapons and jewelry — were recovered from tombs located in large, perhaps tribal, burial grounds throughout the land.

The *Middle Canaanite (Bronze) Age* (2000–1550 BCE) — parallel to the Middle Kingdom in Egypt and the Old Babylonian period of King Hammurabi in Mesopotamia — saw the resurgence of city-states, whose main urban centers were surrounded by massive earthwork fortifications. Contrary to what such ramparts would lead us to expect, destruction layers are conspicuously lacking in archaeological strata of this era, until its last century that is. The impression is generally one of peaceful coexistence. Commerce — with Egypt, Mesopotamia and the Aegean region — was on a larger scale than ever before; this was truly a period of internationalism.

The Middle Bronze Age is represented in the Museum by exhibits such as a model of the astonishing, intact arched mud brick city-gate and paved street at Tel Dan. The pottery of this period is among the most beautiful ever made; the full potential of the potter's fast wheel was realized and the results are often fabulous in their technique and aesthetic sense. Zoomorphic (animal-shaped) and anthropomorphic (human-shaped) vessels are fairly frequent finds from this period, though each is marked by an individual touch. Scarab and cylinder seals, inspired by and sometimes imported from Egypt and Mesopotamia respectively, recur frequently and help date the archaeological contexts. Written material makes its first appearance at this time in the form of Egyptian hieroglyphs on scarab seals and statuettes, and cuneiform tablets in Akkadian from Hazor, Shechem, Ta'anach, Gezer and Hebron. Essentially, this is the first truly historical period in Canaan.

The Middle Bronze Age also came to an end under somewhat mysterious circumstances. Some scholars suggest that an internal social and political implosion was responsible. Others point to Egypt, which ejected Canaanite rulers known as the Hyksos from their capital in the Nile delta and then besieged them in southern Canaan at Sharuhen. Still others infer that a Hurrian warrior class from north Syria migrated to Canaan and brought with them turmoil and conquest. A combination of these factors may have been responsible.

Through much of the *Late Canaanite (Bronze) Age* (1550–1200 BCE) Canaan was subjected to Egyptian rule. The exhibits from this period include numerous imported luxury goods – pottery, metals, jewelry – from Egypt, Greece, Cyprus, Syria, Anatolia and Mesopotamia. These have been found throughout the country in tombs, temples and palaces. All this glitter once induced scholars to see the Late Bronze Age as a period of great prosperity. But there is another aspect to this period; the number of settlements decreased markedly from the previous period and extremely few rural settlements are known. This tells us that a large section of the population had reverted to nomadism once again. It seems quite clear that while the élite class had access to wealth, and while international trade was extensive, the majority of the population was disenfranchised and poor. The Egyptian rulers certainly had something to do with this. The anthropomorphic coffins and exquisite jewelry and metal vessels from Deir el-Balah, an Egyptian settlement uncovered beneath the dunes of the Gaza Strip, are a prominent expression of Egyptian influence and presence in Canaan.

By this stage the earliest Semitic alphabet had been invented, probably in Sinai (the origins of this alphabet are dealt with in the separate Pavilion of Hebrew Script and Inscriptions described below). Glass began to appear in larger quantities and in more complex forms.

The *Early Israelite Period* (Iron Age I, 1200–1000 BCE) has traditionally been associated with the conquest of Canaan by the Israelites, and the settlement of the tribes under the leadership of the Judges. It is now thought that much of the Israelite population was already present in the form of nomadic and semi-nomadic groups living in the rugged central hills of Samaria. These groups subsequently consolidated control over this region, and united under a single ruler (Saul, then David, according to the Bible) to counter the threat of the Philistines (one of the 'Sea Peoples' origi-

Philistine pottery with its characteristic decorations, 12th–11th century BCE.

Tomb reconstructed for the exhibition of finds from 'Ketef Hinnom, Jerusalem,' 1986. A major discovery in the tomb was the silver amulet bearing the inscription of the Priestly Benediction, 7th–6th century BCE.

nating in the Aegean region) living on the coast, and the Canaanites of the lowlands. Gradually prevailing against their enemies, the Israelites expanded into Judah, the Galilee, the Negev and across the east bank of the River Jordan.

The permanent display of this period thus reflects the various peoples who occupied different parts of the land: Philistine pottery decorated with birds and fish in metopes indicating its Aegean inspiration; Canaanite cult stands, pottery and tools showing continuity from the Late Bronze Age; and the simple, utilitarian pots and large storage jars made by the inhabitants of the central hill country — the early Israelite settlers. Iron tools and weapons occur at this time, if only in small numbers, first in Philistine and then at early Phoenician sites.

The *Israelite Period II* (Iron Age II, 1000–587 BCE), also called the First Temple period, starts with the United Kingdom under David and Solomon and ends with the destruction of the divided kingdoms: Israel by the Assyrians in 722 BCE, and Judah by the Babylonians in 586 BCE. There is a special significance in the finds exhibited from this period as nearly all are associated in some way with events and information described in the Bible, especially from the Books of Kings, Prophets and Chronicles. Among the highlights are the decorated architectural elements from large royal structures at Jerusalem, Hazor and Megiddo, ivories from the palace of Ahab in Samaria, and ostraca and seals written in Paleo-Hebrew, some of which mention names familiar from the Old Testament. Such inscriptions often look unimportant, but they can be momentous. The 'House of David' stele inscription from Tel Dan, and two minute silver scrolls inscribed with the Priestly Benediction (cf. Numbers 6:24–26, Psalms 67:2) found recently in a Jerusalem tomb, are both of great import for historical and biblical studies.

One section of the display is dedicated to finds revealed in excavations carried out in Jerusalem. It depicts material culture from the eve of the Babylonian conquest. Another section focuses on material found at Lachish. The conquest of Lachish by the Assyrian king Sennacherib in 701 BCE is recounted in the Bible (II Kings 17:13). Visitors to the Iron Age Hall can view a giant, life-size replica of a relief from Nineveh, the Assyrian capital, showing how the Judahites of Lachish defended themselves against the Assyrian attack, and how the Assyrians viewed the Judahite defeat. Fortunately, the museum also possesses an Assyrian clay prism which refers to the same story, again from an Assyrian perspective. Also on display are arrow-heads, slings, remains of Assyrian helmets, armor scales and chains used for suspending a battering ram.

Just beyond the Iron Age gallery lies the Pavilion of Hebrew Script and Inscriptions. The development of the Hebrew alphabet is traced from its genesis in the second millennium BCE to its progression into the Phoenician, Aramaic, Greek, and Latin scripts. The inscribed artifacts themselves — whole jars, sherds (called ostraca), stamp seals and bullae (impressions in the clay used to seal the knot on bound papyrus or parchment documents) are also on display. The script characteristic of the First Temple period was replaced in the Second Temple period by the Aramaic script still used in modern Hebrew.

Jerusalem was devastated and its temple razed in 586 BCE, terminating the Kingdom of Judah. A significant portion of the Jewish population was taken into exile, repeating the expulsion of part of the Israelite population 136 years earlier. Despite the social trauma caused by the loss of their homeland and cultic center, Jews thrived in captivity. Shortly after the fall of Judah, the Babylonians were defeated by the Persians. The declaration of the Persian king, Cyrus, in 539 BCE, resulted in the return of the Jews to Zion and the building of the Second Temple, in 520 BCE.

The Second Temple Period

Archaeological strata from the *Persian Period* (538–333 BCE) tend to be incoherent and highly disturbed due to later building or erosion subsequent to the sites' abandonment. The resulting scarcity of finds once led scholars to believe that this was a period of relative poverty when the country had still not recovered from the ravages of the late Iron Age. But it is now

The Samaria Hoard

Jug, 39 coins and jewelry
Mid-4th century BCE
Diameter of coins 4 – 9 mm (¼ – ½ in)
Gift of Abraham Bromberg, London and Shraga Qedar, Jerusalem

According to the Bible (2 Kings 17 : 24) the inhabitants of Samaria after 722 BCE consisted of populations brought by the Assyrians from remote places and settled there. Some historians, however, suggest that the bulk of the people of Samaria after 722 were the descendants of the Israelites. There is some truth in both theories and it seems that due to the high percentage of Israelites in the area, the conglomerate of people who lived there had accepted the Hebrew Law.

For a long time, the Samaritans tried to be accepted as a legitimate part of the Jewish people, willing to take part in the ceremonies of the Temple in Jerusalem. Despite their continuous efforts, they were rejected by the Jews. The final separation between the Samaritans and the Jews probably took place in the last years before Alexander the Great conquered the area (332 BCE).

This jug, discovered in the vicinity of Samaria, originally contained 334 minute silver coins, as well as several pieces of jewelry. Of the coins, 182 were Samaritan, 86 were Tyrian, and 66 were local imitations of Athenian prototypes. According to the dated coins, the hoard was hidden in 346-5 BCE. The Samaritan coins bear Aramaic inscriptions mentioning the name 'Shamryn' (Samaria), as well as the private names of several governors. The hoard is one of the main sources for our knowledge of the Samaritans during the late Persian Period.

recognized that the Persian period was a time of prosperity, particularly in the coastal cities, bolstered by a burgeoning maritime trade. Cities grew rapidly, under the guidelines of Hippodamian (grid) planning. Although the Persians were the supreme power, commerce and contact were mainly oriented toward the Aegean and Phoenicia. One indication of this is that coins introduced into the local markets were Greek and Phoenician, not Persian. Imported pottery of different styles abounds in this period: East Greek, Corinthian, and Attic wares.

The *Hellenistic Period,* starting with the conquest of Alexander the Great in 332 BCE, marked another turning point for the inhabitants of Eretz Israel. Greek influence was now stronger than ever, with political and cultural institutions such as the polis and the gymnasium spreading a new world view, that of Hellenism. Under Alexander, new cities were established and populated by Macedonian veterans, Greek mercenaries and traders, and elements of the local population. At the same time, many of the core values were retained from the original culture – cultic institutions and civil law for example. Moreover, though Greek became the lingua franca of administration and international commerce, Aramaic remained the first language for many inhabitants, especially those in rural areas. In sum, the artifacts on display from this period tend to show an amalgamation of eastern and western features. It was, indeed, this amalgamation that provided fertile ground for the growth of new ideas and new religious movements.

Following the death of Alexander and during the first part of the third century BCE Judaea was ruled by the Ptolemaic kings of Egypt. Later it came

Detail of a floor mosaic from a Roman villa, Nablus, 3rd–4th century CE.

under the Seleucid kings of Syria. In the mid-second century BCE the Hasmonean family (the Maccabees) defeated the Seleucid armies and an independent Jewish kingdom emerged. Jewish life and culture now experienced a renaissance; sumptuous buildings and tombs were constructed, displaying mixed oriental and Hellenistic styles. Independent coinage was minted bearing cultic and propagandist themes. While the Hasmonean revolt was to some degree a rebellion against Hellenism, the institutions and ideals of that culture retained much of their original force.

The *Roman Period* in Judaea can be said to have begun in 37 BCE when the Hasmonean dynasty was replaced by the rule of Herod under Roman patronage. In Israel this period is divided into earlier and later sub-periods — the Herodian Period (37 BCE — 135 CE), and the Late Roman Period following the destruction of the Second Temple or the Bar-Kokhba Revolt (135 CE — c. 326 CE).

The Museum's Herodian period exhibit emphasizes the rich finds yielded by systematic, large-scale excavations carried out in Jerusalem after 1967, mainly from the Jewish Quarter renovations, from the area south and west of the Temple Mount, and from Jewish tombs in the necropolis surrounding the city in antiquity. The villas of well-to-do priestly families situated in the area of the modern-day Jewish Quarter, destroyed in 70 CE by the army of Titus, rendered a wealth of finds from everyday life buried under burned and collapsed debris. Among these finds are the numerous stone and glass vessels that bear eloquent testimony to the observance of new Jewish laws pertaining to ritual purity (the ritual cleanliness of stone

Ossuary of Caiaphas, The High Priest, bearing the inscription 'Yehosef bar Qafa' (Joseph, son of Caiaphas), Second Temple Period.

and glass was considered renewable while that of pottery was not). Pseudo-Nabatean pottery gives some indication of that southern people's aesthetic influence (Herod was of Idumean, i.e. Nabatean stock. His father had converted to Judaism.) Examples of Roman *terra sigillata* pottery imported from different places in the Mediterranean basin hint at widespread trade relations.

Herod greatly enlarged and beautified the temple and its surrounding podium, making it one of the wonders of the ancient world. In the final days of the Great Revolt of 66–70 CE the Temple was decimated by Titus' men who tossed fragments originating in the magnificent sanctuary over the platform's side. Many such pieces were found in the thick conflagration debris at the base of the Temple Mount and some are on display in the Second Temple Period hall. One of these is an inscription indicating the place where the priests would trumpet the *shofar* to announce the onset of festivals and the new moon. Perhaps this very inscription was seen by Jesus as he walked the temple precinct. The ossuary (a rectangular stone casket for the secondary interment of bones) inscription of 'Simon the Temple Builder' should also be mentioned in this context. Another find of historical and theological importance – one of very recent vintage – is now on view: the inscribed ossuary of Joseph Caiaphas, the high priest who, according to the New Testament, disparaged Jesus and had him transferred to Pontius Pilate for judgement. Pilate's name, too, was carved in a dedicatory stone inscription found at Caesarea.

The first century CE was the heyday of Jewish art, for both the Hasmoneans and Herod did their utmost to restore the glory of the First Temple Period. Ornamented architectural elements, decorated ossuaries and lamps, coins, jewelry and other objects all expressed an aesthetic akin to the sensuality of Roman art, albeit tempered by Jewish motifs and restrictions.

The Rise of Christianity and Islam

With the destruction of the Second Temple in 70 CE, and especially after the Bar-Kokhba revolt of 132–135 CE, the Roman style asserted itself throughout the land. The exhibition halls housing material from the second to fourth centuries CE are full of mosaics, sarcophagi, statues, and pottery bearing the human form, and at times even depicting erotic scenes. One of the Museum's world-renowned masterpieces is the evocative bronze bust of the Roman emperor Hadrian, found in a field not far from Beth Shean. At the same time, however, Jewish culture and learning continued to flourish in Palestine. At the beginning of the third century CE the *Mishna* (the first written compilation of the Oral Law) was compiled under Rabbi Judah the Patriarch, establishing a normative Judaism that dominated Jewish life for centuries, and still holds sway amongst many Jews today.

The *Byzantine Period* (326–636 CE) saw the building of numerous churches and synagogues. Though Jerusalem appears to have been off-limits to Jews, the two monotheistic religions Christianity and Judaism existed side by side, in competition, but with much in common. Comparing the techniques and motifs in contemporary ecclesiastical architecture, mosaics, oil lamps and coinage one finds a tremendous variety of imagery and even some ideological crossovers. Decorated mosaic floors in synagogues often contained people, animals and even ostensibly pagan symbols, such as the zodiac. Several such mosaic pavements are vertically displayed along the museum's long entry forecourt. Other synagogue floors, usually in more rural settings, maintained stricter observance of the Jewish prohibitions of figurative representation. The most common symbols portrayed in synagogue floors and oil lamps of this time were temple furnishings (*menorahs* and *shovels*), synagogue fixtures (the ark) and the *lulav* and *etrog* used for the Festival of Succoth. From this period on, these attributes were maintained in Jewish art as the emblems of Judaism itself.

Bronze oil lamp decorated with Jewish symbols, 4th century CE.

Having traversed the Roman-Byzantine halls, the visitor comes to the broad corridor in which the evolution of the oil lamp can be followed from its beginnings in the Early Bronze Age until the Islamic period. The display includes several items of unusual decoration or elaboration, such as multi-spouted lamps, and others featuring religious insignia and inscriptions.

The *Islamic Period* began officially with Palestine's conquest by the Ummayad dynasty in 636 CE. Initially, the trappings of Byzantine culture such as art, architecture, and Greek language continued to hold sway. Eventually, however, an indigenous Islamic culture evolved; inscriptions came to be written in Arabic and the mosque became a more prominent component in both urban and rural settings. In some areas the Jewish and Christian population gradually dissipated, converting or leaving the country, abandoning their churches and synagogues to the ravages of time. In other regions — the Galilee and Jerusalem for example — these communities seem to have sustained themselves. The Islamic exhibit includes local finds such as colorful glazed pottery, rich coin hoards and elegant jewelry from the Early Islamic period, preceding the Crusader conquest. A separate Islamic display in the center of the Museum presents art of various periods from Egypt, Syria, Iran and India.

Neighboring Countries Pavilion

Ancient Canaan/Israel/Palestine existed in the midst of other, usually wealthier and more powerful neighbors. As noted in the introductory paragraphs of this chapter, much in the culture of Eretz Israel derived from these neighboring civilizations. Hence, four years after the Museum`s opening, the curators decided to display the finds that originated in these neighboring countries, from its still-fledgling collection. The Neighboring Countries Hall is divided into Classical, Western Asiatic and Egyptian sections and exhibits artifacts from Greece, Turkey, Cyprus, Egypt, Syria, Jordan, Mesopotamia, and Iran. It is intended to allow the visiting public to form an idea of these regions' material cultures and to compare their cultures with that of Eretz Israel.

The Glass and Numismatic Pavilions

The Pavilion for the Ancient Glass Collection contains highlights of ancient glass manufacture from the mid-second millennium BCE to the Ottoman period. The display is arranged chronologically and includes important finds from archaeological excavations. A particularly impressive group of Jewish glass from the Roman-Byzantine period is on view, often decorated with the *menorah*, as well as two gold-glass vessel bases from the Jewish Catacombs in Rome.

The newly inaugurated Numismatic Pavilion exhibits coins and related objects by theme, such as ancient banking and hoarding, means of payment, inflation, Jerusalem through coins, and non-numismatic uses of coins. The Museum is fortunate to own the world's richest collection of Jewish and non-Jewish coins struck in Eretz Israel.

Group of Roman-Byzantine glass vessels, 3rd–5th century CE.

The Dead Sea Scrolls in the Shrine of the Book

In 1947, a Bedouin shepherd boy searching for a lost kid at Qumran, on the shores of the Dead Sea, entered a cave and chanced upon what is perhaps the most significant archaeological find ever made in the Holy Land: a pottery jar containing a group of scrolls inscribed with extraordinarily early biblical and extra-biblical manuscripts. This first group of scrolls, also comprising the most complete ones, were acquired shortly after by Professors Sukenik and Yadin for the State of Israel and transferred to the Israel Museum's Shrine of the Book when it opened. Following this astonishing find, surveys and excavations were undertaken which revealed further written material of an early date. The material recovered in these later investigations is now administered by the Israel Antiquities Authority. As a whole, the 'Qumran library' now comprises a large collection of Jewish writings that includes all the books of the Hebrew Bible, except for the Book of Esther, as well as many other texts of an apocryphal, pseudoepigraphical and sectarian nature. The documents appear to have been written over a period of approximately 300 years – from the third century BCE to 68 CE (the date of the destruction of Qumran).

The scrolls and other finds are exhibited in a separate building, The Shrine of the Book – D. J. and Jeane Gottesmann Center for Biblical Manuscripts. Its roof in the form of a scroll-jar lid mantled with white glazed

Interior of the Shrine of the Book housing the Dead Sea Scrolls.

ceramic bricks symbolizes the Sons of Light, who, according to one of the scrolls, are designated to do battle with the Sons of Darkness, represented by a large black wall adjacent to the dome.

An entirely new branch of biblical studies has grown out of the Qumran discoveries: Qumran Scroll research. Thousands of scholarly (and some not so scholarly) works have been written and much debate has ensued. Some questions are still open: who were the people who lived at Qumran? Did they practice what they preached? Were they Essenes? Were they related to early Christianity?

The Shrine of the Book exhibits only the first and most complete scrolls found: the Books of Isaiah and Psalms and hitherto unknown Hebrew manuscripts, such as the Manual of Discipline and the Temple Scroll (acquired after 1967). According to the sectarian texts, such as the Manual of Discipline and the Temple Scroll, the biblical commentaries and apocalyptic visions, it is clear that while most of the writings are imbued with concepts akin to the rabbinical law *(Halakha)* that crystallized in the later *Mishna,* this library belonged to a sect with a somewhat different approach. Most scholars maintain that these were the Essenes, a sect disgusted with the leadership of the Hasmonean priests in Jerusalem, who removed themselves both physically and spiritually from normative Judaism, leaving Jerusalem to live a communal life of ascetism and hard discipline in the desert under the leadership of a 'Teacher of Righteousness.'

The Shrine of the Book also exhibits archaeological artifacts (pottery, leather sandals, basketry, textiles and metal utensils) and important documents found in the Judaean desert dating from the beginning of the second century BCE: wedding contracts, lease contracts and letters written by Bar-Kokhba during the revolt of 132–135 CE.

The Shrine of the Book is the most frequented section of the Israel Museum and for many has become the symbol of the institution itself.

Ubeidiya
Lower Palaeolithic
1,500,000 years old

Handaxe (*top*)
Basalt
H 19.5 cm (7 ¾ in)
W 12 cm (4 ¾ in)
IAA

Pick (*right*)
Flint
H 12.9 cm (5 in)
W 7.8 cm (3 in)
IAA

Spheroid (*left*)
Limestone
8.5 cm (3 ½ in) diameter
IAA

Chopper (*bottom*)
Flint
H 7.4 cm (3 in) W 8 cm (3 ¼ in)
IAA

Homo erectus expanded from Africa into Eurasia through the Syrio-African rift, Eretz Israel providing the bridge between the two continents. Ubeidiya, located on the shore of an ancient lake in the Jordan Valley about 3km (1 ¾ miles) southwest of today's Sea of Galilee, is the oldest archaeological site outside Africa, being 1,500,000 years old.

Competition with animals for survival and defense stimulated man's outstanding adaptive capabilities. The tools manufactured at this early stage do not indicate hunting activity, therefore it is most likely that meat was acquired by scavenging.

The tools were made with a hard hammer from various raw materials. Man learned to choose the proper stone for the required tool: flint was used for producing chopping tools, limestone for spheroids, and basalt for hand-axes. Chopping tools were used to break bones and obtain the nutritious marrow. Spheroids could have been used as projectiles for defense. The hand-axe was probably used as a cutting tool.

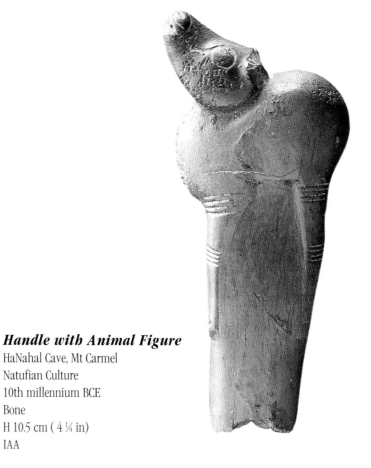

Jewelry
Various Sites
Natufian Culture
10th–9th millennium BCE
Animal bone and teeth, shell, stone, ostrich egg
IAA

In every society, even today, jewelry is used not only for adornment, but also as an amulet, as a demonstration of physical and material position in society, or as a means of payment. The earliest known extensive use of jewelry in Eretz Israel appears at the time of the Natufian culture (10,000 – 8,000 BCE). This was also the first culture to produce jewelry whose form was not dictated by the shape of the material, for instance, bone pendants. The variety of materials used, the shape of individual pieces, and the positioning of the adornments on the body, combine to give this jewelry a distinctive character. Much of it was made from the canine teeth of predatory animals, as well as from animal bones, various shells, coloured stones, and ostrich eggs. Delicate cutting, and the piercing and polishing of the jewelry, which was done using simple tools, all bear witness to a high standard of technical achievement. Certain materials were apparently considered so important that they were brought from as far afield as the Red Sea and the Mediterranean.

The burial of certain individuals adorned with jewelry might attest, for the first time, to different ranks in human society.

Handle with Animal Figure
HaNahal Cave, Mt Carmel
Natufian Culture
10th millennium BCE
Bone
H 10.5 cm (4 ¼ in)
IAA

This masterly carving was found in 1928 in HaNahal Cave, on the western face of Mount Carmel, during archaeological explorations following quarrying for the construction of Haifa harbor. Subsequent excavations revealed a group of Early Natufian burials immediately below the spot where this animal figurine had been found.

Originally described as a 'young deer,' this identification is by no means certain. The figurine is complete, carved from a long bone that had been split in two. Employing the natural protuberances of bone articulation, the upper part was used to carve the head in three dimensions and the lower part to depict the body and legs. Details such as the mouth, muzzle, eyes, and horns – one of which is broken – are all depicted with great skill, making this one of the most beautiful examples of prehistoric art.

The beginnings of the cultivation of cereals and legumes, the transitional period from hunter-gatherers to farmers, took place some 12,000 years ago, early in the Natufian period, within the 'Levantine Corridor,' the area stretching from the middle Euphrates through the Damascus Basin into the Lower Jordan Valley. The earliest agricultural tools from this period consist of grinding and pounding tools and sickles. It is assumed that this piece once formed the end of a sickle handle.

Modeled Skulls

Plastered Skull
Beisamoun
Pre-Pottery Neolithic B
7th millennium BCE
H 18.9 cm (7 ½ in) W15.2 cm (6 in)
IAA

Decorated Skull
Nahal Hemar Cave
Pre-Pottery Neolithic B
7th millennium BCE
H 18.5 cm (7 ¼ in) W 16.5 cm (6 ½ in)
IAA

During the Pre-Pottery Neolithic B period (7th millennium BCE) one of the common burial customs was the separation of the skull from the skeleton. In several sites in the Levant such skulls had the facial features modeled in layers of plaster. They were found in secondary burials below house floors, probably reflecting a form of ancestor worship. Ancestor worship may have reinforced the sense of land ownership during a period that witnessed a shift to sedentary villages.

Another type of skull, unique to the Nahal Hemar cave, near an asphalt source, has a coating of asphalt on its back. This layer is decorated with rolled cords of asphalt placed on the cranium in a net-like pattern resembling hair or a woven headdress. Perhaps these skulls also represent ancestor worship. The absence of facial features suggests the possibility that the masks found at this same site were meant to be attached to the skulls. If so, then the Nahal Hemar skulls may express a different cult practice than that of the plastered skulls.

Animal Figurines

Various Sites
Pre-Pottery Neolithic B
7th millennium BCE
Limestone, clay
L 3.5 – 13.6 cm (1 ½ in – 5 ¼ in)
IAA

Animal figurines are numerous during the Neolithic period when man started to domesticate animals. The smaller figurines were naturalistically modeled in clay; larger ones were carved out of stone. The figurines represent animals familiar to man at that time.

The earliest domesticated animals were sheep and goats, but non-domesticated species such as cattle, deer, frogs, birds and mice were also sculpted. Judging by their relaxed postures or humorous expressions, some were probably used as toys, like the 'bull' from Horvat Minha. Others, however, have a clearly ritual nature. Cattle figurines from Ein Ghazzal (in Jordan) were found beneath cattle bones. A few had been 'ritually killed' by flint bladelets inserted into the heart and chest while the clay was still wet, and others were found with a groove around the neck resulting from a twisted fiber lead. This latter feature may indicate the aspiration of early man to control or tame cattle by haltering.

The figurine of a rodent (possibly a mouse) from the Nahal Hemar Cave, carved from an elongated, pointed lime-stone pebble, may likewise have been intended as a magical measure to curb the threat of mice to stores of grain and other foodstuffs in an agricultural society.

Mask

Nahal Hemar Cave
Pre-Pottery Neolithic B
7th millennium BCE
Stone
H 26.5 cm (10 ½ in) W17 cm (6 ¾ in)
IAA

This mask was found in a cave on the bank of Nahal Hemar, a dry river-bed in the Judaean Desert, its name derived from the Hebrew word for asphalt (*Hemar*), which wells up near the Dead Sea. It is made out of limestone and is the largest of the four Neolithic stone masks found thus far in Israel and the only complete example found within a confirmed archaeological context.

Though the back is hollowed out, the thickness of the mask is uniform and symmetrical throughout. The chin is painted, the small mouth open, with four teeth in both the upper and lower jaw. Both cheekbones are prominent and the high forehead is domed, producing an overall skeletal impression. A radial design has been made with red, green and possibly also white paint, while thin red and white lines outline the round eyes. Eighteen irregular holes are cut into the side of the mask. Masks serve many functions, but primarily invest the wearer with mystery and supernatural powers.

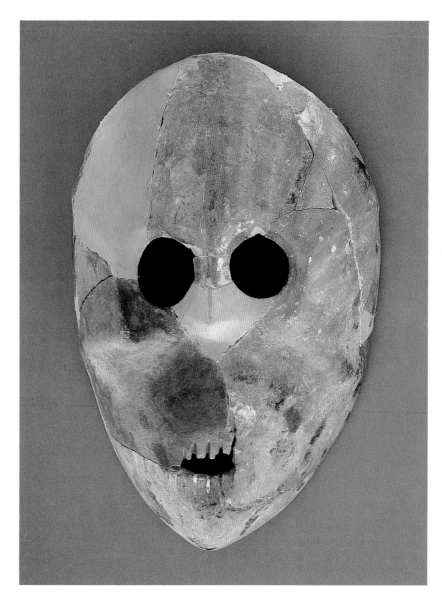

Seated Woman

Horvat Minha (Munhata)
Neolithic
6th millennium BCE
Pottery
H 11 cm (4 ¼ in) W 6.5 cm (2 ½ in)
IAA

Though depictions of the human form are known from the beginning of the Neolithic period (8th millennium BCE) in the Levant, this female figurine from 2,000 years later is the most impressive example of its kind as yet uncovered.

The cult of the Mother Goddess was widespread among ancient civilisations and, in keeping with other early female representations, the fertility aspects af this figurine have been emphasized: wide hips and enlarged buttocks. Her triangular head rests directly on her shoulders while her bent left arm supports her relatively small breasts. The right arm, now restored, hung straight down.

The construction of the sculpture involved wrapping a layer of clay around a cylindrical clay core, and adding the separately made parts of the body. Details, such as the garment covering the shoulders and back, oblong pellet-shaped eyes ('coffee bean eyes'), and the ears, are indicated by applied bits of clay.

Archaeological evidence places it within the Yarmukian culture, which flourished in the sixth millennium BCE, when agriculture and pasturage were beginning to develop in the Levant. Though found during an excavation of Horvat Minha (Munhata), south of the Sea of Galilee, parallels exist in a figurine from Kefar Giladi and other sculptures from Shaar HaGolan, Megiddo, Tel Aviv and Byblos.

Gold Circlets
Nahal Qanah Cave
Chalcolithic period
Late 5th – 4th millennium BCE
Average outer diameter: 4.6 cm (1 ¾ in)
IAA

The Nahal Qanah Cave, located in western Samaria, has yielded a remarkable collection of archaeological finds. An active karstic cave, containing a dazzling array of stalactites and stalagmites, it was created almost one hundred million years ago, and served during the Chalcolithic period as a burial site for at least twenty individuals.

Eight circlets, weighing a total of nearly one kilogram (2 ¼ lb), were found scattered throughout the perpendicular tomb cavity. They constitute the earliest find of gold in Eretz Israel and one of the earliest occurrences of this precious metal in the world. Six are electrum (70 per cent gold, 30 per cent silver), and two are 100 per cent gold, cast within open molds made of clay or sand. The surfaces were intentionally enriched with gold and hammered to heighten the sheen.

The function of these circlets is not completely understood. They do not appear to be bracelets, finger-rings or other ornaments, yet the attention paid to the surface suggests that aesthetic considerations were important. They may have served as ingots to be used in a commercial context.

Selections from the Judaean Desert Treasure
Nahal Mishmar (Cave of the Treasure), Judaean Desert
Chalcolithic period
First half of 4th millennium BCE
Copper and ivory
H of ivory box 38 cm (14 ¾ in)
H of copper bucket 15.5 cm (6 in)
IAA

A breathtaking hoard of Chalcolithic material was discovered in 1961, containing 429 objects which had been wrapped in a woven mat and then hidden in a Judaean Desert cave. Copper is the base for the majority of the objects, with five made of hippopotamus ivory, one of elephant ivory, six of hematite and one of limestone. The hoard represents the largest group of ancient copper objects found in the Near East.

Most objects were made of arsenic and antimony copper, a very durable and malleable material. The technical and aesthetic quality of these tools and vessels, molded using the lost wax process, are so sophisticated that in many cases they still astound modern artisans.

Mace heads, maces, standards, scepters and crowns form the bulk of the copper hoard, yet the variety, shape and decoration of each is so unusual that no two objects are identical. Many are so strange that they defy proper definition. This unusually large collection of seemingly non-functional pieces must have been of a ceremonial or cultic nature. The hoard may have originally been the treasure of a temple, removed in a time of danger and hidden in the cave.

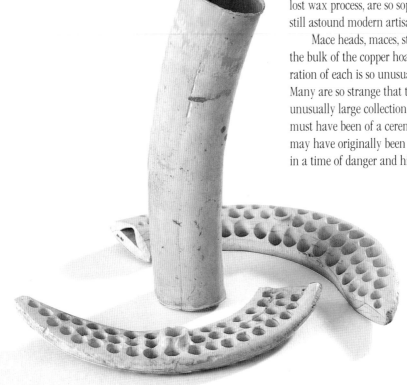

Violin-shaped figurines

Gilat
Chalcolithic period
Mid 5th - mid 4th millennium BCE
Stone
H 22 cm, 7 cm (8 ¾, 2 ¾ in)
IAA

At the site of Gilat in the northern Negev, a 6,500-year-old temple was discovered, which had been the center of worship for the agricultural settlements in the vicinity for over 1,000 years. About sixty stone violin-shaped figurines were uncovered there and curiously this type of figurine is unknown from periods either before or after the Chalcolithic period.

The sculptures have three defined body parts; head-neck, shoulders-waist, hips-thighs, producing an entirely abstract form. The shape is uniform, with only the proportions varying. One (the right-hand figurine) has marks indicating breasts, which may suggest that the figurines represent a type of mother goddess or female fertility deity.

From two remarkable pottery sculptures which were also found at the temple it is clear that the craftsmen were capable of producing detailed, naturalistic objects; the violin-shaped figures, therefore, must have been intentionally made in an abstract manner.

Violin-shaped figurines have also been found on the Cyclades in the Aegean though the earliest in that group are only 5,300 years old, 1,200 years later than the Eretz Israel finds. Unfortunately, this remarkable cultural connection remains a mystery.

Sculptured Pedestal Bowls

provenance unknown
Chalcolithic period
First half of 4th millennium BCE
Basalt
Average height: 25 cm (9 ¾ in)
Gift of Jonathan Rosen, New York to American Friends of the Israel Museum and Dr and Mrs Melvin Stich, Jerusalem

Although the exact provenance of these magnificent stands is unknown, they probably come from the vicinity of Irbid in north Jordan. Fortunately, very similar sculptured bowls with pedestals were excavated in various sites in the Golan. They come from the Chalcolithic culture and were found only in dwellings. It appears that they were often placed on wooden shelves built along the walls of houses.

The stands are one-piece pedestals with shallow, bowl-shaped tops. They are often decorated on their bases with schematic human faces, consisting of eyes, an additional pair of protrusions possibly, a prominent nose, and sometimes a beard or horns. Mouths are almost never indicated. These pedestal bowls may have been used as portable home altars, on which incense offerings were burned.

It is assumed that these sculptures represent household gods. Those with horns, for example, symbolized the 'sheep gods' while those without horns signified the 'gods of the fields.' The offerings, most probably milk, seeds, and grains, were placed in the bowls at the top of the stands, to ensure the fertility of the land and livestock. Alternately, the stands may have been used as portable home altars, on which incense offerings were burned. The fact that the stands did not have any fixed location seems to support the latter theory.

Ram

Azor
Chalcolithic period
c. 3500 BCE
Stone
H 9.3 cm (3 ¾ in) L 17.5 cm (6 ¾ in)
IAA

This ram figurine, carved from a flat, squarish stone, represents a remarkable combination of both abstract and naturalistic expression. The stone is elegantly shaped with soft curves and lines that subtly give the sense of the animal's body, without actually representing its limbs. Only the head is indicated, also with gentle curves, while two incised lines mark the animal's stubby tail. In contrast to this abstract treatment, the curved horns are vividly and naturalistically depicted in high relief. The emphasized horns point to the prominent role this animal played in the everyday and religious life of the period. The figurine was found by accident in 1895 by farmers ploughing land near the village of Azor. Based upon parallel finds, it would seem that it can be dated to the Chalcolithic period.

Bowl with Pair of Ibex

Beth Shean Valley
Early Canaanite period
Mid 4th – 3rd millennium BCE
Basalt
H: 20 cm (7 ¾ in) Diameter 34.5 cm (13 ½ in)
IAA

This elaborate bowl was discovered along with other, less ornate basalt bowls in a burial cave in the Beth Shean Valley. While it is the largest of its type ever to have come to light, it nonetheless fits in well with the other basalt bowls from the Early Canaanite period in Eretz Israel. These bowls are characterized by one remarkable feature – their perfectly round bodies rising from square bases.

The basalt industry, which owing to the hardness of the stone required great skill, dates back to Chalcolithic times. Even then craftsmen had already achieved impressive results. The 'guilds' of the Chalcolithic period may very well have continued into the Canaanite period.

On two of the vessel's four sides, an ibex is carved in relief. The ibex was one of the most common animals in Eretz Israel, decorating numerous objects from the Chalcolithic period. This bowl was undoubtedly used in a cultic ceremony, perhaps of a funerary nature, as it was found in a burial cave.

Statuette of a Calf and Model Shrine

Tel Ashkelon
Middle Canaanite period
First half of 2nd millennium BCE
Statuette: Bronze with silver plate
H 10.5 cm (4 in) L 11 cm (4 ¼ in)
Model shrine: Pottery
H 25 cm (9 ¾ in) W 12 cm (4 ¾ in)
IAA

During the Middle Canaanite period Ashkelon was a pre-eminent port city on the eastern Mediterranean coast. Recent excavations of a temple at Tel Ashkelon uncovered a pottery model shrine in which a silver-plated bronze statuette of a calf had been placed. This model shrine and calf are the only instance known in which the statue of an animal was actually discovered within its shrine.

Literary sources reveal that the bull and calf were attributes of *El* and *Baal*, the chief gods of the Ugaritic and Canaanite pantheons. Syrian cylinder-seals of this period show *Baal Hadad*, the storm god, riding on the back of a bull. It would be natural for the storm god to be worshipped at the temple in Ashkelon since his blessing would be especially important to a city situated so close to the sea, with its economy greatly dependent on the climate.

The bull and the calf are later mentioned in the Bible in the stories of the golden calf made during the Israelites' exodus from Egypt (Exodus 32), and Jeroboam's commissioning of two golden calves to be placed in the temples of Dan and Bethel (1 Kings 12) which the prophets vehemently condemned as a symbol of idolatry.

Canaanite Fertility Figurine

Near Tel Miqne (Revadim)
Late Canaanite period
13th century BCE
Clay
H 11 cm (4 ¼ in)
IAA

This unique, mold-made clay figurine is decorated in relief
with a wealth of detail, which simultaneously depicts the
outside and inside of a woman's body.

The two arms create a roundish frame (possibly a
womb), in which twin embryos can be seen, each one clutch-
ing at a breast. In the lower part of the figurine is a rather
graphic depiction of the woman opening her vagina in prepa-
ration for childbirth. Each of her thighs is embellished with
the 'tree of life' motif. The figurine may have been used as a
charm by women in childbirth. In Canaanite texts from
Ugarit, *Ashera*, the wife of the god *El*, is mentioned as
mother of seventy divine sons. She is also called *Qudshu* –
goddess of fertility, and *Rahmay* – the one of the womb. As
Rahmay she appears in an Ugaritic myth giving birth to a
pair of 'gracious and beautiful gods.' It is possible that the
figurine illustrates this mythological tale.

Incense Stands

Tel Nami, near Haifa
Late Canaanite period
13th century BCE
Bronze
Average height: 25 cm (9 ¾ in)
IAA

The site of Tel Nami, located on a peninsula some 15 km south of Haifa, functioned as a harbor from the beginning of the 2nd millennium BCE. Excavations carried out in the sand dunes east of the peninsula revealed a large Late Canaanite cemetery, which yielded a rich variety of objects reflecting the cultures of the Eastern Mediterranean basin. Among them were three bronze incense stands, one of which has three opium poppy pods hanging like bells from the bottom of the bowl. An imported vessel from Cyprus, which still contains traces of opium, proves that the opium poppy was known in Eretz Israel in the Late Canaanite period. The second stand is in the shape of a woman (caryatid) carrying an incense bowl on her head. The third is decorated with petals. All three consist of a base, made of cast bronze sections soldered together, and a bowl, hammered from bronze sheet and attached with bronze nails.

Combinations of incense, such as myrrh and frankincense, were originally placed in the bowls of these stands. The use of such burners is illustrated by an Egyptian relief depicting a Canaanite ship on which a merchant can be seen offering incense to the gods in order to ensure a safe voyage.

Anthropoid Sarcophagi

Cemetery at Deir el-Balah
Late Canaanite period
14th–13th century BCE
Pottery
Average height: 190 cm (6ft 3in)

South of Gaza city, at Deir el-Balah, over fifty pottery sarcophagi were unearthed from a large, ancient cemetery. Located near the sea, the site had been protected from plunder by heavy sand dunes.

The sarcophagi were fashioned by hand using the coil technique, the method employed for creating large vessels. They were then fired, with their lids, in an open fire. The lids were later refired in kilns located nearby, and this accounts for the color discrepancy between lids and bases.

Similar cemeteries were also discovered in the vicinity of the Nile Delta. The mummy-coffin shape of the Gaza sarcophagi shows clear signs of Egyptian influence. The lids bear depictions of mummy-like figures, indicating the face, wig, arms, and hands of the deceased. Many of the faces have a small beard on the chin, perhaps symbolizing the beard of Osiris – the Egyptian god of death, into whose realm the deceased was about to enter.

The bodies of the dead, usually more than one, were laid unembalmed in the coffin, along with funerary gifts which included pottery food bowls. If the deceased was wealthy, elaborate jewelry and vessels made of stone and bronze were also added.

Necklace strung with beads and pendants

Apparently from the cemetery at Deir el-Balah
Late Canaanite period
14th century BCE
Spacer 1.8 × 2.1cm (¾ × 1 in)
Carnelian, gold and jasper
Gift of Tamar and Teddy Kollek

The beads and pendants on this necklace have been restrung. Most of them are similar to the type of jewelry found in the anthropoid sarcophagi of the cemetery near Deir el-Balah, hence the assumption that they originated there. The site at Deir el-Balah contained one of the richest finds of jewelry from the Canaanite period. Most of the ornaments were probably made by a local artist, although with a strong Egyptian influence. For example, the cornflower-shaped pendant or the bead in the form of an Egyptian scarab.

Of the 237 items in the necklace, of special interest is the unique gold spacer (a spacer is a plaque which separates the threads on which the beads are strung – in this case only two threads). The spacer bears the face of the Egyptian goddess, Hathor, the goddess of love and joy. It is made of gold and decorated with a design made in the repoussé technique. While spacers of this kind are familiar from the hoard of jewelry found at Bet Shemesh, spacers decorated with a woman's face are known only from a later period, from Cyprus. This plaque is particularly beautiful and well-made, significantly enhancing the collection of jewelry Deir el-Balah.

Gold Jewelry

Provenance unknown
Late Canaanite period
13th century BCE
Shown actual size
Gift of Jonathan Rosen, New York

This important and rich collection of gold jewelry was made in Canaan in the Late Bronze Age, with gold from mines in the eastern desert of Egypt or from Nubia. The difference in color is due to the addition of other elements, such as silver, since ancient gold work was seldom pure gold. Gold has a high degree of malleability and a fairly high melting-point, allowing craftsmen to heat a piece to the glowing point, to create or add designs without risking damage.

Relatively simple tools were effective in working this soft metal even in a cold state. Hammers, bronze chisels and puncheons, and various tracers of bone or ivory were commonly used. These would be applied to sheet-gold and gold wire. Sheet-gold was made by hammering a small bar, and it was finished by the sheet being beaten between two pieces of leather.

Wire was also made from sheet-gold. A narrow strip was cut from a thin sheet, twisted spirally, then rolled between two polished stones or perhaps plates of bronze. Granulation, another ancient technique, involves applying tiny granules of gold to the surface in order to create an optically pleasing, textured exterior in contrast to the smooth surrounding areas.

Although Late Canaanite jewelry was receptive to various influences, principally from Egypt, the particular character of this jewelry is mainly to be found in the distinctive Canaanite style.

'Ashdoda' Figurine
Ashdod
Israelite period
12th century BCE
Pottery
H 17 cm (6 ¾ in)
IAA

Excavations at Ashdod, one of the five major Philistine cities, have yielded a rich assemblage of figurative art from the Early Iron Age. Among the finds was a female figurine nick-named 'Ashdoda' by its excavators.

This hand-modeled, schematically-rendered figurine represents a seated woman merging with the throne on which she sits. The long neck with its bird-like head rests on the straight back of the four-legged throne. The black and red decoration on a background of white slip is characteristic of Philistine pottery.

This type of stylized female figurine is unknown in the local repertoire of representational art in both the Late Canaanite and Early Israelite periods. Its prototype is to be found in the Mycenaean seated female figurines believed to represent the 'Mother Goddess.' It seems likely that this 'Ashdoda,' found next to a cult place, represented a votive offering.

Model Shrine
Vicinity of Mt Nebo, Transjordan
Israelite period
9th–8th century BCE
Pottery
H 29 cm (11 ½ in) W 31 cm (12 ¼ in)
Gift of the Reuben and Edith Hecht Trust, Haifa

This gracefully executed model shrine consists of a small cubiculum attached to a tall façade. Rectangular in shape, the cubiculum's floor extends forward to produce a threshold. The two freestanding columns flanking the entrance to the cubiculum are surmounted by capitals decorated with a row of drooping petals, a popular motif in the art and architecture of the period. Large rectangular blocks rest on the capitals, and above them is a broad rectangular entablature.

Models of houses from Mesopotamia and the Levant, some bearing symbols attributed to specific deities, date back to the third millennium BCE, and are believed to represent the houses of deities. Sometimes they contain a figure in the cubiculum, presumably that of the deity. They were probably presented to the gods in their temples, or kept at home for private cultic use, or placed in tombs.

This model shrine, found in Transjordan, and similar ones from Eretz Israel no doubt reflect the Canaanite-Phoenician tradition of temple architecture. The large façade recalls the entrance to Solomon's Temple which, according to the Bible, also had two freestanding bronze columns, referred to as 'Yakhin' and 'Boaz' (1 Kings 7:21).

Cult Stand with Musicians

Ashdod
Israelite period
Late 11th–early 10th century BCE
Pottery
H 34.7 cm (13 ¾ in), Diameter at base 14.2 cm (5 ½ in)
IAA

This unusual pottery stand, found in the excavations of
Ashdod, consists of a deep carinated bowl mounted on a tall
cylindrical pedestal. Five figures of musicians stand in rectangular 'windows' cut into the pedestal. Four of the figures are
modeled in the round, with the lower parts of their bodies
merging into the vessel. The fifth figure is larger than the
others and cut out of the wall of the pedestal.

Each of the figures plays a musical instrument – one
strikes the cymbals, two play double pipes, a fourth performs
on a stringed instrument, probably a lyre, and a fifth shakes a
tambourine.

Above the row of musicians runs a procession of three
crudely executed animals, partly incised and partly worked in
relief. The stand bears traces of white slip, and a lattice pattern
in red and black is visible on the bowl. This reflects a mixture
of Mycenaean and Canaanite decorative traditions, characteristic of Philistine ceramics.

Musicians played an important role both in court life and
in cultic ceremonies throughout the ancient Near East.
Although the depiction of musicians was common in the
Levant, this is the only known instance of an orchestra
modeled in the round.

Striding Sphinx

Samaria
Israelite period
9th–8th century BCE
Ivory
H 7.5 cm (3 in)

The art of ivory carving had a long tradition in the ancient Near East and was a specialty of the Phoenician artists. Ivory was as highly valued as gold or silver and this plaque probably once decorated splendid wooden furniture in the palace of the northern Israelite kings in Samaria.

The 'ivory palace' that King Ahab built in Samaria is mentioned in the Bible (1 Kings 22 : 39). To the prophet Amos writing a century later, the 'ivory beds' symbolized the corrupt society of the Samarian aristocracy that he so abhorred (Amos 6 : 4). This new life-style may well have been introduced by Queen Jezebel, Ahab's wife and the daughter of the king of Tyre.

The plaque was discovered together with a large group of ivories. It represents a winged sphinx striding through a thicket of lotus blosssoms. Most of the Samaria ivories are carved in the so-called 'Phoenician' style which is marked by a preference for Egyptian motifs.

Ivory Pomegranate

Jerusalem
Israelite period
Mid-8th century BCE
H 4.3 cm (1 ¾ in) Diameter 2.1 cm (¾ in)
Acquired with a donation by a Friend of Culture in Israel, Basel, Switzerland

This beautifully carved ivory pomegranate has a rounded body, with a small round hole at its bottom, indicating that it was probably mounted on a rod. Around the shoulder of the pomegranate is a carefully incised inscription in early Hebrew characters, part of which is broken off, which reads: 'qodes kohanim l-beyt [yahwe]h'. 'Sacred donation for the priests of (in) the House of [Yahwe]h'. 'House of Yahweh' most probably refers to the Temple in Jerusalem.

The juicy pomegranate fruit with its multitudinous seeds was a popular symbol of fertility and fecundity in ancient times, and was widely used in the sacred and secular art of various cultures throughout the ancient Near East. The pomegranate is frequently mentioned in the Bible and is counted among the seven kinds of fruit with which the Land of Israel is blessed (Deuteronomy 8 : 8). It was a favorite motif in the Temple of Solomon, and decorated the capitals of the two freestanding columns at the entrance to the Temple (1 Kings 7 : 21).

This thumb-sized pomegranate is believed to be the only known relic from Solomon's Temple in Jerusalem. It probably served as the decorative head of a ceremonial scepter used by the Temple priests during one of the ceremonies.

The 'House of David' Inscribed on a Victory Stele

Tel Dan
Israelite period
9th century BCE
Basalt
H 32 cm (12 ½ in) W 22 cm (8 ¾ in)
H 20 cm (8 in) W 14 cm (5 ½ in)
H 9 cm (3 ½ in) W 10 cm (4 in)
IAA

This fragmentary monumental inscription from the First Temple period, discovered in the excavations of the ancient city of Dan, is the only extra-biblical reference to the Davidic dynasty ever to have come to light. The large fragment was uncovered in 1993. Later the two additional pieces were found, shedding new light on the original interpretation of the inscription.

The inscription appears to have been a victory stele erected by Hazael king of Aram. The inscription boasts of the king's many battles, in which he killed "seventy kings," among them Yehoram king of Israel and Ahazyahu king of Judah. While this corresponds to the biblical account in II Chronicles 22, which describes the war between Hazael and the kings of Israel and Judah, Yehoram and Ahazyahu, it contradicts the version in II Kings 9, according to which the two allied kings were murdered by Yehu.

Written in Aramaic, the stele was engraved in alphabetic script, the words separated by dots, on a large stone that had been smoothed for writing. It was smashed in ancient times, and its fragments were found in secondary use. Based upon the location of the fragments at the site, it seems that the stele had already been destroyed by the early 8th century BCE. It was probably smashed by Yehoash, Yehu's grandson, who battled the Arameans and struck Ben Haddad son of Hazael three times.

'Astarte' Figurines
Judah
Israelite period
8th–early 6th century BCE
Pottery
H 12.5 – 17 cm (5 – 6 ¾ in)
IAA
On loan from the Reifenberg family, Jerusalem

Clay figurines of this type were found, mainly in private dwellings, in settlements throughout Judah. Their upper parts were designed in the shape of a woman's body with over-sized breasts, often supported by the hands. The heads of many of the figurines were made in a mold, some with wig-like head-dresses and others with conical hats. In the so-called 'bird-faced' Astarte figurines, the noses were formed by pinching the soft clay between the fingers.

The figurines were regarded as having magical properties and were kept as household cultic amulets to enhance fertility and ensure abundance. They are commonly identified with the well-known Canaanite deities *Astarte* or *Ashera*. The use of such objects were vehemently condemned by the prophets of Israel. Indeed, in excavations of the City of David in Jerusalem, more than two thousand cultic figurines were found, all of which had been smashed to bits. This may have been connected with the religious reform of Josiah in the late /th century BCE, the primary aim of which was the abolition of idol worship and establishment of the centrality of the Temple in Jerusalem.

Phoenician Jugs
Akhziv
Israelite period
9th–7th century BCE
Pottery
H 19–29 cm (7 ½ – 11 ½ in)
IAA

These vessels were uncovered in the excavation of two cemeteries at Akhziv, a site on the northern coastal strip of modern Israel. This region was home to the Phoenicians, political and economic allies of the Israelites and best known for their pursuit of maritime trade.

Noted for their precise and clean-cut form, these Phoenician jugs are also distinguished by a highly burnished surface of red slip. They fall into two categories: the first is characterized by its long handle and trefoil mouth which clearly imitates in pottery the bronze and silver vessels found at Phoenician sites. The jugs of the second type have a long and narrow neck, a small handle, and a broad, splaying mushroom like rim. The body has an angular shoulder and widens towards the bottom, imitating, no doubt, the most popular Israelite jug – the decanter. This last group thus represents a cross between the pottery-making tradition of the Phoenicians and that of their Israelite neighbors.

Vessels similar to the 'Akhziv group' have been found along the Mediterranean coast wherever a Phoenician settlement or trading post existed – on the coast of Phoenicia (now Lebanon and northern Israel), in North Africa, and in Spain.

Balustrade

Ramat Rachel
Israelite period
Late 8th–early 7th century BCE
Limestone
H 37 cm (14 ½ in) L 125 cm (4ft 1 in)
IAA

Little has survived of royal architecture and decorative art from cities of the Israelite and Judaean monarchies. However, some sites have yielded the remains of architectural ornamentation, of which this window balustrade is one of the finest examples. It was uncovered in the ruins of a Judaean palace at Ramat Rachel, situated near Jerusalem.

The balustrade consists of a row of identical colonettes, joined to the capitals by metal clamps inserted into holes, and surmounted by a lintel, which has not survived.

The design of the voluted capitals, derived from the stylized palm-tree motif, is a scaled-down version of the monumental Proto-Aeolic capitals that often crowned door-jambs or pilasters.

The architecture at Ramat Rachel and other royal centers reflects Phoenician influence, which began in the time of Solomon, who brought in Phoenician builders and artisans for the construction of the Temple and the royal palace. Elements of this style were incorporated into local traditions, thus creating a distinctive architectural style that became the hallmark of the Judaean and Israelite royal cities.

Inscribed Hebrew Seals

Various sites and unknown provenance
Israelite period
8th–6th century BCE
H 0.5 – 2 cm (¼ – ¾ in)
Gifts of Norman P. Schenker Collection of Hebrew Seals;
Dr Reuben Hecht; Esther Lamport; Shoshana Richman

In ancient times, when only a small minority of people could read and write, the seal impression was used as a mark of ownership and as a means of authenticating documents, just as the signature is used today. The seals are usually made of semi precious stone or hard limestone, and a few are carved from bone, glass, bronze, or silver.

Archaeological evidence shows that pottery vessels containing wine, oil, or valuables were closed with clay stoppers which were then stamped with a seal. Papyrus documents were rolled up, tied with a string, and secured with a lump of wet clay on which a seal was impressed (*bulla*). Great importance is ascribed to the seal in the Bible: it was the symbol of the king's authority, appearing on all royal edicts (1 Kings 21:8).

Seal inscriptions were carved in mirror writing, so as to appear correctly in the seal impression. The seals bear the name of the owner, generally with the father's name appended, used as a sort of 'family name.' Some seals also bear an ornamental design. A particularly important group of seals is inscribed with the names of ministers or other royal functionaries, many bearing titles or names that are mentioned in the Bible.

'House of God' Ostracon

Arad
Israelite period
Early 6th century BCE
Pottery
H 6.2 cm (2 ½ in) W 4.3 cm (1 ¾ in)
IAA

This ostracon (potsherd inscribed in ink) was written by a professional scribe in the ancient Hebrew script. It was found in Arad, a frontier fortress of the Judaean monarchy which also served as the administrative center of the region during the ninth–sixth century BCE. Written in the early sixth century BCE, this letter is among the earliest epigraphic references to the Temple in Jerusalem.

The letter is addressed to Elyashib, probably the commander of the Arad fortress. It was sent, presumably from Jerusalem, by one of his subordinates whose name is unknown, who was in Jerusalem on a mission of inquiry about a certain person. Elyashib is informed that all is well with the man about whom he had inquired: the individual is in the 'House of God' where he probably found refuge. 'To my lord Elyashib, may the Lord seek your welfare . . . and as to the matter which you command me – it is well; he is in the House of God.' Elyashib is also asked to supply some goods to someone named Shemaryahu and to an unknown person referred to as the 'Kerosite.'

The Priestly Benediction on a Silver Amulet

Jerusalem, Ketef Hinnom
Israelite period
Late 7th century BCE
H 3.9 cm (1 ½ in) W 1.1 cm (½ in)
IAA

This silver plaque, along with another silver scroll found next to it, together constitute the earliest known fragments of a biblical text. They predate the oldest biblical scrolls from Qumran by over 300 years. Inscribed in ancient Hebrew script and rolled up into a tiny scroll, both the scroll and its companion were uncovered in a burial cave at Ketef Hinnom. The inscription was written in the cursive style by a non-professional scribe.

The inscription was very difficult to decipher as it was very shallowly incised by a sharp instrument, and there are also many cracks and breaks in the plaque. Its lower part is most striking, being an abbreviated version of the biblical verses in Numbers 6:24–26: 'The Lord bless you and protect you. The Lord make his face to shine upon you and be gracious to you. The Lord lift up his countenance to you and give you peace.' This text, which forms part of the Prayer Book to this day, is known as the Priestly Benediction.

Menorah

Synagogue of Hammath by Tiberias
Byzantine period
4th–5th century CE
Limestone
H 46 cm (1 ft 6 in)

The *menorah*, the seven-branched candelabrum, was a national and religious symbol as early as the end of the Second Temple period. After the destruction of the Temple in Jerusalem (70 CE) the motif seems to have taken on an apotropaic connotation (was believed to have the power of warding off evil). The symbol began to be widely used in the third century and has continued in popularity ever since. *Menorahs* were drawn, incised or fashioned in mosaics; they also appear in relief carved on marble or made in molds.

The *menorah* from Hammath by Tiberias, excavated in 1921, is unique in that it has special hollows on top for holding oil lamps, probably small beakers of glass. This is the only stone *menorah* presently known which was made to be used. The unfinished rear and sides of the stone may indicate that it was placed against the wall. This rare *menorah* is well designed and has been made according to a recognized pattern. The branches, carved with alternating pomegranates and flowers, are probably inspired by the biblical description of the *menorah* in the sanctuary, 'with a knop and a flower in one branch.' (Exodus 25:33)

Gold-Glass Bases

Roman Catacombs (?)
4th century CE
Glass and gold leaf
Diameters 10, 11.7 cm (4, 4 ½ in)
Gift of Mr Jacob Michael in memory of his wife Erna Sondheimer-Michael
Previously in the collection of Castle Goluchow

Gold-glass bases were first discovered in catacombs in Rome in the seventeenth century, embedded in the walls as a signal to the family of the deceased. These small disks are in fact the bases of bowls or cups. They were prepared by a complicated process in which gold leaf was glued onto a glass disk, and the design incised into the gold. A glass bubble was then blown on top of the gold leaf, thus encasing it between two layers of glass.

Of the hundreds of known bases, many bear Christian motifs, while some are decorated with biblical or general scenes. Only about a dozen have Jewish features, incorporating most of the characteristic motifs of Jewish art in the late Roman and Byzantine periods, commemorating the Temple, its ritual appurtenances, and its ceremonies.

Here, an upper register contains the Holy Ark or Torah Ark, its open doors revealing three shelves of scrolls shown in profile, while in the lower register there is a seven-branched candelabrum (*menorah*) in one base and two *menorot* in the other base. Additional symbols include a palm branch (*lulav*), a citron (*etrog*), a ram's horn (*shofar*) and an amphora. The Greek inscription written in Latin characters in the complete base, above the frame, reads: 'Pie Zesis Elares' (Drink, live, Elares).

Jewish Sarcophagus (below)

Beth She'arim
Roman period
First half of the 4th century CE
Lead
L 1.96 m (6 ft 5 in)
IAA

Lead coffins, popular in the eastern Mediterranean countries, were cast in sheets on wet sand imprinted with large stamps bearing various designs. The mold was good for only one casting, but the stamps were re-used, thus producing variations in the same decoration on different coffins. Here, the Jewish theme is represented by the characteristic motifs of Jewish art of the period: the seven-branched candelabrum (*menorah*), the ram's horn (*shofar*) and incense *shovel* on one side, and the palm branch (*lulav*) and citrus fruit (*etrog*) on the other, are placed in rectangular frames under an arch supported on two columns.

The coffin was found in the necropolis of Beth She'arim in the north of the country together with four other lead sarcophagi in single cist graves, dug on a steep slope. The style indicates that this coffin seems to have originated in a workshop in Sidon. The coffins may have served to carry Jews from Sidon for burial at Beth She'arim, an important Jewish necropolis in the late Roman period.

Jewish Ossuaries

Jerusalem
Second Temple period
1st century BCE – 1st century CE
Stone
Sarcophagus: H 51.5 cm (1ft 8 ¼ in) L 189.5 cm (6 ft 2 ½ in)
Largest ossuary: H 68.6 cm (27 in) L 84 cm (33 in)
Smallest ossuary: H 43 cm (17 in) L 58 cm (23 in)

Stonework was a well-developed craft in Jerusalem of the late Second Temple period. The monuments erected above the tombs in the Valley of Jehoshaphat and in northern Jerusalem superbly demonstrate a distinctive local style.

In Judaea during this period, besides burial in elaborate sarcophagi, it was customary to practice secondary burial using stone caskets, called ossuaries. The deceased was laid to rest in a niche of a burial cave for a year. After the flesh decayed, the bones were collected into an ossuary which was placed in the cave.

The ossuaries were made of soft limestone, their length determined by the longest human bone, the femur. Ornamentation was often a six-petaled rosette, set in a geometric border, or stylized architectural motifs such as columns, pillars, arches and gates, in an attempt to reproduce the façades of tombs and buildings in Jerusalem. Some bear inscriptions with the name of the deceased in Greek, Aramaic, or Hebrew.

Roman Jewelry

Nahal Raqafot, Jerusalem
Roman period
First half of 3rd century CE
Gold inset with pearls and semiprecious stones
Ring: L of seal 2.5 cm (1 in)
Earring: H 4.1 cm (1 ½ in)
Brooch: H 5.3 cm (2 in)
IAA

This jewelry was found in a rock-cut tomb in Jerusalem, which contained a decorated lead sarcophagus. The ring, one of two found inside the coffin, has an elliptical loop and a flattened oval bezel set with a blue onyx intaglio showing a cuirassed elephant, a familiar subject from the public shows of Rome, where this intaglio may have been made.

The earring consists of a rosette soldered to a horizontal bar of juxtaposed animals, hammered from sheet-gold. A baroque pearl is enclosed in the rosette. Attached to the bar are three pendants, each composed of a garnet in a gold bezel setting from which hangs a baroque pearl.

The brooch consists of a sheet-gold oval frame enclosing an onyx cameo of four light and dark layers showing the bust of a helmeted Minerva, her nose chipped in antiquity, holding a round shield with a gorgoneion in the center. Eight bezel settings in the frame hold two emeralds and five garnets. The brooch's style suggests that it probably originated in the Southern Russian steppes and may have been brought to Jerusalem by a Roman soldier. The earring and brooch, found on top of the coffin, were probably torn off mourners' garments at the time of burial as an expression of grief, and placed on the coffin as an offering to the deceased.

Statue of a Young Satyr

Caesarea
Roman copy of an Hellenistic original from the 3rd century
BCE
Marble
H 132 cm (4ft 4in) W 58 cm (1ft 11 in)
IAA

This freestanding figure of a young satyr was found at
Caesarea Maritima, the seat of the Roman governors during
Herodian times. It is an excellent example of the Greco-
Roman aesthetic tradition, prevalent in the country since the
Hellenistic period. Almost life-size, the satyr is cross-legged,
twisting his upper body as if dancing. Not entirely drunk, but
perhaps fatigued from dancing, he has placed his musical
instrument, a syrinx (Pan's pipes), on a tree trunk, and is
looking down at a small panther at his feet. His round grin-
ning face is clearly non-human: he has prominent cheeks, a
flattened nose, eyebrows scowling in a deep frown, small eyes
and a short tail.

Young satyrs and old Silenus figures were popular motifs
in Greek art as early as the Archaic period, but the earliest
freestanding sculptures can be dated to the fourth century
BCE, when the masters Praxiteles and Lysippos first made
statues on this theme. A development of the theme during
this period was the dancing satyrs with crossed legs.

Various other Hellenistic types, widely copied during
Roman times, were produced from these examples. The
panther is included since he is the sacred animal of Dionysos,
the satyr's patron.

Statue of Hadrian

Tell Shalem, Beth Shean Valley
Roman period
2nd century CE
Bronze
Head: H 37 cm (14 ½ in)
Breastplate: H 52 cm (1 ft 8 ½ in)
IAA

This bronze statue was found by chance, some 12 km (7 ½ miles) south of Beth Shean (Scythopolis), at a site that was once a camp of the Sixth Roman Legion. It was apparently set up there, as was the custom in camps of the Roman legions.

The statue is one in a series of representations of standing cuirassed emperors, most of them carved in marble. Of the many bronze statues that must have existed, only a few heads have been preserved. Hence the importance of this find, which is further enhanced by its high aesthetic quality. The head, cast in one piece and found intact, is one of the finest portraits of Hadrian. The breastplate depicts a mythological battle, a subject not often seen on cuirassed statues.

Although Hadrian is regarded as one of the most enlightened of the Roman emperors, his attitude toward Judaea and the Jews was hostile, and his oppressive measures provoked the outbreak of the Bar-Kokhba Revolt (132-135 CE).

Head of Athena

Beth Shean
Roman period
2nd century CE
Marble from the island of Thassos
H 55 cm (1ft 10 in) W 29 cm (11 ½ in)
IAA

The Greek goddess Athena, Minerva in the Roman pantheon, was the daughter of Zeus, king of all gods. Goddess of war, patron of the arts and artisans, she is traditionally portrayed wearing a helmet and holding a spear and shield. Unearthed at the north end of Beth Shean (Scythopolis), this sculpture probably adorned one of the magnificent public buildings or temples that stood in the center of this Roman city. The helmeted head is all that remains of a marble statue that once reached a height of 2.5 m (8 ft).

With head tilted somewhat to the left, full lips, and almond-shaped eyes whose details would probably have been painted, she exhibits an impressive demeanor. Her wavy hair is parted in the middle and gathered at the back, exposing a good portion of her ears. Two wavy locks flank the thick neck and traces of red paint are visible in the grooves of the hair.

The schematic and rough design of the helmet and hair contrasts with the smoothly-carved and naturalistic rendering of the face, as if the work was unfinished. This difference in finish is typical of the second century CE. The sculpture is a Roman copy of a Greek prototype, probably carved at one of the sculpture centers in the eastern Mediterranean and imported to Beth Shean.

Mosaic Pavement

Kissufim
Byzantine period
576-578 CE
Stone and glass
H 130 cm (4 ft 3 in) W 153 cm (5 ft 3 in)
IAA

Uncovered in the fields of Kibbutz Kissufim in the western Negev, this pavement once formed part of the mosaic floor of a sixth-century Byzantine church. Although there is a tradition of mosaic work going back to the Hellenistic period (second century BCE), the craft flourished and achieved a wide popularity in the Byzantine period (fourth to seventh centuries CE), when mosaics were used to pave synagogues, churches, and secular buildings.

The two scenes reproduced here are of a lioness with her cub and a horseman spearing a leopard. The Greek inscription above the horseman scene reads: 'The deeds of Alexander,' perhaps referring to Alexander the Great, whose exploits were renowned throughout the ancient world. An inscription in the mosaic indicates the exact date of the completion of this pavement in 578 CE, during the reign of the Byzantine Emperor Justin II (565-578 CE).

The Kissufim mosaic, displaying an excellence of design and execution, is unparalleled among the many mosaic pavements known in Israel. The western Negev, where it was found, is rich in contemporaneous mosaic floors. Literary sources also mention magnificent wall mosaics in Gaza, which was apparently an important center for mosaic workshops of different styles in the fifth and sixth centuries CE.

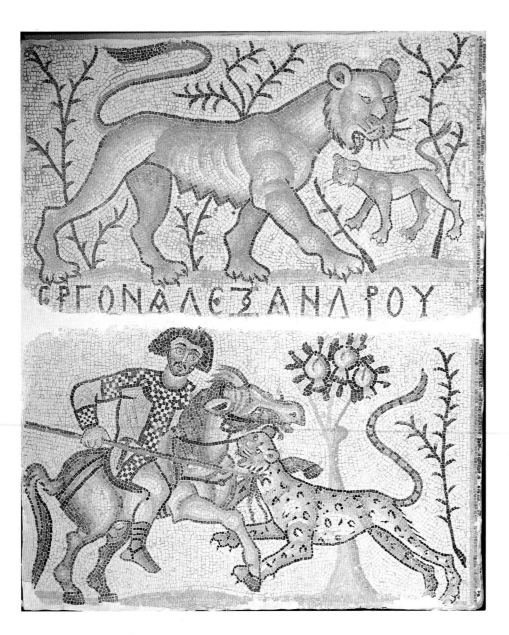

דויד

King David Playing the Lyre

Mosaic from the floor of the ancient synagogue at Gaza
Byzantine period
6th century CE
H 3 m (9 ft 10 in) W 1.90 m (6 ft 3 in)
Courtesy of the staff officer of archaeology in Gaza

This mosaic floor once decorated a large, early sixth-century synagogue in Gaza. An inscription states that the floor was donated in 508-9 CE by two brothers, both of whom were merchants.

Two aspects of King David are incorporated here – that of the King, and that of the Sweet Singer of Israel. Executed with great skill, the crowned figure sits on a royal throne, a stool at his feet, playing the lyre. Written in Hebrew near his head is the name 'David.'

The animals gathering before David suggest an affiliation with Orpheus, the mythological hero who enchanted wild animals with his music. He was usually depicted as a shepherd playing to animals in a pastoral setting. Orpheus, popular in Roman and Byzantine art, symbolized the hope for redemption and the struggle against the forces of the underworld.

Music is the element common to David and Orpheus, and in this unusual rendering, the traits of both heroes were combined to produce a crowned figure of King David, appearing as a haloed Byzantine emperor, charming the animals with his music.

Years after the 1960s excavations at the site were completed, part of the figurine was damaged and the head was skillfully restored in the Israel Museum laboratories.

Three Glass Bowls and their Packing

Cave of the Letters, Judaean Desert
Roman period
2nd century CE
Dia 33.8 cm, 14.5 cm, 12.9 cm (13 ¼ in, 5 ¾ in, 5 in)
IAA

During the second war of the Jews against the Romans in 132-135 CE, a group of people escaped from the Dead Sea settlement of Ein Gedi to find temporary refuge in a neighboring cave, where they ultimately perished. When the site was excavated in 1961, public and private documents, everyday objects and personal effects taken by these people in flight were discovered.

One parcel, consisting of palm fibers tied with a cord, contained a glass bowl and two small plates, remarkably well-preserved. The bowl was made in a mold and the facets and decoration of the rim were carved using the engraver's wheel. The vessels were highly polished to a sheen which is still apparent.

Popular during the second half of the first century and the first half of the second century CE, these molded and wheel-cut vessels made of colorless glass were found all over the ancient world, yet probably emanated from one center – the glass workshops of Alexandria in Egypt.

One of the refugees in the cave was an affluent woman named Babatha, whose personal documents were found in a leather pouch. It seems that Babatha was not only a keen businesswoman, but was also concerned about aesthetics, as these beautiful works of art demonstrate.

Finds from the Cave of Letters
Judaean Desert
Roman Period
2nd century CE
IAA

The Cave of Letters is named after the letters of Bar-Kokhba, leader of the Second Revolt, which were found there.

The exceptional climate of the cave and the fact that, because of its inaccessibility, it was hardly disturbed for almost two thousand years preserved not only the letters and a private archive of papyri but also a unique group of uninscribed objects. Many of these objects are made of organic materials which usually perish with time and thus are unparalleled in the archaeological records.

The objects (clockwise from left): A mirror shaped like a ping-pong bat; a basket made of palm fibers; knives; a basket made of willow twigs; keys; wooden bowls and a spoon; and a dome-shaped jewelry box with sliding bottom.

The Great Isaiah Scroll *(detail)*

Chapters 58, 6 – 65,4
Qumran Cave 1
c. 100 BCE
parchment
L 7.34 m (24 ft)

The Isaiah manuscript A is one of seven scrolls discovered in
Qumran in 1947.

In subsequent years some 800 scrolls, most of which are
fragmentary, were found in this region. Of these, 200 are
biblical (i.e. Old Testament) and represent all the books of the
Bible, many in numerous copies, except the book of Esther.

This scroll is the largest, the best preserved and the only
biblical book that survived in its entirety. The 54 columns
contain all 66 chapters, without a marked division between
what modern scholarship regards as First and Second Isaiah.

The scroll is one of the oldest Dead Sea Scrolls — it dates
from about 100 BCE and is older by about 1000 years than the
oldest biblical manuscript known prior to the Qumran finds.

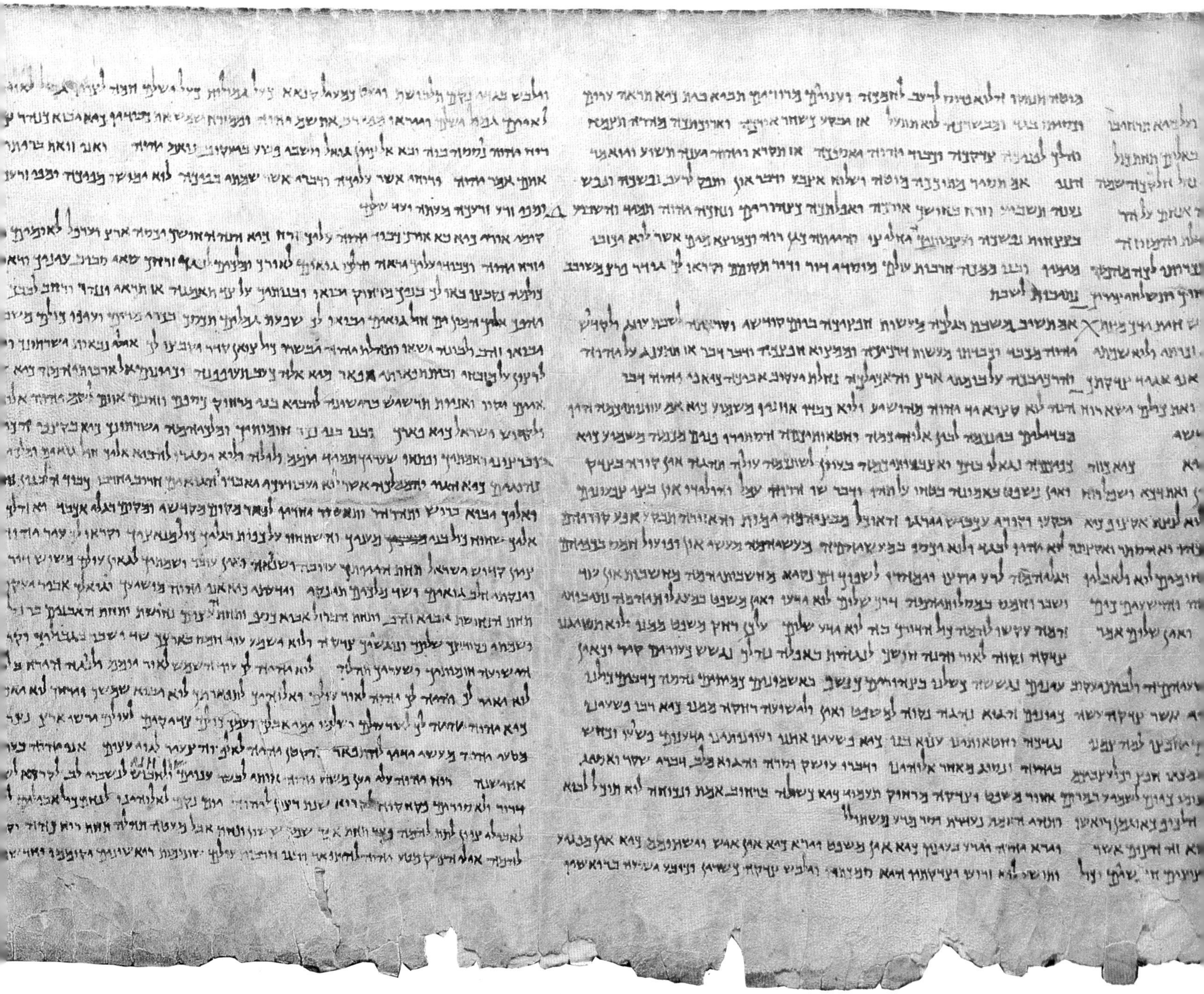

The Temple Scroll (*details*)
Qumran Cave 11
2nd century BCE
parchment
L 8.75 m (28 ft 9 in)

The Temple Scroll is a halachic composition dealing with
laws as they were interpreted by the Dead Sea sect. In it the
Lord speaks in the first person singular and the style tries to
emulate the language of the book of Deuteronomy. However,
despite the author's endeavors, numerous slips betray the
scroll's late origin (probably second century BCE).

Five major subjects are dealt with in the Temple Scroll:
the Temple, the king's statutes, the feasts and their sacrifices,
the Temple City, and laws of purity. More than half the scroll
is devoted to the Temple and the Temple City and hence its
name.

The Temple described is an ideal edifice of gigantic
dimensions that was never built.

The Temple Scroll is the longest Dead Sea Scroll.

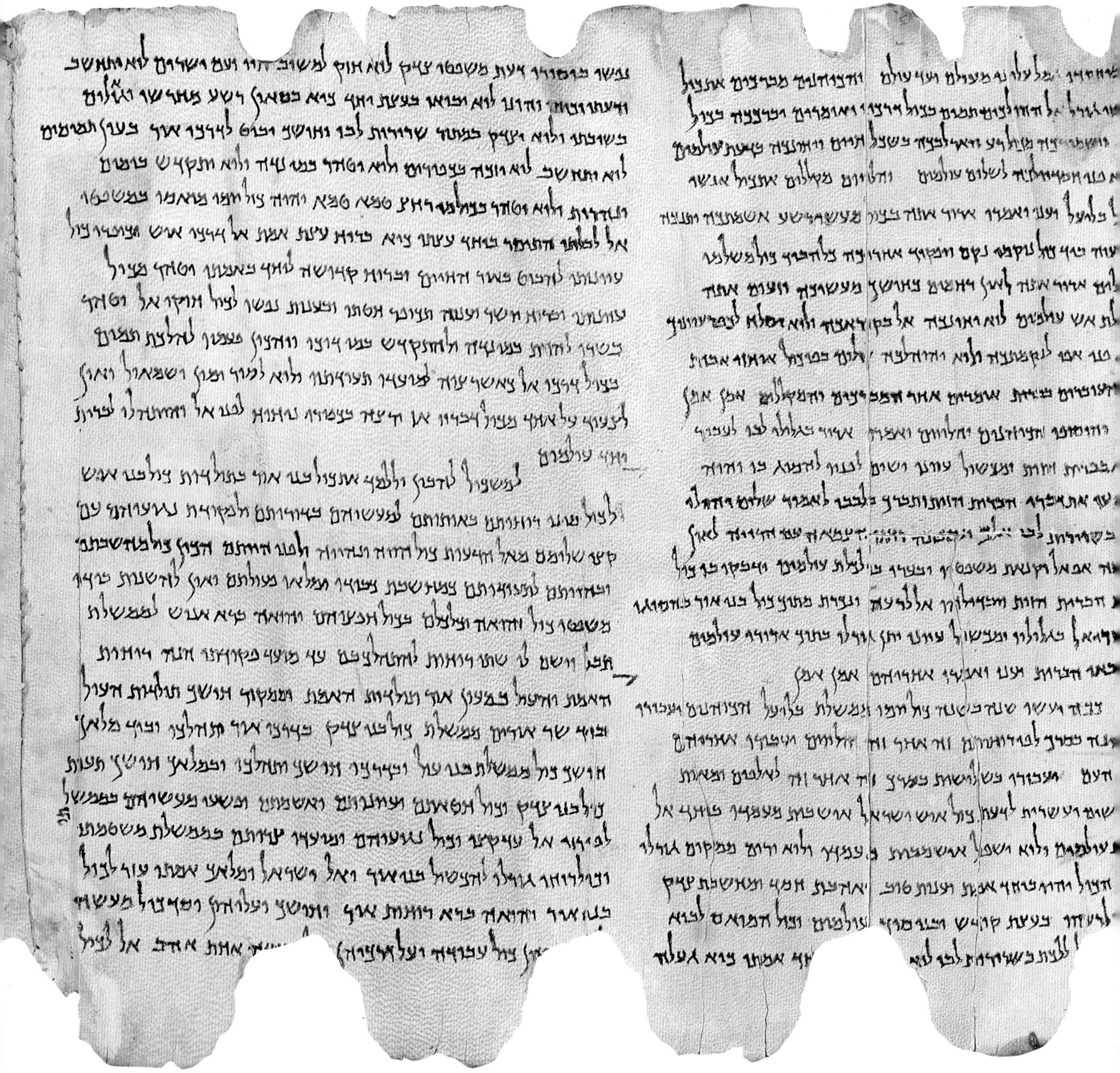

The Manual of Discipline (detail)

Qumran Cave 1
100-75 BCE
parchment
L 1.86 m (6 ft 1 in)

The Manual of Discipline is the book of regulations of the Jewish Community that lived in Qumran on the north-western shore of the Dead Sea from sometime in the first century BCE until 67 CE.

At that time, there existed in Qumran the first monastic community in the Western world that used to '…eat in common, pray in common and deliberate in common.' The scholarly consensus is that these people were Essenes, belonging to one of the three major Jewish religious movements of that period.

The scroll deals with such matters as acceptance of new members, conduct at communal meals and assemblies, punishment for infringements of the rules, etc. A long passage elaborates the Essenes' main theological principle in which they differed from normative Judaism — their belief in predestination.

The caves preserved no less than 11 copies of this book, of which this is the most complete.

Jerusalem Through Coins
Unknown provenance
Silver and bronze
Gifts of Abraham Bromberg, London,
Bessin Family, Ottawa and acquisitions
Diameter 8.5 – 26 mm (¼ – 1 in)

While coins were struck throughout Eretz Israel during
various periods, the mint of Jerusalem was always more
important than other mints, owing to the city's special role.
Many coins were struck in the city, mainly by the Jewish
authorities, from the end of the Persian period and Ptolemaic
rule until the Jewish War against Rome. The coins of
Bar-Kokhba, although not struck in the city itself, were
dedicated to Jerusalem by their inscriptions and symbols.

Even after Jerusalem ceased to be the capital of Israel it
continued to serve as a mint: coins were struck during the
Roman period, when the city was called Aelia Capitolina, and
later, at the end of the Byzantine period, and during the early
Arabic and Crusader periods. Minting in Jerusalem continued
intermittently for some 1600 years, from c.380 BCE to c.1200
CE. During this long period the name of Jerusalem was
changed several times, each time using the current language.
In modern times, after a long cessation, minting was resumed
by the State of Israel, which issued its first coins in 1948.

Yahud (Hebrew)
c. 350 BCE

Yerushalayim (Hebrew)
68 CE

Aelia Capitolina (Latin)
130 CE

Zion (Hebrew)
69 CE

Iliya (Arabic)
660–680 CE

Jerusalem (Latin)
1163–1174

City of the Cross (Latin)
1187 CE

The 'Judea Capta' Coins

Aureus (gold coin)
struck in Lugdunum
unknown provenance
c.70 CE
18 mm (¾ in), 7.26 gm (¼ oz)
Gift of Abraham Bromberg, London

Obv.: Laureate head r. of Vespasian; around inscription:
IMP CAESAR VESPASIANVS AVG TR P ('Imperator Caesar
Vespasianus Augustus, with Tribunician Power')
Rev.: Triumphal quadriga, in exergue: TRIVMP AVG
('Triumph of the Emperor')

The victory of Rome over Judea and the destruction of
Jerusalem in 70 CE were commemorated by the Romans in
various ways. Among these was the minting of numerous
gold, silver, and bronze coins depicting the victorious emperor,
mourning Jewesses, and the trophy – Jewish weapons that
had fallen into Roman hands after the defeat.

Friendship and Alliance between the Jews and the Romans mentioned on a Coin Struck in Sepphoris, Galilee

unknown provenance
Bronze
c.215 CE
31 mm (1 ¼ in), 17.70 gm (½ oz)
Gift of Rena and Robert Lewin, London

Obv.: Bust of Caracalla r., laureate; around, Greek inscription:
('Imperator Augustus Antoninus')
Rev.: Greek inscription in five lines surrounded by wreath:
('Diocaesarea the Holy, City of Shelter, Autonomous,
Loyal (a treaty of) friendship and alliance between the
Holy Council and the Senate of the Roman People')

This important coin has a long inscription which commemorates a pact of friendship between the Senate of the people of Rome, and the Holy Council of Sepphoris. Sepphoris, at that time known as Diocaesarea, was then the seat of the Sanhedrin, the Jewish spiritual leadership.

Many stories are found in Jewish sources concerning the friendship which is said to have existed between a Roman emperor Antoninus and Rabbi Judah the Patriarch, who codified the *Mishna*. According to these stories, the emperor openly admired the Jewish sage and even humbled himself before him. These legends, though obviously intended to glorify and exalt the figure of Rabbi Judah, undoubtedly contain some historical truth. The emperor in question is Caracalla, who is known to have been well-disposed towards the Jews, and to have endeavored to develop the Roman East. Indeed, during his reign, this country progressed and flourished. The coin illustrated here shows that an actual treaty existed between Caracalla and Rabbi Judah, or rather, between the people of Rome and the people of Sepphoris.

The First Hebrew Shekel

unknown provenance
66 CE
Silver
21 mm (¾ in), 14.26 gm (½ oz)
Gift of Reuven Hecht, Haifa

Obv.: Temple vessel surrounded by border of dots; above it, letter Aleph; standing for (Year) 1 = 66 CE; around inscription: 'Shekel of Israel.'
Rev.: Stem in three pomegranates surrounded by border of dots; around inscriptions: 'Jerusalem is holy.'

The Jewish War against Rome began in the summer of 66 CE. Silver shekels and half-shekels were minted in Jerusalem immediately after the outbreak of hostilities. This particular shekel was struck during the late summer/early fall of 66 CE. It is assumed to be the first coin type of the Jewish War, a prototype or pattern shekel for later issues. Only two exemplars of this experimental issue are known.

The first motivation to strike coinage was political: autonomous minting suggested independence. The striking of Hebrew shekels was thus a declaration of both war and political sovereignty. The second motivation was primarily internal and theological; silver shekels were still required for the payment of the annual tribute to the Temple in Jerusalem. It is interesting to note that the shekel was originally not a coin, but a measure of weight as mentioned in the Bible: 'And Abraham hearkened unto Ephron; and Abraham weighed to Ephron the silver, which he had named in the audience of the sons of Heth, four hundred shekels of silver, current money with the merchant.' (Genesis 23:16)

Caesarea Jewelry Hoard
Fatimid period
11th century
gold, silver, semiprecious stones, glass
Vase: H 11cm (4 ¼ in)
IAA

This hoard contains jewels of various types, the finest piece
being a gold necklace consisting of six oval beads of sheet-gold
decorated with granulation. Three other beads, designed in
filigree, are set with small granules, and ten smaller beads
serve as spacers.

A second group, of silver jewelry, is decorated in niello
and includes pendants in the shape of amulet cases and
earrings, and a third group contains a necklace of glass beads
and semiprecious stones.

The jewelry pieces from this hoard differ not only in
material but also in function. While the sole purpose of gold
jewelry was to adorn and establish the social status of the
woman who owned it, her silver jewelry served as a talisman,
worn as protection against the 'evil eye' and other misfortunes.

The hoard dates from the period of the rule of the
Egyptian Fatimid dynasty in the country, and may have been
buried during the Crusader attack on Caesarea in 1101 CE.

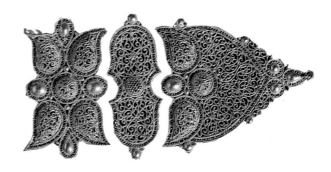

Gold Jewelry
Ashkelon
Fatimid period
11th–12th century
H 6.5 cm (2 ½ in)
IAA

These remarkable jewelry parts may have belonged to a belt
or served as an ornament on a garment. The four pieces
include one terminal element shaped as a pointed arch, one
violin-shaped piece, and two flower-shaped components. It
seems likely that several additional pieces would have been
needed to complete the set. Both the technique and motifs are
characteristic of the Fatimid period. Each line of filigree is
made of two twisted gold wires soldered together along the
face of the piece. The space between the wires was concealed
by granulation, variously sized 'grains' which artistically fill in
the intersections as well as providing additional support for
the whole composition. Along the back, the whole surface is
covered in tiny thin strips which join and reinforce the filigree
threads.

Decorated Jug (Minai Ware)

Iran
12th-13th century
Pottery, overglaze and painted
H 13 cm (5 in)
Gift of Mr and Mrs Edward Warburg, New York

The jug is decorated with four hunters on horseback alternating with a design of five falcons, a princely motif which derived from popular contemporary Persian manuscript illustrations. Four strips of inscriptions, executed in foliated Kufic, are visible on the inner surface, on the outside near the base, and on the handle. Unfortunately, they are indecipherable.

The group of luxury items to which this piece belongs is called 'Minai ware,' after the Persian word for enamel, referring to the highly polished glaze on the figures. The uniqueness of this pottery lies in its richly painted decoration and its extensive palette, often employing as many as seven colors. This jug used six colors: blue and turquoise are under the glaze while the overglaze consists of black, red and brown, with gold used for accented details. Minai pottery pieces are considered some of the most remarkable creations of the Persian ceramic masters of the twelfth and thirteenth centuries.

Zoomorphic Incense Burner

Iran, Khorasan
12th-13th century
Cast bronze, openwork and incised
H 36 cm (14 ¼ in)
Gift of Ayoub Rabenou, Paris

This incense burner is a rare example of those zoomorphic incense burners which have survived intact from the Seljuk period. It consists of three lion-shaped legs fastened to a round container which holds the incense. The handle is formed in the shape of a bird. The various decorative elements – incised palmettes, half-palmettes and interlace – are in openwork technique, thereby allowing the fumes from the burning incense to escape.

Incense burners were very popular during the Seljuk dynasty, and the zoomorphic form was particularly common.

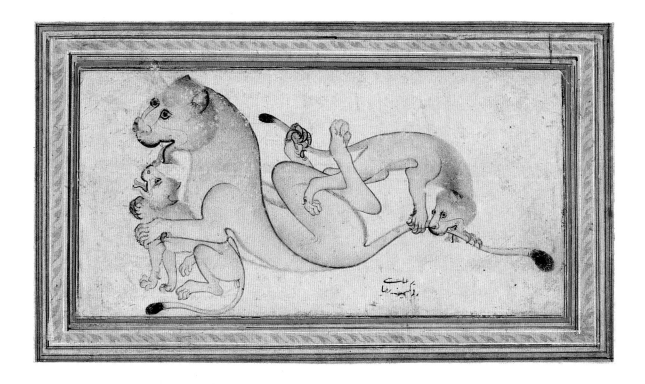

Lioness and cubs

Signed by Riza Abbasi
Isfahan
Late 16th century
Ink and gouache on paper
H 13.9 cm (5 ½ in) W 6.8 cm (2 ¾ in)
Bequest of Prof. Yuhanna Dawud, London

This representation has been reduced to the barest of essentials. A smooth, buff-toned, polished paper acts as the support for the washes of dark brown pigment contained within gray and red-brown lines.

The many seemingly spontaneous drawings of lionesses, either alone or with mates or cubs, done during this period might lead to the false conclusion that predatory felines were common in daily life. This, however, was not the case. The popularity of lion drawings stems from the supple feline body movements and languorous postures which allowed the artist to exercise his ability and mastery of the calligraphic line.

By manipulating perspective to show both the profile in the upper portion of the lioness' body and the upturned rear portion, allowing the undulating line to act as a dividing line, Riza Abbasi has managed to unite the three cats. He has thus achieved a symmetrical, visually balanced composition, allowing the mother to play with both cubs simultaneously.

Young Nobleman holding a glass vessel

Signed by Riza Abbasi
Isfahan
First half of 17th century
Ink and gouache on paper
H 17.5 cm (6 ¾ in) W 8.5 cm (3 ¼ in)
Bequest of Prof. Yuhanna Dawud, London

In the decades around 1600 a newly flourishing Persian
middle class demanded paintings and book illustrations, a
luxury previously reserved for royalty. Riza Abbasi was the
master of this genre, often departing from standard representations to inject elements of whimsy, debauchery or intimate
spontaneity. His ability to use a single pen- or brush-stroke of
varying thickness to convey volume and solidity gave him
great artistic range within the limited and rather conservative
medium of Persian painting.

 The Persian concept of beauty was an idealized one.
Thus, this nobleman's facial features are not represented real-
istically, but according to the canons of the time: full face,
small bud-shaped lips and almond eyes set beneath heavy,
arched eyebrows. Riza attempts to convey an elegant, if somewhat effete, young man enjoying his dilettante existence.
Dressed in color-coordinated finery, he stands against a
mythical landscape background painted in washes of gold.
His buff-colored silk pants are embellished with scenes of blue
birds flying amidst gold trees and leaves, while his splendid
blue-plumed hat echoes the overall color scheme as does his
blue-and-gold sash. He holds a gilt-glass bottle which is part of
the apparatus used for smoking.

An Attic Red Figure Kylix
by the Antiphon Painter
490-480 BCE
Pottery
H 12.7 cm (5 in) Diameter 39.7 cm (15 ½ in)
Bequest of N. Schimmel to American Friends of the Israel
Museum

The decoration on this wine cup *(kylix)* is attributed to the
Antiphon Painter, a major cup painter of the Late Archaic
Period. The Antiphon Painter's style is characterized by his
predilection for oversized heads, adorned by curly hair with
heavy scalloped edges, a black broken line that divides the
torso, muscles rendered with great delicacy in a dilute glaze,
and the use of relief lines.

The festive drinking party *(symposium)*, and the revel
(komos), well-known aspects of life in Athenian male
society, are illustrated on this exquisite *kylix*. Displays of
excess and exhilaration are conveyed by a dancing youth
holding a staff; a drunken, bearded reveler clasps his head
while vomiting, as another supports himself precariously on
his staff. Various receptacles associated with wine are depicted:
an open bowl for mixing wine and water, a deep cup held by
a youth, and a wine pourer.

Several inscriptions are present: the word 'handsome'
(kalos) above the staff of the vomiting man and on the
krater; the word 'the end' *(telos)* beside the drunken man,
which seems to refer to his empty cup or the fact that the
participants are in the final stage of a drunken revel. *Kalos* is
also used in an inscription in the interior of the vessel praising
the beauty of a contemporary Athenian aristocrat named
Aristarchos.

Attic Red Figure Neck Amphora with Lid
by Polygnotos
c. 440 BCE
Pottery
H 50.5 cm (1 ft 8 in)
Gift of Jan Mitchell, New York to American Friends of the
Israel Museum

Amphoras, used for storing and carrying wine, oil and other
commodities, were two-handled vases with a wide body,
narrower neck and a lid. In earlier times they also served as
storage urns for cremated ashes.

The decoration on this amphora is ascribed to the well-
known Athenian artist Polygnotos. The front is decorated with
a scene from the battle of the Amazons, a popular artistic and
literary theme representing the triumph of the civilized world
over barbarism. Theseus, the Attic youth-hero of the Athenian
democracy, is attacking an Amazon. He is supported by
Antiope, his Amazon wife who, according to legend, fought at
his side until she fell in battle. Inscriptions next to their heads
identify the principal figures. The other side of the amphora,
decorated with a scene of an elderly man holding a staff,
between two young women, exhibits less confident draftsman-
ship. Palmettes below the handles separate the two scenes.

The large size of the vase, the composition using only
three figures, the illusion of volume and movement conveyed
by the elongated figures, and the dramatic interrelation of
their positions, are all characteristic of Polygnotos's classical
style. Indeed, this elaborately painted vase is a superb example
of the high aesthetic quality and iconographical complexity of
classical Greek pottery.

Dionysos Mask

Greece, Boeotia
c. 450 BCE
Clay
H 30.6 cm (12 in)
Bequest of N. Schimmel to American Friends of the Israel
Museum

This life-size mask belongs to a small group of terracottas
from Boeotia, Greece, made in a mold and representing the
wine god Dionysos. Remains of white, blue, red and yellow
can still be seen on the mask, indicating that it was originally
polychrome. Its style is close to Boeotian terracotta works from
the mid-fifth century BCE, dating it to the Classical period.

The use of masks was characteristic of the Dionysian
cult, in which even the god's votaries donned masks. Here the
god is depicted as a bearded man wearing a crown. The holes
in the mask and the downward glance of the face indicate
that this mask was elevated, mounted high above the viewer. It most probably served as a cult image, such as the
ones known from Boeotia where, in the rural rituals, the
god's image sometimes consisted of a mask and garment
hung on a pole. Women played the main role in the ecstatic
cult of Dionysos, during which they were said to abandon
their duties, homes and children in favor of wandering in the
mountains, dancing, and reveling in the presence of the god,
who probably appeared before them in the form of a mask
like this one.

Hydria

Greece
c. 400-325 BCE
Bronze
H 44 cm (17 ¼ in)
Gift of T. Goldman, New York to American Friends of the
Israel Museum

Hydriai are one of the most impressive types of ancient Greek
bronze vessels, used primarily for carrying water, but also
serving as athletic prizes, sanctuary dedications, and cinerary
urns. Having two horizontal handles for carrying and a large
vertical handle for pouring, they were produced in both
ceramic and bronze versions, the latter probably reserved for
special occasions.

As was usual in the bronze hydriai the thin body of this
vase was hammered from sheet-bronze, while the handles and
base were cast and elaborately decorated with leaf pattern and
scrollwork. At the base of the fluted vertical handle, and cast
with it as a single piece, there is a siren, the mythological half-
woman, half-bird. Here she is seen full face, with outspread
wings, feet together and talons gripping the end of a palmette.

The appearance of the siren is not merely a decorative
motif. In antiquity, sirens were often placed on top of funerary
stelae as the symbolic guardians of the tomb, and presumably
also on hydriai intended for funerary use. The mourning
sirens on grave reliefs are often depicted with arms for tearing
their hair and beating their breasts, as is this unusual siren.
The shape of this hydria, its subject and style, suggest that this
example is rather late, probably dating to the late fourth
century BCE.

Gold Earring

Greece, from Trebizond
Late 4th century BCE
H 8.3 cm (3 ¼ in)
Bequest of N. Schimmel to American Friends of the Israel
Museum

This elaborate gold 'boat' earring belongs to a type that was
extremely popular in the late fourth century BCE. At the top
of the earring is a disk, missing the central ornament, and on
the other side of the disk is the ear hook. A richly decorated
boat-shape below the disk supports bud pendants, little chains
with rosettes and miniature jugs suspended from it. Above the
boat rises a mixture of scrolls, palmettes, tendrils and plant
forms. Over this, attached with wires, are two flying nude Eros
figurines with long wings, giving emphasis to a new sense of
space and tri-dimensionality characteristic of early Hellenistic
objects.

The earring is decorated using the traditional techniques
of filigree and granulation, combined with attached decorative figures and ornaments. It is outstanding because of the
quality of richly detailed workmanship, exemplifying the skill,
imaginative diversity and inventiveness of Greek jewelry
craftsmen in gold.

Other earrings of this type have been found in Southern
Russia and Asia Minor, but the majority of the examples, like
this piece, come from the northeastern part of the Greek
world.

Figure of a Worshipper

Northern(?) Sumer, Mesopotamia
Early Dynastic period
c. 2600 BCE
Copper, cast
H 14 cm (5 ½ in) W 5 cm (2 in)
Gift of P. Klutznick, New York

Figures of mortals in gestures of reverence or prayer were prominent in the visual art of ancient Mesopotamia. This worshipper stands with his hands clasped before his chest in a gesture of supplication typical of Sumerian sculptures of the mid-third millennium. Naked figures displaying this type of posture are sometimes regarded as representing priests. However, the priestly figures are usually shown bald, in contrast to this worshipper, whose hair falls down below his shoulders. The long beard reaching down to his chest is also unusual, since it parts into two sections at the bottom.

Unlike most statues of this period, which are made of stone and tend to be somewhat geometrical and ponderous, this copper figurine is more refined and even naturalistic in expression, for example in the rendering of its slightly bent legs. It is similar to pieces found near the Diyala river, east of Baghdad, namely two statuettes from Tell Agrab and three figurines adorning offering stands from Khfaje. All five figurines were found in temples and it is therefore likely that this piece was also dedicated to the divine and was placed in a temple by an anonymous believer.

Rock Relief of Iddin-Sin, King of Simurrum

Northeastern Iraq
c. 2100-2000 BCE
Limestone
H 103 cm (3 ft 5 in) W 98 cm (3 ft 3 in)

This rock relief is one of a group of similar works that were carved on the high cliffs of the eastern border of Mesopotamia. It was made to commemorate the victories of Iddin-Sin, King of Simurrum, probably located along the Little Zab river, which flows westward from the Kurdistan Mountains into the Tigris. This area was marked by numerous battles between the Mesopotamian cities, among them Ur, and their opponents, during the last two hundred years of the third millennium. Despite the long and well-documented rivalry between Ur and Simurrum, the rock relief exhibits features typical of the Mesopotamian tradition, namely the depiction of an apparently young king trampling his enemy in front of a goddess and carrying a scepter surmounted by two volutes. The inspiration for this theme of a victorious ruler was the stele of Naram-Sin, King of Akkad (2254–2218 BCE). The scene occurs not only on later rock reliefs, but also in miniature art, such as cylinder seals. The seven-column inscription in the background ends with a call to the great gods to bestow terrifying curses upon anyone daring to erase Iddin-Sin's name from the monument.

Wall Relief
Nimrud

Reign of Ashurnasirpal II (883-859 BCE)
Alabaster
H 157 cm (5 ft 2 ¾ in) W 203cm (6 ft 9 in) D 1.7 cm (¾ in)
Gift of Baron and Baroness Edmond de Rothschild, Paris

A stylized date-palm tree flanked by two winged human-headed genies appears on many wall slabs decorating the North-West Palace of King Ashurnasirpal II, built in his newly-founded capital, Nimrud (Biblical 'Calah'). The numerous repetitions of this pictorial theme throughout the royal buildings testify to the significance of the scene, despite the lack of related written sources. The motif of a tree with two genies may be a symbolic representation of the pollination of date-palm trees, implying the bestowal of abundance on the entire kingdom.

Three aspects of this slab are of special interest: its relatively small size, its 26-line cuneiform inscription stretching from shoulder to midcalf, and its large characters. These, along with the ending of the 'Standard Inscription' in the middle of a sentence, suggest that the slab belongs to a phase in which the relations between the pictorial and textual components of the wall reliefs were not yet fixed.

The exact placement of the slab is unknown; however, the above evidence suggests that it originated either from the east wing of the North-West Palace or in the Temple of Ninurta north of it, both probably dated early in the building process of Nimrud.

Stele of Tiglath-Pilesar III, King of
Assyria (745-727 BCE)

Zagros mountains, western Iran
Dolomite (hard limestone)
H 2.4 m (8 ft)
Gift of Ayoub Rabenou, Paris

Tiglath-Pilesar III's régime had a decisive impact on the ancient Near East and for the people of Israel. Under his rule, an unprecedented policy of mass deportations changed the face of the ancient Near East for generations to come. The inscription commemorates the king's campaigns in 738 BCE in the territories west of the Euphrates and in Iran. The mention of tribute paid by Menachem, son of Gadi, King of Israel (747–737 BCE) is significant, being referred to in the Bible: 'King Pul of Assyria invaded the land, and Menahem gave Pul a thousand talents of silver that he might support him and

strengthen his hold on the kingdom. Menahem exacted the money from Israel: every man of means had to pay fifty shekels of silver for the king of Assyria. The king of Assyria withdrew and did not remain in the land' (II Kings 15:19-20). Subsequently, Tiglath-Pilesar returned to southern Syria and Israel and in 734--732 BCE, during the rule of Pekah, King of Israel, he conquered the Aramaic kingdom of Damascus and territories of the kingdom of Israel, an event which is also mentioned in the Bible (II Kings 15:29).

The king, clad in a robe, is wearing the royal headgear of the Assyrian kings and holding a mace, an emblem of authority. Symbols of the main Assyrian deities are seen above him. The stele was reconstructed from two original fragments. The third, which includes the king's garment, is a modern replica.

A Wine (?) Goddess Plaque
North Syria or Southern Anatolia
8th–7th century BCE
Electrum
H 7.2 cm (2 ¾ in) W 6.6 cm (2 ½ in)
Gift of S. Lamon, New York, through the American-Israel Cultural Foundation

Frontal depictions of women wearing long dresses open in front to reveal their nudity, usually thought of as fertility goddesses, were common in Syria from the first half of the second millennium BCE. The mountain-like podium on which the figure stands confirms her divine identity, since mountains were regarded as the abode of the gods. However, precise identification of this sensual figure is problematic. The decorated circles adorning her dress recall similar garments of first-millennium Mesopotamian deities, among them *Ishtar*, an astral goddess. The richly decorated background of the plaque, filled with star-like patterns, suggests a connection with *Ishtar*. However, the wings probably rule out such an identification, as prominent Mesopotamian gods were usually depicted without wings. Wings were restricted in Mesopotamian art to semi-divine beings or demons, although in regions adjacent to Mesopotamia, such as Urartu in Eastern Anatolia or North Syria, winged gods and goddesses do occur.

The grapes carried by this figure are rarely found in association with nude, winged frontal depictions, but appear among Anatolian representations of the first millennium BCE. Iconographic features such as the wings and the grapes, as well as the material, a natural alloy of silver and gold, plus the variety of techniques applied here, suggest a North Syrian or Southern Anatolian origin for the plaque.

101

Female Offering-Bearer

Unknown provenance
Early Middle Kingdom, 11th Dynasty (c.2100–2000 BCE)
Painted wood
H 59 cm (1 ft 11 ¼ in) (including base)
Gift of Curtis Katz, Great Neck NY, to American Friends of the Israel Museum

Wooden models illustrating daily life, along with a supply of provisions for the deceased, were common in Egyptian tombs of this period. They provided detailed representations of houses, gardens, granaries, army troops, boats, workshops and people.

This type of female offering-bearer was found in the tombs of this period guaranteeing provisions for the deceased. Often larger than the models of daily life, they are usually depicted carrying a basket on their head, filled with food stores such as meat, bread, wine or flour. The basket is always supported by the left hand, and in many cases a live duck is held in the right hand. They can appear singly or in pairs, either in the tomb chapel or in the burial chamber.

This figure wears a white dress held by a strap over the left shoulder. Her black wig is cut below the ears at the sides, left long at the back and surrounded by a white fillet tied at the back. Her skin is painted yellow, as was customary in representations of women in ancient Egypt, while the flour in her basket is painted white.

A live duck, fashioned from a separate piece of wood, is held by the tail. Its wings, which were attached, have not survived.

Scarabs

Unknown provenance
Second and first millennia BCE
Glazed steatite, faience, glass, semiprecious stones, ivory and gold
L 1 – 3cm (½ – 1 ¼ in)
Gift of Dr Kurt Stern, London

The scarab, an amulet shaped like the Scarabaeus Sacer (dung beetle), hence its modern name, was a primary symbol of regeneration in ancient Egypt. The beetle rolling its ball of dung was associated by the Egyptians with the sun-god rolling the sun-disk, reborn every day in heaven. Moreover, the mistaken notion that these beetles were self-engendered, generated the association of the beetle with the primary god of creation. Scarabs thus became very popular funerary amulets, thousands of them originating from Egyptian tombs or habitation areas of the second and first millennium BCE

The flat base of the scarabs, often inscribed or decorated,

misled early scholars to regard them as seals. Some scarabs did bear royal names, private names, and titles of officials, and for a short period were actually used for sealing, as attested by clay seal-impressions. However, it is now clear that scarabs were primarily used as amulets, and that their use as seals was secondary and limited to a short period of time.

Scarabs were made of a variety of materials, many of them believed to possess magical properties. The most common were glazed steatite and faience, but semiprecious stones such as amethyst, jasper, carnelian, lapis lazuli, agate and felspar were also used, and, less frequently, gold, silver, bronze, glass and ivory.

A Game of Senet

From the Tanis area.
The New Kingdom, 19th Dynasty (c. 1300–1200 BCE)
Faience
L 33.5 cm (13 ¼ in)
Gift of Norbert Schimmel, New York, to American Friends of the Israel Museum

The board game most favored by the ancient Egyptians was *Senet,* the game of 'passing.' Boards and other equipment for the game were found in tombs of commoners, nobles and kings from the earliest dynasties, and remains of elaborate boards, as well as crude grids or sketches, reflect its popularity among all classes of society.

Two people played *Senet* on a board marked with thirty squares arranged in three parallel rows of ten. The number of playing pieces varied from five to ten, and each opponent advanced by throws of marked sticks, used in the same manner as dice. The object of the game was to advance along the board, passing an opponent by blocking or eliminating the latter's pieces.

During the New Kingdom, tomb walls bore representations of *Senet* players, for the game had acquired a religious-magical meaning, symbolizing the passage of the deceased through the netherworld, his resurrection dependent upon his winning a *Senet* game. The last five squares were given new markings, reflecting the desired arrival in the divine domain of eternity. This board is an example of such a funerary *Senet.*

Faience was the most common material for *Senet* boards, but examples made of wood also exist, some including drawers for the pieces.

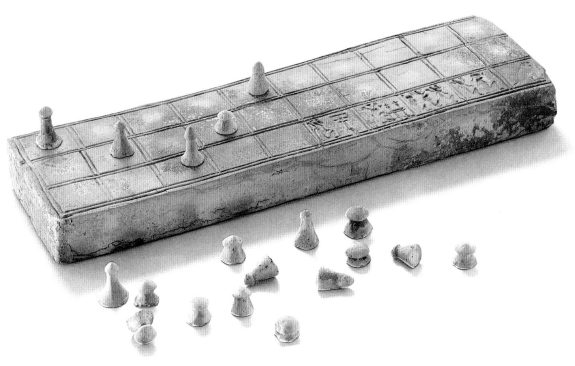

Fragment of a Funerary Scene Decorating a Tomb Wall

The Theban necropolis
The New Kingdom, 18th Dynasty (c. 1400-1350 BCE)
Painted plaster
H 15.6 cm (6 ¼ in)
Gift of Norbert Schimmel, New York, to American Friends of the Israel Museum

Representations of rituals performed during funeral processions commonly decorate 18th-Dynasty tomb walls. This fragment depicts part of such a scene taking place in the funeral barge which carried the deceased to his tomb in the Theban necropolis.

Two priests perform the ritual. The one on the right, clothed in leopard skin, pours a libation from a vase held in his right hand, while his left hand is raised offering incense (missing in the fragment). The other priest, wearing a white skirt, recites funerary texts from the open roll of papyrus held in his hands.

The fragment originated in the west wall of the Theban tomb chapel of the king's chief sculptor Nebamun, a man of high position, who lived during the reign of Amenhotep III. During this period Egypt was at the height of its power and wealth, its prosperity reflected by the splendor of the art of the period.

Votive Statue of the Singer Imeni

Probably from Cusae in Middle Egypt
The Middle Kingdom, Late 12th Dynasty (c. 1850-1800 BCE)
Granite
H 29.3 cm (11 ½ in)
Gift of Norbert Schimmel, New York, to American Friends of the Israel Museum

This remarkable sculpture exhibits the newly acquired privilege of non-royal officials to place their statues in temples, a prerogative previously reserved only for the royal family.

The man is portrayed in the conventional idealized style, common in depictions of people of high position in ancient Egyptian art. The type of wig and large ears are typical of representations of 12th-Dynasty officials, and the rolls of fat below the chest reflect his elevated status. His left hand is placed on his right breast in a gesture of devotion before the gods.

The inscriptions on the skirt and upper part of the base reveal the identity of the owner of the statue. On the skirt is the traditional offering formula, ensuring provisions for the deceased in the netherworld. Here it invokes the goddess *Hathor* of Cusae in Middle Egypt, where she was revered as the goddess of the local necropolis. The man, identified as 'Director of the singers, *Imeni*,' may have performed in the local temple of *Hathor* in Cusae.

From the short inscription on the base we learn the name of his father, *Sesi*, who is mentioned without a title, indicating a man of humble origin. However, the fact that *Imeni* could afford a granite statue of such quality and was granted the privilege of placing it in a temple, reflects the high position of musicians during the Middle Kingdom.

Judaica and Jewish Ethnography

Rivka Gonen

The Jewish world has long been held in fascination by both its own people and the world at large. The long life-span of Judaism — the oldest religion still practiced today — its monotheistic principle and strong moral character, the fact that it gave birth to both Christianity and Islam, and perhaps, above all, the stubborn survival of the Jewish people despite millennia of persecutions, pogroms and exiles have throughout time inspired feelings of awe, admiration, and love, but also of envy and hatred. What is it about this religion and the people who adhere to it that has carved for them such a unique place in the history of the world? Wherein lies the enigma of survival? These far-reaching questions may be asked also of the objects which represent Jewish material culture. These objects, both ritual and secular, hold in themselves stories of survival and testify to the Jews' continuity as a people despite all perils. They also convey a spirit of optimism and hope, a love of beauty in the face of hardship and persecution. They are worthy representatives of the people themselves.

The Judaica-Jewish Ethnography Wing is devoted to the collection and display of these very objects that in themselves reflect the story of the Jewish people, their dispersal to the four corners of the world, and their religious practices. They illustrate a basic unity manifested in the performance of the same religious practices, and simultaneously a great diversity of life-styles, the result of the long history of Jewish dispersal. But it is the stories of individual objects — some rescued from the ashes of destroyed communities, others the last remnants of greatly dwindled ones, yet others obtained from immigrants in Israel, — encapsulating sagas of individual people who left their homes, wandered near and far and found a new home in this country that make this wing so exciting.

For many centuries, certainly since the destruction of Jerusalem in 70 CE but even earlier than that, the Jewish people have been dispersed in many parts of the world, with large communities in the Middle East, North Africa and Europe. During the long exile, living in different geographical and historical situations under the rule of pagans, Christians or Muslims, Jews have strictly adhered to their religious heritage while adapting themselves to the customs and styles of their host countries. With the passage of

Hanukkah lamps from different countries and periods; foreground: *Hanukkah* lamp from a synagogue in Poland, 18th century.

time, the Jewish religion itself has undergone changes, some resulting from theological considerations, others merely from differences in the interpretation and practice of some of the laws. Being open to the world in which they lived, Jews everywhere were influenced by customs and ceremonies practiced by their neighbors, and often incorporated some of them into their own religious life. Each community thus developed a unique blend of Jewish life – an amalgam of what was absolutely essential to their Jewishness and what they could without hesitation adopt from their neighbors. Jewish life in recent centuries, as manifested by the Museum's collections, thus incorporates a vast span of intriguing possibilities.

An interesting distinction exists between the basic philosophies of the

Italian Esther scroll decorated with the signs of the Zodiac and symbols of the twelve tribes, 18th century.

two departments that form the Jewish wing. The Department of Judaica deals with the formal aspects of Judaism, namely ritual and the objects used in its performance both in the synagogue and at home during the Sabbath and holidays. The department stresses the unity, the universal Jewish ritual as it was and still is observed to a greater or lesser extent by the majority of traditional Jews around the world. The Department of Jewish Ethnography, on the other hand, is interested more in the local color of the various ethnic communities that constitute the Jewish people, resulting from their long interaction with their host societies. The department collects objects and information relating to ceremonies adopted from neighbors, to beliefs in the supernatural world and means used as protection against it, and local costumes, home furnishings and personal belongings that, interestingly, are as representative of the regions where they were produced as of the Jews who used them.

Building the collections

The basic goal of the wing is to save the material remnants of Jewish life. Under this general definition, the collection of each department demonstrates its own point of view and means of obtaining objects. Objects of Judaica, many of which are made of materials such as silver and velvet, have long been considered items of value and were collected by both private individuals and public institutions who ultimately became the major source of objects for the Museum. This was not the case with the most mundane and simple objects that represent the ethnographic side of Jewish existence. These objects did not attract the attention of collectors, and to this day have to be obtained directly from the very people who made them or who own them. Indeed, Judaica, rather than ethnographic objects, have comprised the core collections of Jewish museums since such institutions were established at the very end of the nineteenth century, and remain the hallmarks of these museums around the world.

Bird-shaped hat pin worn by married Jewish women of Izmir and Rhodes, 20th century.

The Israel Museum collection began with an assemblage of Judaica which from the beginning of this century was housed at the Bezalel Museum until its incorporation into the new museum. The collection was greatly enlarged by thousands of objects gathered in Europe after the Holocaust, as well as by gifts and purchases of large and small private collections and individual objects. This is now the most comprehensive and varied collection of Judaica ever assembled anywhere, covering almost the entire Jewish world from Singapore to the United States, from the Yemen to Germany, and ranging in content from complete synagogues to tiny *mezuzot* from exquisite illuminated medieval manuscripts to simple, homemade *Hanukkah* lamps. It acts as a major repository for Judaica and continues to obtain and preserve as many examples as possible of the various material expressions of Jewish ritual.

The collections of the Department of Jewish Ethnography stress the everyday aspect of Jewish life throughout the Diaspora, and bring together anything that Jews made use of both on a day-to-day basis and on festive occasions. Special emphasis is placed on items crafted by Jews, such as exquisite pieces of jewelry produced by Jewish Yemenite jewelers who, in fact, dominated the craft in that country, or large hangings and blankets

Tombstone in a Jewish cemetery in Cochin, from a field trip to India in 1984.

woven by Jewish men in Kurdistan. There are also items that were used exclusively by Jews, examples being articles of clothing required by religion such as a *tallit* and a head covering, or others imposed on the Jews by the authorities in various countries, such as dark overcoats for streetwear to hide colorful dress, or specially shaped hats. Many objects, however, could easily fit into non-Jewish collections, their 'Jewishness' being established only by the undoubted identity of their users.

The majority of the ethnography collections, itself the largest of its kind in the world, was obtained through fieldwork carried out by members of the Department in homes throughout Israel. The keen interest in the everyday objects which were brought to this country by immigrants was not always shared by their owners. They often considered these objects unworthy remnants of a past that should be quickly forgotten if a new life was to be built in Israel. They therefore not only did not come forward with their possessions, but were on the whole greatly surprised when the Museum showed interest in them. The Department's field workers traversed the country, visiting every village and neighborhood where members of a certain community lived, and, whenever possible, also traveling to its country of origin. In this way outstanding collections from Jewish communities such as those of Morocco, Kurdistan, Turkey, Afghanistan, Alsace, Germany, Eastern Europe, India, Libya, Yemen and Ethiopia were assembled, and became sources of pride for the members of the various communities whose unique cultures are fast disappearing as they are integrated into the general Israeli environment. The extensive collections assembled over the years range from colorful and well-executed embroidered wall-hangings to crude blacksmiths' tools, from exquisite pieces of jewelry in gold and precious stones to plain wooden washboards.

The Department's activities are not limited solely to the collection of Jewish artifacts, but also include research into, and acquisition and display of costumes and items of everyday life representative of the Muslim, Christian and Druze communities in Israel.

In addition to its collections of objects, the Judaica-Jewish Ethnography wing has assembled an impressive collection of photographs, slides and videos of people, scenes and objects. Many of the photographs capture a vanished past, especially in Europe, but also in places where Jewish communities no longer exist; others were taken more recently during fieldwork in Israel and abroad. This collection, which serves to provide the objects with their vital background and context, is extensively used both in exhibitions and in publications, and will form the basis for a planned Judaica-Jewish Ethnography study-center.

The Exhibitions

Permanent displays center on the most important subjects on the agenda of the two departments, using the best objects in the collections. They convey the message that beneath the almost bewildering array of styles and materials lies a unity of Jewish belief and ritual, and that the variety of life-styles represents the many faces of but one people.

The Judaica exhibition, glittering with precious objects made of metal, especially silver, is centered around five major themes, four of them representing the main pillars of centuries of Jewish religious practices throughout the world: the Sabbath; the synagogue, represented by three complete, original examples installed in the exhibition; the *Torah* scroll and its embellishments; and the yearly cycle of holidays. In the fifth section beautifully illuminated manuscripts are on display.

The Jewish Ethnography exhibition is rich in complete and partial reconstructions of environments and ceremonies, with numerous exquisite objects, mainly finely woven and embroidered textiles. It dazzles the viewer with the amazing wealth of Jewish experience in the Diaspora during the nineteenth and early twentieth centuries. The exhibition as it is today centers around three subjects: the Jewish life-cycle from birth to death; the Jewish home, or rather homes Jews lived in; and festive costumes and jewelry. In all these subjects there is a marked and interesting tension between aspects, ceremonies and objects that are definitely of Jewish origin and those that were absorbed into Jewish practice from the various neighbors among whom Jews lived in the Diaspora. Many basic questions relating to this tension are raised by the exhibition. For example, why did several Jewish communities start to perform the *Henna* ceremony which is definitely not an original Jewish practice? What are the objects, articles or otherwise that make a home in which Jews live a Jewish home? How widespread, among Jews, was the use of amulets and other supernatural protective measures,

Silver *Torah* ornaments from the exhibition, 'The Stieglitz Collection: Masterpieces of Jewish Art,' 1987.

strongly resented both by the scriptures and by most Rabbinic authorities? And perhaps the biggest question of all — if Jews everywhere wore the same costumes as their non-Jewish neighbors, decorated themselves with the same jewelry, lived in homes that resembled all the others in the same region — is there indeed such a thing as Jewish material culture? These and many other questions are not meant to be answered by the exhibition. They are there for the visitor to contemplate.

The series of temporary exhibitions that have been mounted by the wing over the years have focused attention on certain well-defined subjects such as marriage contracts, or have highlighted specific issues. One of the main concerns of the Department of Judaica has been the collection and preservation of the ritual remnants of the lost Jewish communities of Europe. In 1990 it mounted a large-scale exhibition of treasures from the Jewish Museum in Prague, a museum that was intended by the Nazis to represent the culture of the, as they planned, extinct Jewish race. The Nazis assembled in Prague exquisite ritual pieces such as richly embroidered *Torah* Ark curtains and *Torah* decorations from Czechoslovakia and other East European countries that were under their yoke. Following World War II, these pieces remained in the Jewish Museum, but after the fall of the Soviet régime in Eastern Europe which facilitated diplomatic contacts with Israel, a selection of objects was allowed to travel to the Israel Museum for a display that aroused strong emotional reactions.

Examples of alms boxes, both traditional and modern, as presented in a special exhibit.

Another concern of the department is its encouragement of the creation of contemporary Jewish ritual objects. This was manifested by the exhibition, 'Judaica Here and Now' (1989) that displayed objects made by contemporary Israeli craftsmen.

Most of the exhibitions of the Department of Jewish Ethnography have centered around the life of various Jewish communities in the Diaspora, based on field research carried out by members of the department. These exhibitions — the Jews of Bokhara (1967), Morocco (1973), Kurdistan (1981), the Ottoman Empire (1989), Alsace (1992) and Eastern Europe (1994) — have had a monumental impact on the social fabric of Israel. When the various communities arrived in Israel, especially in the early years of statehood, the prevailing sentiment in the country was to absorb the newcomers into Israeli culture with great haste. The immigrants were encouraged quickly to study Hebrew, shed their traditional costumes, and adopt the Israeli way of behaving, of arranging their private surroundings, and of

Jewish costumes from different regions
in Morocco as shown in the exhibition,
'Jewish Life in Morocco,' 1973.

performing customs and ceremonies, all mainly based on European models. In an effort to become part of newly-created Israeli society, these immigrants lost their unique identity, even becoming ashamed of their past, a situation that created personal tension and stress and feelings of alienation and hostility. The exhibitions at the Israel Museum, centering around the secular and religious life of these new immigrants in their countries of origin, with vignettes of homes and kitchens, workshops and marketplaces, and displays of costumes and jewelry, ritual objects, books and manuscripts, helped members of the communities thus represented to regain some of their self-esteem and advance their prestige in Israeli society. The exhibitions 'Jewish Life in Morocco' and 'Jews of Kurdistan' were particularly meaningful from this point of view, as these communities in particular had suffered from low status in Israel. Throngs of people flocked to the Museum and were able to view aspects of their former lives with pride and nostalgia. Now they could show the young generation of native-born Israelis that their stories were true, that indeed life abroad had had value and substance. Groups of folk dancers and musicians performed in the Museum, continuing these activities even after the shows were dismantled.

Through these exhibitions the Department of Jewish Ethnography and the Museum in general fulfilled some of its major goals. Apart from its aim to collect and preserve precious relics of the past, it aspires to contribute to a better appreciation of the various communities in Israel, and to the understanding of the culture that has developed here out of the meeting of so many different traditions.

Birds' Head Haggadah

Southern Germany, c. 1300
Scribe: Menahem
Parchment, pen and ink, tempera; handwritten
47 leaves
27 × 19 cm (10 ½ × 7 ½ in)

The so-called Birds' Head *Haggadah* derives its name from the images featured in the manuscript. Most of the human figures are depicted as having birds' heads with pronounced beaks. Some figures also have short, pointed animal ears. All male adults in the manuscript wear the conical 'Jew's hat,' which was compulsory for Jews in Germany from the time of the Lateran Council in 1215.

The practice of distorting the human face may have arisen from the growing asceticism among the Ashkenazi Jews of the period, and their strict observance of the biblical prohibition of creating graven images.

The Birds' Head *Haggadah* is the earliest Ashkenazi illuminated *Haggadah* to have survived as a separate book. It is richly illustrated in the margins with biblical, ritual and eschatological scenes.

Sassoon Spanish Haggadah

Spain, c. 1320
Parchment, pen and ink, tempera and gold leaf
Handwritten
21 × 16.5 cm (8 ¼ × 6 ½ in)
On deposit from the State

The Sassoon Spanish *Haggadah,* as it is known, is one of some twenty Spanish illuminated *Haggadot* which survived the Expulsion of the Jews from Spain in 1492.

Its colorful and rich decorative style points to Catalan origins around the first half of the fourteenth century. Written on parchment in square Sephardi script, the *Haggadah* displays a blend of local and foreign stylistic influences such as the Spanish Gothic grotesques framing the margins, the elongated figures betraying a French influence, and the coloring and design of the floral scrolls, recalling Italian manuscripts of that period.

Interspersed with the text throughout the *Haggadah* are numerous illustrations of biblical passages, and motifs connected with the Passover festival, some of which are quite literal. The passage 'And he went down to Egypt,' for example, is illustrated by a depiction of a man descending a ladder.

The splendor of the Sassoon *Haggadah* evokes the flourishing Spanish Jewish communities of the time, who generally lived in harmony with their Christian neighbors.

The Vittorio Veneto Synagogue

Vittorio Veneto, Italy, 1700
L 10.50 m (34 ft 5 in), W 5.80 m (19ft)
Gift of Jakob Michael of New York, in memory of his wife
Erna Sondheimer-Michael

In 1965 the interior of the synagogue of the north Italian town of Vittorio Veneto (formerly Ceneda and Serravalle) was transferred intact to the Israel Museum, where it has been faithfully reconstructed.

The synagogue was used by the local Ashkenazi community for more than two hundred years. During the nineteenth century the community dwindled in size, and by the end of World War I the magnificent synagogue was no longer in use.

It originally occupied the second and third stories of a plain stone building, with the women's gallery in the upper story, running along all four walls, overlooking the main hall and partitioned by a screen. Separation of men and women during prayer for reasons of modesty appears to have existed in synagogues since the Middle Ages.

The synagogue is designed in a typical north Italian baroque style. The *bimah* (raised platform for reading the *Torah*) is situated within a niche on the western wall at the end of the hall, flanked by the two entrance doors. The Ark of the Law, carved in wood and gilded, stands before the eastern wall (the direction of Jerusalem). The worshippers' seats run along the length of the synagogue, the northern and southern walls, facing the center.

Bridal Casket (Cofanetto)

Northern Italy, second half of the 15th century
Silver, cast; engraved, niello; partly gilt
H 6.6 cm (2 ½ in) L 13 cm (5 in) W 6 cm (2 ¼ in)
Gift of Astorre Mayer, Milan

This unique casket appears to have been a gift presented to a Jewish bride by her bridegroom. On the front are illustrations portraying the three duties *(mizvot)* specifically incumbent upon Jewish women. From right to left these tasks are: *hallah,* setting aside a portion of the dough; *niddah,* ritual immersion at the end of the menstrual cycle; and *hadlakat ha'ner,* kindling of the Sabbath lights.

The function of the small casket is somewhat enigmatic. On its lid are eight dials arranged in two rows. Each dial has a single hand, surrounded by Hebrew letters that are the numerical equivalent of one to twelve. The inscription on the dials are written in Hebrew letters, but the words themselves are Italian, indicating names of the household linen, including sheets, tablecloths, shirts, etc. The hands on the dials could be turned to indicate the number of each of the household possessions, and thus may have been used to keep an inventory.

It has been suggested that wealthy women put all the keys to their linen caskets in one small casket, perhaps like the one featured here. Then the key to this small casket made of silver or gold was fastened with a pin to their garment on the Sabbath to avoid carrying it.

Torah Mantle

Mogador (?), Morocco, 1926
Velvet and silk, metallic thread embroidery
H 67 cm (26 ½ in) Diameter 29 cm (11 ½ in)
Gift of Shlomo Zini, Moshav Yad Rambam, Israel

Torah scroll case

Iran, 1973
Wood, velvet, silver repoussé and glass beads
H 107 cm (42 in) Diameter 30 cm (11 ¾ in)

Torah Ark Curtain (Parochet)

Mannheim, Germany, 1728
Velvet, silver thread embroidery, and raised appliqué
200 × 140 cm (6 ft 6 ¾ × 4 ft 7 in)
Gift in memory of Asher and Kate Judith Angel, London, by courtesy of their grandchildren

The art of embroidering *Torah* Ark curtains reached a peak during the first decades of the eighteenth century in Bavaria, and was carried out by Jewish male embroiderers. All the Bavarian curtains of this type seem to have had an upper valance *(kaporet)*, but unfortunately the valance of the Israel Museum curtain has not survived.

The curtain is characterized by a central panel (mirror) embroidered with a rich geometric and floral design. The design is flanked by a pair of twisted columns entwined with grapevines and surmounted with vases of flowers. On top, two rampant lions support a crown inscribed: 'Crown of Torah' (Sayings of the Fathers 4:17). Between the lions is the donors' inscription. In its form, the *parochet* repeats the form of the Ark, and its central mirror reflects the curtain hanging in front of the Ark. At the bases of the columns the actual shape of the Ark's drawers are depicted, including the rings for drawing them out.

The donors mentioned on the Bavarian curtains are in most cases married couples, and the inscription here mentions Feis Oppenheim of Kaub and his wife Rechie, daughter of Baruch Rheinganum, who are known to have lived in Mannheim.

Because of their sanctity, *Torah* scrolls, handwritten on parchment by an expert scribe (*sofer stam* - scribe of *Torah* scrolls, phylacteries and *mezuzahs*), are never left without some kind of cover in order to assure their protection. In Ashkenazi synagogues the scroll is covered by a mantle, often richly decorated, but in most oriental communities the *Torah* scroll is traditionally kept in a wooden or metal case. The style and decoration, however, varied considerably according to the origin of each community and the artistic milieu in which they were created. In Morocco, for example, where a large community of exiles from Spain resided, a richly gold-embroidered *Torah* mantle with a hard round top was often used instead of a case, probably following the custom practiced in Spain. The decoration on this example consists of a very stylized flowering vase, as well as the *hamsa* (hand amulet).

Spiceboxes

Spiceboxes are used in the *havdalah* ceremony that marks the end of the Sabbath. The ceremony is generally performed at home by the master of the house, and includes blessings recited over a cup of wine, spices, and a burning candle. After the benediction, the spices are passed around to be savoured by all members of the family.

The spices used in the *havdalah* ceremony were traditionally kept in beautifully decorated containers.

From left to right:

Russia or Poland, 19th century, silver; H 17.9 cm (7 in) W 6.9 cm (2 ¾ in)
The Stieglitz Collection, donated to the Israel Museum, with the contribution of Erica and Ludwig Jesselson, New York

Poland, late 18th century, silver, semiprecious stones; H 29.5 cm (12 in) W 5.5 cm (2 ¼ in)

Austro-Hungary, 18th century, silver, partly gilt; H 18 cm (7 in) W 5 cm (2 in)

Central Europe, 18th century, silver, filigree, partly gilt, semi-precious stones; H 40.5 cm (16 in) W 10.5 cm (4 in)
The Feuchtwanger Collection, purchased and donated to the Israel Museum by Baruch and Ruth Rappaport of Geneva

Cracow, Galicia, 1818-1843, silver, filigree; H 17 cm (7 in) W 6.1 cm (2 ½ in)
Maker: Stanislaw Westafalewocz
The Stieglitz Collection, donated to the Israel Museum, with the contribution of Erica and Ludwig Jesselson, New York

Nuremberg, Germany, 18th century; silver; H 32 cm (13 in) W 8 cm (3 in)
Maker: Johann Conrad Weiss
Gift through the Jewish Restitution Successor Organization, 1952

Rome, Italy, 1824-1865, silver; H 25 cm (10 in) W 8.5 cm (3 ¼ in)
Maker: Angelo Giannotti

Austro-Hungary, dated; 1817, silver, partly gilt; H 29.3 cm (11 ½ in); W 6 cm (2 ¼ in)

Front row (fish), left to right:

Germany, 19th century, L 10 cm (4in) W 3.5 cm (1 ½ in)
The Stieglitz Collection, donated to the Israel Museum, with the contribution of Erica and Ludwig Jesselson, New York

Poland, 19th century, silver; L 13.5 cm (5 ¼ in) W 2.5 cm (1 in)

Prayer stand (Tevah)

San'a, Yemen, 18th century
Wood, carved, painted, and lacquered
H 100 cm (3 ft 4 in) W 34 × 30 cm (1 ft × 11 ¾ in)
(top: 68 × 57 cm; 2 ft 3in × 1ft 10 in)
Purchased with the help of Florence and Sylvain J. Sternberg, Jerusalem

This prayer stand, or *tevah* (*teboh* in the Yemenite idiom), is an example of the portable stand on which the *Torah* scrolls are placed for reading in the Yemenite synagogue.

The *tevah* usually stood next to the *heykhal,* a niche in the northern wall - the direction of Jerusalem - in which the *Torah* scrolls were kept. For the reading from the *Torah* the *tevah* was moved to the center of the synagogue.

A bench which could be drawn out for little boys to stand on while reciting the Aramaic translation *(tarjum)* of the Hebrew text was an integral component of the *tevah*.

Until recently this *tevah* served the congregation of a small private synagogue in Jerusalem, where it was treated with great pride and esteemed as a precious legacy from the past.

(Overleaf)
Painted Wooden Synagogue from Horb

Horb am Main, Germany, 1735
Artist: Eliezer Sussmann
H c. 213 cm (7 ft) L c. 625 cm (20 ft 6 in) W c. 480 cm (15 ft 9 in)
On permanent loan from the Bamberg Municipality, reconstructed through a donation from Jakob Michael of New York, in memory of his wife Erna Sondheimer-Michael

Between c. 1732 and 1742 Eliezer Sussmann from Brody, in the Ukraine, appears to have painted the wooden interiors of at least seven synagogues in the present Bavarian region. The painted ceiling of Horb is the most complete surviving example of Sussmann's work.

The Horb Synagogue occupied the second floor of a half-timbered building typical of the region. The Jewish community which owned and used the synagogue moved away in the 1860s. When rediscovered in 1908, it was unfortunately being used as a hayloft. The wall paintings were partly damaged and faded. Only the wooden barrel-vault ceiling and the Torah Ark were rescued.

The walls and ceilings of the synagogue were covered with quotations from prayers along with a carpet-like design of floral and animal motifs, including a unicorn, a deer, rabbits and an elephant with a castle on its back. On the eastern wall above the Ark, Sussmann painted a curtain symbolizing the Tent of Meeting; while on the western tympanum, a pair of rampant lions blowing trumpets flank the inscription from a prayer recited on the day of the Jewish New Year *(Rosh ha-Shanah)* , crowned by a set of Ram's horns *(shofar)*, with a basket overflowing with fruit and greenery reminiscent of the four species used during the Feast of Tabernacles *(Sukkot)* to the right. There is a stereotyped depiction of the city of Jerusalem to the left.

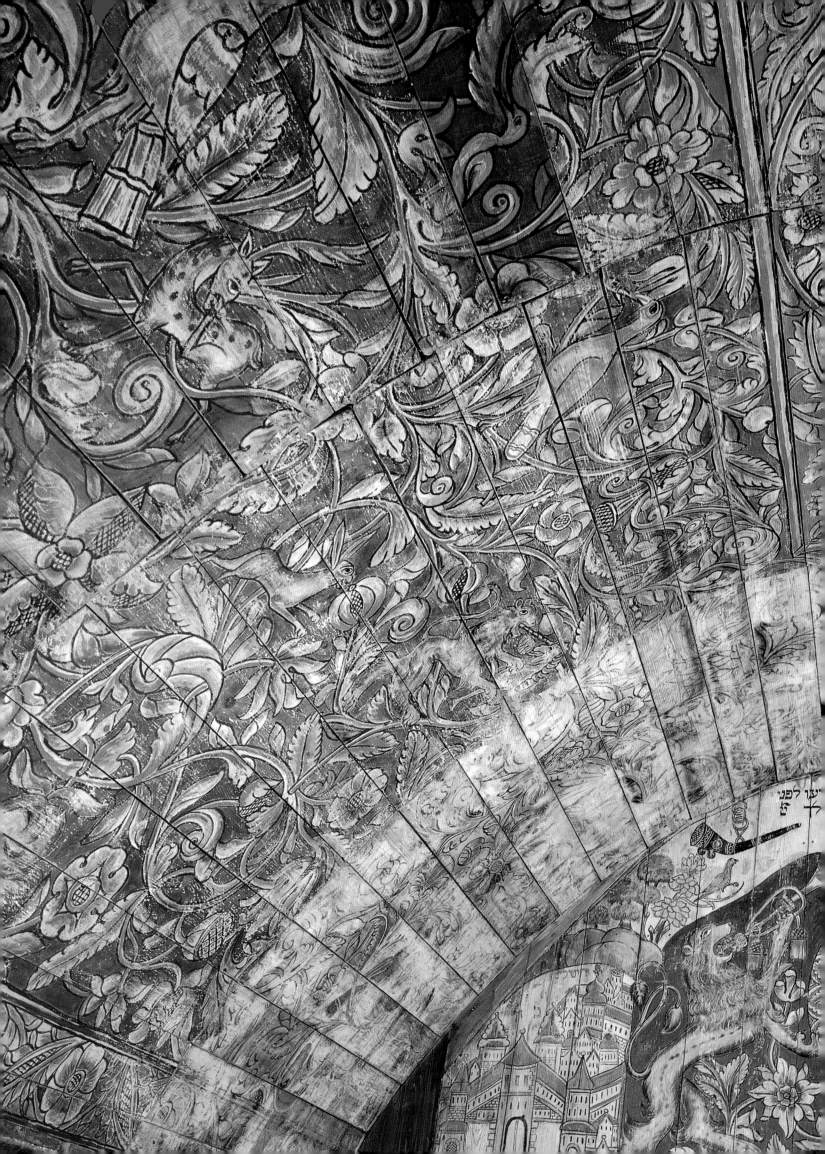

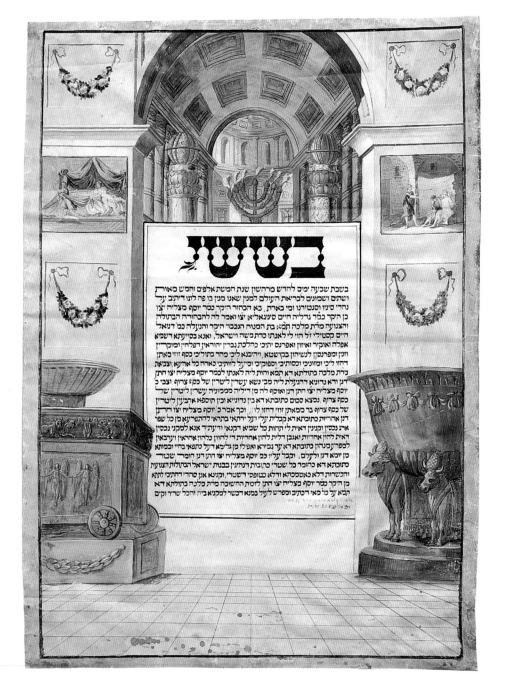

Marriage contract (Ketubbah)

Lugo, Italy, 1821
Parchment, watercolor, pen and ink
65 × 47 cm (25 ½ × 18½ in)

This splendid *ketubbah* originated from Lugo, a town in the
north central region of Emilia Romagna, in Italy, where a
small, affluent Jewish community resided. It is very unusual
in style and iconography and does not conform to the traditional decorative scheme of the Italian marriage contracts.
The text, placed within an architectural framework, is flanked
on the upper part by a three-dimensional depiction of the
interior of the Temple of Solomon, and on the right and left
border, by two massive columns. The large copper basin standing on the back of oxen on the right alludes to the 'tank of
cast metal' that Solomon made, while, on the left, the laver
and laver-stand on wheels allude to one of the ten laver
stands also made by Solomon (1 Kings 7:23-26). The miniature scenes from the life of Joseph relate to the name of the
bridegroom, Joseph.

Sukkah

Fischach, Southern Germany, c. 1837
Wood, oil paint
Gift of the Deller Family with the help of Dr Heinrich
Feuchtwanger
H 210 cm (6 ft 11 in) L 290 cm (9 ft 6 in)
W 290 cm (9 ft 6 in)

The Fischach *sukkah* was discovered in 1935 by Dr Heinrich
Feuchtwanger, stored in the attic of the Deller family resi-
dence in the village of Fischach, near Augsburg, Germany. The
painted wooden boards were numbered so that they could be
easily reassembled every year on the Feast of Tabernacles. It
was used until the beginning of the twentieth century and
then stored in an attic to prevent further deterioration.

The artist who painted this *sukkah* incorporated motifs
inspired by both everyday scenes from traditional German
folk art, and Jewish religious sources. On the walls of the
sukkah one can see a genre hunting scene and a view of the
village, including the synagogue and the Deller house. Five
vignettes relating to the major Jewish festivals are interspersed
on the walls, the immediate model for which seems to have
been a *mahzor* (High Holiday and Festival prayer book),
which was printed in Sulzbach in 1826.

The wall opposite the entrance to the *sukkah* bears a
monumental vista of the Holy sites of Jerusalem as seen from
the west, based on a lithograph dated 1836-7 drawn by the
Jerusalem scholar Yehosef Schwartz.

Hanukkah lamps

Foreground: Morocco, 19th Century
Brass, H 22 cm (8 ¾ in) W 13 cm (5 in)
Anonymous gift

Left: Fez, Morocco, 19th–20th Century
Brass, H 30.1 cm (11 ¾ in) W 24.2 cm (9 ½ in)

Right: Algeria, early 20th century
Copper, brass, H 30.1 cm (11 ¾ in) W 28.7 cm (11 ¼ in)
Anonymous gift
Maker: Simon Kalif Partuche

Background: Morocco, 18th–19th Century
Brass, H 51 cm (20 in) W 44 cm (17 ¼ in)
Loan from Shalom Asch Collection, Bat Yam

The Israel Museum collection of *Hanukkah* lamps is one of the largest in its variety of examples from different countries. The structure and design of each different group reflects the style typical of the milieu in which they were created. Thus in these examples of North African lamps, the influence of local Islamic art can be seen. The arabesque style, with stylized floral patterns melding with the architectural motif of the

horse-shoe arch, recalls the influence of the thriving Hispano-Mauresque tradition in those countries. In Islamic countries, most of the artisans and silversmiths were Jews and the ritual objects were commissioned from them.

Hanukkah is celebrated for eight days, commemorating the rededication of the Temple in Jerusalem by the Maccabees (Hasmoneans) in 164 BCE. A *Hanukkah* lamp, as a rule, consists of eight lights, and in most cases, an additional light, called a *shamash,* is added.

Passover Haggadah
Scribe: Nathan ben Shimshon of Mezeritz,
Moravia, 1732
Parchment, pen and ink and gouache
29 × 20.5 cm (11 ½ × 8 in)
Fol. 25 - The Temple of Jerusalem

Essentially an account of the Egyptian bondage and Israel's redemption, the *Haggadah* is recited at the Seder ritual on the Eve of Passover. This *Hagaddah* belongs to a group of similar eighteenth-century Hebrew books, hand-written and handpainted on parchment. These luxurious manuscripts were intended for private use, and were often presented as personal gifts. They must be considered as part of the phenomenon of the revival of Hebrew manuscript illumination in the eighteenth century, long after the invention of printing.

This book was written and painted by Nathan, son of Shimshon of Mezeritz, in Moravia (today part of the Czech Republic), where the revival of manuscript production began. He was a rather prolific scribe, and a number of manuscripts written by him are known. He wrote at least seven Passover *Haggadot,* all of which include colorful illustrations, and display a similar, recognizable style.

The illustration of the Jerusalem Temple, featured here, is modeled after the printed edition of the Amsterdam *Haggadah.*

Passover Set, 1989

Artist: Amit Shor
Aluminum, spun; brass, gilt
Tray W 36 cm (14 in) D 24 cm (9 ½ in)
Height of Elijah cup 16 cm (6 ¼ in)

Amit Shor was born in Kibbutz Kinneret in 1965. Since her graduation from the Bezalel Academy of Art and Design, she has dedicated herself to the field of Jewish ritual objects. During the past decade, she has produced an impressive number of bold and innovative objects. When designing this Passover Set, Amit Shor employed unconventional materials and unexpected forms, in her constant search for fresh solutions to a traditional Jewish object.

Shor experimented here by casting the blank images of the traditional Passover foods into the aluminum blocks.

While creating new forms and ideas, Amit Shor always makes reference to the traditional Jewish sources.

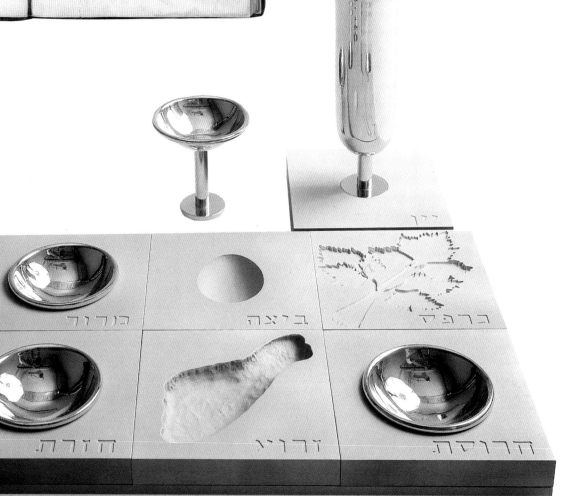

Salon in an urban Jewish home

Fez, Morocco

Gifts of Mr Raphael Benazeraf, Paris; Mr and Mrs Edward Toledano, London; Mr Rafi Moscuna, Tel-Aviv; Baroness Alix de Rothschild, Paris; Société des Amis du Musée de l'Homme, Paris; The Jerusalem Foundation

Loan by Carmit and Alex Gatman, Tel-Aviv

The Jewish presence in Morocco goes back many centuries. Historically, local Muslim rulers engaged the skills of Jewish doctors, financial advisers and diplomats for the court, thus ensuring stable relations. During the Christian *Reconquista* in Spain, both Jews and Muslims fled to Morocco and took with them Spanish styles in architecture, crafts and costume.

Receiving guests was an important tradition among Jews and among Muslims. Most homes had a special room for this function. It was typically furnished in Muslim style. Viewed through a highly ornate wooden grill separating it from the house's inner courtyard, it includes low seating on mattresses placed on wooden benches. The elements for afternoon tea are present: silver and tin kettles, brass samovars on coal stoves, tea glasses on tin trays, containers for tea leaves, mint and sugar, and vibrantly painted wooden cake containers with conical covers. Colorful textiles such as the velvet wall-cover, embroidered curtains and mattress coverings, woolen carpets, and gold-embroidered velvet cushion covers, create a joyful atmosphere.

The seated woman wears the 'Great Dress,' the green velvet, gold-embroidered ceremonial gown of Jewish women from the Fez-Sefrou region. This Spanish-style dress is worn also by Jewish women of other north Moroccan towns, where it is made of black, dark blue or violet velvet.

Two rural-style necklaces and amulet case

Sous region, Atlas mountains, Morocco
Early 20th century

Situated between the Mediterranean, the Atlantic Ocean and the Sahara Desert, Morocco has absorbed a variety of cultural traditions, expressed, among other things, in a surprising variety of traditional jewelry which varies from fine gold pieces in the north, to heavy, almost barbaric-looking pieces in the south and inner regions.

The two necklaces and amulet case shown here, of the bold rural type from southwestern Morocco close to Mauritania, are good examples of a mixture of styles. They are made of silver and are decorated with yellow, green and blue cloisonné enamel, a technique introduced to Morocco by Jewish jewelers expelled from Spain at the end of the fifteenth century. The main elements of the necklaces – large balls in one, three amulet cases in the other – are influenced by African styles. Between the principal components are clusters of coral beads and coin pendants.

Sephardi Bridal Couple

Jerusalem
Early 20th century
Bride's dress, gift of Nurit Na'aman, Jerusalem
Bridegroom's suit, gift of Sapir Family, Jerusalem

Many Jews expelled from Spain in 1492 migrated directly to Eretz Israel, then part of the Ottoman Empire, but more found refuge in western parts of the Empire – present-day Bosnia, Bulgaria and western Turkey. Later, many Sephardim joined the earlier exiles, settling in the Holy cities, especially in Jerusalem. In fact, until the middle of the nineteenth century, the Sephardim were not only the largest but also almost the exclusive Jewish community in the country.

When these fashionable wedding costumes were worn, the Sephardim had already become westernized, but still spoke Judeo-Espagnol (Ladino), a fifteenth-century Castilian dialect. The bride wears a white, European-style gown, her head covered with a white lace kerchief and a wreath of flowers. The bridegroom wears a European suit, his headgear a black felt version of the fez, the red hat most commonly worn in the Ottoman Empire.

In spite of westernization, the couple wed, according to the Sephardi custom, under a *talamo*, not the European *huppa*. The *talamo,* a temporary structure, has three walls and a roof of *Torah* Ark curtains. A Turkish rug, a carved table inlaid with mother-of-pearl in the style typical of Damascus work, and a brass bowl add an eastern Mediterranean flavor.

'Applying the Henna' Ceremony (Mendi)
Bene Israel Community in India
Gifts of Mrs Ita Aber, New York; Mr Baruch Birwadkar,
Or-Akiva; Mrs Diana Jacob, Bombay; Nora and Shelim
Dandekar, Yavne; Mrs Marion Sofaer, New York;
Baroness Alix de Rothschild, Paris; Sir Jacob Sassoon Charity
Fund, Bombay

There were three distinct Jewish communities in India – the
Cochin Jews, the Baghadadi Jews and the Bene Israel from the
Bombay area. From their Hindu and Muslim neighbors, the
Bene Israel adopted the custom of 'applying the Henna,' a
ceremony performed on the evening before a wedding.

Henna, a dye produced from the roots and leaves of a
sweet, pungent flowering plant which produces reddish-
orange stains, was believed to ward off evil spirits. The
ceremony was conducted separately for the bride and groom.
Each family received some henna paste from the other family
to mix with their own, the mixture, spread on the ring finger
and feet of the bridal couple, signifying their union.

Other symbolic objects present were an oil lamp with
seven wicks to repel evil spirits, rice symbolizing fertility and
riches, lumps of sugar depicting sweetness and pleasure, a
coconut promising both food and fuel, and money symbolizing wealth and economic security.

The bride's green sari connotes freshness and rejuvena-
tion. Wreaths of jasmine flowers and silver chains, placed on
the bride's forehead and temples after first being attached to
the foreheads of five healthy women, further insured fertility
and wealth.

Jewish Bride

San'a, Yemen
Early 20th century
Reconstruction made by Rabbanit Bracha Kapah and the
Zadok family, Jerusalem

Yemenite Jews lived a traditional life, practicing age-old customs. For women, the prearranged wedding was doubtless the most important event of their life, often taking place before puberty.

The bride's costume is typically Jewish; Muslim brides, as Muslims in general, wore different attire. The luxurious garments, part hers and part brought by a woman specializing in dressing brides, included a sumptuous coat-dress of fabric brocaded in gold thread, and trousers with leggings decorated with star motifs made of red and silk threads, an exclusively Jewish embroidery pattern. Her headgear was a tall, towering, pearl-embroidered triangular piece framed by fresh flowers and branches of rue, believed to ward off the evil eye.

On no other occasion was the Yemenite woman so lavishly bedecked with jewelry: earhangings dangled from the pointed pearl headgear to her chest, which was completely covered with multiple rows of necklaces made of silver and coral beads, pearls, amulet cases and silver bells. Both her arms were adorned with filigree bracelets arranged in a specific order, and her fingers accommodated up to twenty filigree rings. All the jewelry was crafted by Jewish silversmiths, a specifically Jewish occupation in the Yemen.

Festive Setting for a Mother after Childbirth

San'a, Yemen

In societies such as the Jewish communities in many parts of the world where tradition and religious observance were important, childbearing was considered a great blessing. In the past lack of proper medical assistance and inadequate sanitary conditions made it a life-threatening endeavor, prompting special treatment for the new mother. In San'a, Yemen's capital, a mother spent a post-partum period of forty days in a specially prepared room. Being ritually impure and also endangered by evil spirits, she sat in one corner, behind a triangular wooden structure. This ensured her symbolic separation from female guests who came to congratulate her, drink coffee, eat raisins and nuts, and smoke the *narguileh*. Incense would be burned to sweeten the air and drive away evil spirits.

Significantly, the same embroidered dress she is wearing would subsequently be included in her burial clothes, implying her sucessful escape from the perils of childbirth. She wears her jewelry, especially her rings – wedding gifts from her husband. The room is adorned with a special wallhanging, green bottles, glass balls, aromatic plants, dried fruit and tasseled ostrich eggs. All provide decoration but are also thought to enhance fertility and bestow magical protection.

While Yemenite wedding customs have seen a revival in modern Israel, this protection of the new mother has been almost abandoned, due to greatly improved medical care and better supervised deliveries.

A *mezuzah* is a rectangular piece of parchment inscribed with verses from Deuteronomy (6:4-9; 11:13-21). On the outer side of the parchment the divine name '*Shaddai*' appears, often accompanied by the words 'The Lord our God the Lord' in a cryptogram. The parchment is rolled so that the name *Shaddai* is visible and placed within a case which is then affixed to the doorpost.

Aimed to protect the dwellers of the house, a Jewish home is recognized first and foremost by the *mezuzah* at the door. *Mezuzah* cases are fashioned from various materials, and styles and design vary according to local traditions and taste.

Men's caps

Morocco, Bokhara, Afghanistan, Yemen, Persia and Eastern Europe

Although not a specific religious obligation, a head cover was prescribed by custom and became one of the characteristics of a Jewish man's attire throughout the world. The style of the head cover varied from region to region, and was often pre-scribed by the local authorities in an attempt to segregate the Jews from the rest of the population. Thus in Bokhara Jewish men were obliged to wear a fur hat in the street, and in Morocco a black felt hat.

In all Jewish communities men wore caps at home, and sometimes out-of-doors as well, with the caps differing markedly in shape and decoration. Caps in Afghanistan and Bokhara were hardened by many layers of fabric and embroidered with silk and metal threads on cotton and velvet (right). In Kurdistan there was a wide variety of caps, some made of embroidered cotton and silk, others knitted with colorful woolen threads and further decorated with embroi-dery. In Eastern Europe, the caps were soft and heavily embroidered with metal thread over a fill that created a raised, usually floral design.

Mezuzah Cases (from left to right)

Germany, 19th century
Silver, repoussé, engraved and pierced
Gift of Jakob Michael, New York, in memory of his wife
Erna Sondheimer-Michael

Central Europe, 19th century
Silver, engraved
Gift, E. Burstein Collection, Lugano

Slovakia, 19th century
Wood, carved
Apparently from a synagogue or other public Jewish building.
Stieglitz Collection donated to the Israel Museum with the
contribution of Erica and Ludwig Jesselson, New York

Germany, early 19th century
Wood, carved
Gift of Mr and Mrs Victor Carter, Los Angeles, USA

Bombay, India, 19th century
Brass, cast

USA, 20th century
Silver, pierced
Artist: Ludwig Wolpert
Gift of Mr and Mrs Abraham Kanoff,
New York

H 11.2 – 28.5 cm (4½ – 11¼ in)

Circumcision Amulets

Left: Germany, 19th century
Baruch and Ruth Rappaport, Geneva (Feuchtwanger Collection)
Center: Morocco 20th century
Gift of Baroness Alix de Rothschild, Paris
Top right: Alsace, 18th century
Mr Simon Levi, Paris
Bottom right: Italy, 20th century
Baruch and Ruth Rappaport, Geneva (Feuchtwanger Collection)
Paper amulet 33.3 × 22.3 cm (15 ½ × 8 ¾ in)

According to Jewish custom, a boy is circumcised on the eighth day after his birth, thus becoming a member of the Jewish people. It is believed that man is exposed to evil forces during situations in which he passes from one stage of life to another. Circumcision is such a precarious moment, when the baby receives a new identity.

For protection during this 'rite of passage,' magical means have been employed to safeguard the small, fragile baby. In all Jewish communities, both East and West, amulets of various shapes and materials were attached to the baby, his crib or the walls of his room, containing paraphernalia believed to be of some beneficial effect in subduing harmful forces. The most commonly found are the triangular shape, the fist, teeth, corals, rooster representations and Hebrew writings invoking God.

Style and material are usually influenced by the local cultures in which the Jewish communities lived. For example, the protective hand representation is similar to the Muslim hand of Fatima so widespread in North Africa, and the crystal pendant from Italy could have been a church relic had it not been carved with a Hebrew inscription.

Gold Jewelry

Bokhara

Late 19th century

Forehead decoration: Gift of Baroness Alix de Rothschild, Paris

Traditionally, the bride arrived at her husband's home with jewelry that she had been given by her father, along with pieces bought by her father with funds provided by the bridegroom. Jewelry worn by a woman on public festive occasions such as weddings announced her social standing, determining her position among the guests. It was also believed to protect the wearer against the evil eye and assure her fertility. Most importantly, jewelry was the woman's personal property, securing her economic wellbeing; only she could sell pieces.

Fashioned from high-grade gold and precious materials such as green and pink tourmalines and baroque pearls, the pieces were beautifully designed and expertly crafted. A complete set included bracelets, earrings, and an elaborate necklace and forehead decoration. Two techniques were used: stones inlaid into hammered gold for the forehead piece, and linked, fine, repetitive filigree units for the necklace. Not every woman could, of course, afford such magnificent examples as these brought to Jerusalem by Bokharan Jews around the turn of the century.

Dowry of a Jewish Bride

Bokhara

19th century

For many centuries urban oases along the famed Central Asian Silk Route, especially Bokhara, Tashkent and Samarkand, have had Jewish inhabitants.

One of the richest dowries of any Jewish community is this spectacular Bokharan example, containing items made from expensive materials such as vibrantly dyed silks, gold and gems. It included several sets of dresses, coats, underpants, scarves and ornate leather boots for the bride's future use. Because the bride moved into the bridegroom's family home, only a few items of bedding, copper vessels and china sets were included.

A major clause of the engagement agreement pertained to dowry content and quality, prompting mothers and daughters to begin preparing well before the marriage. During the dowry presentation ceremony held a few days before the wedding, an older, experienced woman, often a widow, assessed the value of each object against an agreed list. The dowry list and each item's value were then included in the marriage contract (*ketubbah*), and a double or triple sum set against the bridegroom as payment in case of divorce. The *ketubbah* was thus an extremely important document which the bride kept throughout her life, and it was often buried with her.

Costume of a Druze Woman
Galilee, Israel
Late 19th century

The Druze are an independent sect, centering around the figure of the prophet El-Hakem, who broke away from Isma'ili Islam in the tenth century. Fleeing persecution, they found refuge in the mountains of Lebanon, the Galilee and the Carmel, where they developed their secret mystical religion. The Druze are strictly observant, and prohibit marriage outside the community.

Shown here is a rare costume, once common among Druze women in the Galilee and Carmel mountains in the second half of the nineteenth and early twentieth centuries. Though first used as a wedding dress, it was later worn on festive occasions. Composed of a sparingly-embroidered long-sleeved cotton dress and short-sleeved coat, and a silk kerchief fastened to the head with a cloth wreath, the costume reflects the quiet elegance of Druze women.

Palestinian costumes from Bethlehem

1930s

Gift of Amir Family, Herzliya

The richly embroidered costumes of Palestinian women vary in their materials and style from region to region, sometimes even from village to village. Outfits were prepared for the wedding and afterwards were worn on festive occasions. The 'royal dress,' from Bethlehem comprises a lavishly-embroidered dress, a short cropped jacket, a high conical hat held by a silver chain under the chin and a shawl (figure on the right). It stands out because of its rich silk and velvet fabrics and spectacular embroidery making use of the unusual couched technique, with gilded and silk threads and cords.

The intricate geometric and floral designs and superior quality of embroidery created a lucrative business for Bethlehem embroiderers who fashioned complete dresses or panels to order. Women from villages surrounding Jerusalem were enthusiastic patrons of Bethlehem embroidered panels, preferring those with red rather than gilded cords, which they attached to their dresses made of Syrian silk. Such is the dress on the left, belted with a Damascus silk fabric.

Bethlehem embroidery, most probably developed from Byzantine ecclesiastical styles, reached its high point between the 1920s and the 1940s, a time of rapid economic development under the British Mandate. This period brought modernization and westernization to Palestine, yet also witnessed the flourishing of traditional styles.

Costume of a Jewish woman
Ethiopia
Recent

Knowledge of Ethiopian Jews is centuries old, yet only in the early twentieth century did they emerge from isolation. By 1991 tens of thousands had arrived to settle in Israel. Ethiopian Jews were farmers, ironsmiths and weavers; the women were potters, basket-weavers and embroiderers. They did not differ much from their neighbors except for the maintenance of religious laws relating to the Sabbath and holy days, Kosher food and family purity.

While in recent times men's costumes followed European fashions, women's dress preserved traditional styles. Their three-part outfit, made of white cotton, was woven by men. The long, wide dress is worn over the head and has a short opening in front. A long embroidered band decorates the front and ends with a large, stylized cross pattern, a design perhaps originating from ecclesiastical robes. After exposure to world Jewry, new motifs such as the *Magen David*, the Tablets of the Law and the *Menorah*, were added to the traditional design. The dress is tied with a fabric belt that has wide, densely embroidered bands at both edges. The outer garment of both men and women is a wrap, draped around the shoulders with one end covering the neck. It may be worn around the waist, or on the head, according to the mood of the wearer.

Costumes of a Jewish couple

Kurdistan, Iraq
Early 20th century

According to their tradition, the Jews of Kurdistan are one of the Ten Lost Tribes of Israel. Living for thousands of years in the mountainous areas neighboring Iran, Iraq, Syria and Turkey, they have preserved ancient Talmudic customs, as well as the Aramaic language.

Weaving and dyeing fabrics were important crafts for Jewish men, while women learned to spin, sew, and embroider garments. A typical woman's garment, represented by this colorful costume from Aqra in Iraqi Kurdistan, includes fully-cut long silk underpants, a wide and long dress with sleeves that have a long triangular addition, a short fitted vest and a long fitted coat. The triangular additions to the dress sleeves were pulled through the coat sleeves and tied behind the neck, to enable the women to work. On her head she would wear a kerchief with many colorful fringes. A wrap would be worn over this costume.

The man's costume includes a white shirt, very wide trousers narrowing at the ankles and held by a wide cloth belt tied several times around the waist, a short fitted vest, a short fitted jacket, and a small cap wrapped around by a kerchief. The embroidery serves either as strengthening for the seams or as decorative amulets.

The Ortenau Room
Munich
Gift of Erich and Poly Ortenau, Munich

Shown here is a highly personal view of the intimate trappings of middle-class German-Jewish life over a period of 150 years from the early nineteenth century to 1938. This room belonged to the Ortenau family of Bad Reichenhall, near Munich. Eric Ortenau's father was a medical doctor and was so appreciated by the people of the town that they preserved the entire contents of the house throughout World War II. This room is thus at the same time a memorial to the victims of the Holocaust, and to those who sought to help them.

An afternoon tea gathering, a ceremony much cherished by German Jews, is the central focus of the room. The two women wear fashionable costumes from the end of the nineteenth century. Among the many family heirlooms is a portrait which hangs on the left of the rear wall representing an early forefather, Samuel Oppenheimer (1630-1703). Oppenheimer was a Court Jew, the 'finance minister' of his sovereign, supplying him with the means to wage his wars and keep his court and retinue intact.

The substantial and solid furniture was purchased in 1863 by Erich Ortenau's grandparents. Of particular interest is the writing desk on the right-hand side of the room, which belonged to the great German-Jewish poet Heinrich Heine (1797-1856), and came into the family's possession through Heine's doctor. Although highly integrated into German culture, the family kept its Jewish heritage and traditions alive, as the *Hanukkah* lamp and spicebox displayed in the vitrine show.

The Art Collections

Yigal Zalmona

If it was the goal of the founding fathers that the new national museum be multi-purpose, providing a comprehensive encounter with the cultural heritage of the Jewish people and Israel through its collections of archaeology and Judaica, and at the same time offering the Israeli public a window on world culture, it fell to the Arts Wing to fulfil the latter obligation. It is no accident, therefore, that the Bezalel Arts Wing comprises nine distinct curatorial departments reflecting this universal approach to its collections: European Art, Prints and Drawings, Israeli Art, Modern Art, Contemporary Art, Design and Architecture, Photography, East Asian Art, and the Arts of Africa, Oceania and the Americas. The Wing is also responsible for the Billy Rose Art Garden.

Like the archaeology, Judaica and ethnography wings, the art collections already began taking shape at the Bezalel Art College, when Boris Schatz collected paintings and objects in order to teach his students to create 'a Hebrew style.' Other works were added to these, to become the collections of the Bezalel Museum. The Arts Wing to this day bears the name 'The Bezalel Wing,' because it is the lineal descendant of that museum, which in 1965 became 'The Israel Museum.'

The 1960s and the early 1970s were the years in which the policy and holdings of the Israel Museum were crystallized and the Museum became a respected member of the world community of modern and innovative museums. Subsequently, during the late 1970s and 1980s, the activities of the Arts Wing increased significantly. Tasks that had been performed by a handful of people in the early stages were parcelled out to newly-recruited curators. New departments — for Design, Asian Art, Art of Oceania, Africa and the Americas — were inaugurated, and the new pavilions, designed by leading architects from Israel and abroad, were established to house collections of Israeli, European, and Twentieth-century art.

The Arts Wing also took under its aegis an information center for Israel Art within the museum and a downtown Jerusalem house containing works by the late artist, Anna Ticho.

The works in the Wing have increased by a factor of twenty, as have the number of exhibitions held under its auspices. The Arts Wing has staged on average about thirty exhibitions a year since the mid-1970s.

Recent catalogues have become extensive and significant publications, unlike the slim booklets of the early years.

The 1980s and 1990s have seen the Wing shift to activities that are 'user friendly' with efforts being made to reach out to a more general audience by means of catalogues, explanatory pamphlets, guided visits, wall texts and audio-visual presentations. During the last couple of decades, large and ambitious exhibitions, some of which have become blockbusters, have been produced in the Museum or imported as loan shows.

A quiet corner in the Art Garden. Left: Alexander Archipenko, *Woman Combing her Hair*, 1914; right: Aristide Maillol, *L'Harmonie*, 1942–3; background: Auguste Rodin, *Burgher of Calais*, 1885–6.

Department of European Art

In the 1960s, the Old Master collection was a focus of attention for those immigrants who arrived with a nostalgia for the European culture that they had chosen or been forced to leave when they came to live in Eretz Israel.

By the 1980s Old Master exhibitions had begun increasingly to attract a wider audience. An exhibition of the Armand Hammer Collection, spanning five hundred years of art, drew the largest number of visitors in the Museum's history. Similar success was accorded the 1993 exhibition of seventeenth-century Dutch biblical paintings, organized by the Israel Museum with the collaboration of the Jewish Museum in Amsterdam, and based on research which shed important light on biblical iconography.

The collections of the Department of European Art have grown substantially and contain a broad nucleus of seventeenth-century Dutch painters, but also include other schools from the fifteenth to nineteenth centuries.

Period Rooms

Near the Old Master galleries is a series of impressive eighteenth-century period rooms including a magnificent French Grand Salon which was originally part of the townhouse of Jacques-Samuel Bernard, one of the leading financiers of the period, and was sold in 1880 to Baron Edmond de Rothschild. He had it lifted practically intact from its setting and installed as the salon of a lavish townhouse he built on the Faubourg St Honoré. In 1969, this splendid salon was inaugurated in its new setting in the Israel Museum and is entered through a lovely, small Empire-style panelled room containing exquisite French porcelain. The other delightful eighteenth-century interiors are a small stuccoed Venetian *salotto* and a much larger English dining-room.

Department of Prints and Drawings

The Museum's collection of prints and drawings grew from 500 items in 1928 (at the Bezalel Museum), consisting mainly of works by artists living in Israel, to about 27,000 in 1936, based largely on donations of immigrants from Germany who came to this country when the Nazis rose to power. Today there are about 60,000 items in the Department's collections.

The Museum owns 80 drawings by Pascin, constituting the most important museum collection of Pascin's works on paper. There are many works by Old Masters in the Department's collections, many of which are based on Jewish or biblical themes, though there are also many collections of prints by important artists including a large group of etchings by Francisco de Goya. The Museum's collection of prints by Picasso numbers more than 600 works. Numerous prints and drawings by contemporary artists have also been donated to the Museum, and every important Israeli artist is represented. Other highlights are works by the artist and painter of stage sets, Boris Aronson, a series of original illustrations for the *Had-Gadya*

Paul Klee, Swiss, 1897–1940
Angelus Novus, 1920
India ink, color chalks and brown wash on paper,
31.8 × 24.2 cm (12 ½ × 9 ½ in)
Gift of Fania and Gershom Scholem, Jerusalem,
John Herring, Marlene and Paul Herring, Jo-Carole
and Ronald Lauder, New York

This drawing was created during a breakthough
year in Klee's artistic career: he had his first large-
scale exhibition in Munich, was about to join the
Weimar Bauhaus, and completed his artistic credo,
'Creative Confession,' in which he set forth his
metaphysical perception of reality.

It is within a metaphysical context that these
supernatural beings which populate Klee's work
must be viewed. It is noteworthy that during the
last years of his life he created some fifty celestial
angels.

This drawing intrigued the German Jewish
philosopher and literary critic, Walter Benjamin
(1892–1940), who purchased it in 1921. Benjamin's
lifelong friend, Gershom Scholem (1897–1982), the
distinguished scholar of Jewish mysticism, inherit-
ed the drawing after Benjamin's death. According
to Scholem, Benjamin, apart from a mystical identification with the _Angelus Novus,_ interpreted it
as the 'angel of history,' expressing his melancholy
view of the historical process as an unceasing cycle
of despair.

by Eliezer Lissitzky, a large collection of original drawings by Chagall for several of his books, and a very extensive collection of Dada and Surrealist documents and rare periodicals, making the Museum one of the most important research centers for this subject in the world.

The Department has held a number of major and influential exhibitions: 'Beyond Drawing,' presented in 1974, is to this day considered the most important exhibition of drawings ever held in Israel. It exhibited the works of artists who sought to cross the boundaries of traditional drawing, and to redefine the concept of 'line.' The exhibition of the collection of drawings belonging to the Duke of Devonshire (1977) and of drawings from the collection of the Uffizi Museum in Florence (1984) enabled the Israeli public to see marvelous drawings by great master painters from the Renaissance to the eighteenth century. 'Tradition and Revolution: the Jewish Renaissance in Russian Avantgarde Art 1912–1928' (1987) was an important exhibition, based on commissioned studies by various scholars, and demonstrating the importance of the Jewish dimension in Russian revolutionary culture. An exhibition of original works by William Blake on biblical themes, and important drawings by Picasso, are among some of the special exhibitions of prints and drawings mounted in recent years.

The Department also holds a large number of exhibitions of Israeli art. During the 1970s, drawing and works on paper in general were a favored medium for many of the world's leading artists, and so it was in Israel. Drawings by Israeli conceptual artists attained recognition and support in various art centers, especially in New York. All these artists had in the first instance been supported by the Israel Museum, and had also often exhibited here.

Ticho House

Anna Ticho, the Israeli draftswoman, was born in Vienna and emigrated to Eretz Israel at an early age. She married the legendary opthalmologist, Dr Ticho, and together they lived in an old Arab-style house which became a Middle Eastern literary salon during the 1920s and 1930s. Anna Ticho was excellent at drawing landscapes, and was considered the *grande dame* of Israeli art. On her death, she bequeathed her home and her 2000 drawings to the museum, which now administers the beautiful house. It contains a permanent gallery where works by Ticho are on show, a display space for temporary exhibitions, and a restaurant. The Ticho House, with its lovely garden, serves the inhabitants of Jerusalem as a venue for cultural events such as concerts and lectures.

Entrance to the Ticho House with garden restaurant.

Department of Photography

The Israel Museum was already mounting exhibitions of photography in the early 1970s, when this was a relatively unusual phenomenon in museums, and when, unlike today, there were no commercial photography galleries in Israel. The Museum very quickly reached the conclusion that there was a need for a curator of photography and chose a candidate to study abroad in order to gain expertise for establishing a proper department for the art of photography, which was then opened in 1978. The Museum's collection of photography is impressive, having been started by New York photographer Arnold Newman who began collecting works for a future Photography Department many years before the Department itself was realized. It totals some 55,000 photographs including rare masterpieces, some of them representing milestones in the history of photography. The Department is committed to Israeli photography, and includes complete and important collections of hundreds of works by the pioneers of photography in Eretz Israel, such as Mendel Diness, the first Jewish photographer who captured images of Jerusalem in the mid-nineteenth century; Yaakov

Contemporary works from the collection in the photography gallery. Right: Andy Warhol, *James Dean T-Shirt*, 1985; center: John Coplans, *Self-Portrait*, 1985.

Ben Dov, a photographer from the beginning of the present century; Yaakov Jack Rosner; S. J. Schweig, who photographed in the 1930s — the Museum owns some 12,000 of his negatives — and Bernheim, one of the great architecture and portrait photographers in Israel, 20,000 of whose negatives are in the Museum's possession.

The Department of Photography holds exhibitions of contemporary photographers, and has mounted a large exhibition of commercial photography in Israel, but among its fields of specialization in terms of both collections and exhibitions is the beginnings of photography in the Middle East. The exhibition 'Focus East; Early Photography in the Near East 1839–1885' (1988) was the climax of much research and became an important event in the sphere of historical photography exhibitions, being shown in major photography centers throughout the world. Other major departmental presentations have been devoted to the work of important international photographers, including Bill Brandt, André Kertesz, Erich Salomon, and Manuel Alvarez Bravo, the latter exhibition having also traveled to venues abroad following its initial showing in Jerusalem.

Department of Israeli Art

It is customary to see Israeli art as beginning with the founding of the Bezalel Art School in Jerusalem in 1906. The teachers who were brought to the school from Europe are considered as the first Israeli artists. The history of Israeli art since then has reflected the upheavals of Zionist and Israeli history and the changes in Israel's sense of identity.

Willem Sandberg, the Museum's first art advisor and ideologist, already marked out the principles of the museum's policy in this sphere: the acquisition of works from a fairly small number of important artists, while preserving the principle of in-depth acquisition and representation of all stages of development of these artists in the Museum's collections; awareness of local artists' work by means of intensive studio visits by curators; and a balanced program of activities that presents the work of veteran artists alongside that of younger artists. The Museum has held exhibitions of veteran artists and of younger artists.

In 1985 a large and beautiful two-storied pavilion was inaugurated for Israeli Art, enabling the Museum to display part of the permanent collection as well as temporary shows, with the possibility also of exhibiting large and ambitious works.

The Israel Museum is committed to the documenting of Israeli art and to the dissemination of information about it. To meet this need, an information center for Israeli Art was opened, containing thousands of artists' files, video films and current information about the local art scene. The Museum also encourages Israeli artists by awarding annual grants.

Department of Modern Art

The Department of Modern Art is responsible for international art from the late nineteenth century (Impressionism) to the 1960s. Over the years the collections have been enriched through the generosity of art lovers who also became friends of the museum. More than 130 sculptures by Jacques

Overleaf:
Works from the collection in the Modern Art gallery. Foreground left: Alberto Giacometti, *Woman of Venice*, 1956; right: Jean Arp, a group of plaster sculptures; background: René Magritte, *Le Château des Pyrénées*, 1959.

Motti Mizrachi, *Angelo, Angelo*, 1986.

Lipchitz were presented to the Museum, making possible a didactic retrospective display of the artist's work. In 1972, an important collection of works by Marcel Duchamp was donated and, more recently, the Museum has received two major collections which include paintings by Picasso, Degas, Kokoschka, Gaugin, Cézanne, Léger, Klee and other prominent modern artists.

Many exhibitions in the field of modern art were held when the Museum first opened. In 1966 one-man shows of Picasso and Klee were mounted, and an exhibition of the Sam and Ayala Zacks Collection (1976) enabled the Israeli public to view a most impressive private collection of international modern art. In recent years, exhibitions in the field have included blockbusters such as 'Monet to Matisse: Modern Masters from Swiss Private Collections' (1988), 'Masterpieces of German Expressionism from the Brücke Museum, Berlin' (1990), 'Marc Chagall: Dreams and Drama' (1993) — paintings by Chagall from collections in Russia which included his famous murals for the Jewish Theater in Moscow — and a retrospective of Camille Pissarro which included 125 works by the Jewish-French Impressionist (1994). These exhibitions have all attracted a very large public to the Museum.

A recent innovation of the Modern Art Department is a project which periodically brings one Impressionist or Post-Impressionist masterpiece to the Museum from important museums around the world — a single work by means of which the public can identify with the spirit and the essence of a specific style or problem in the history of modern art. The *Portrait of Emile Zola* by Manet, from the Musée d'Orsay in Paris, and Gustave Caillebotte's *The Bridge of Europe*, from the Petit Palais in Geneva, are among the first works brought to the country as part of the 'Visiting Masterpiece series.' The halls which house the modern art collections are situated in a beautiful Pavilion for Impressionist Art, which opened in 1979.

Department of Contemporary Art

Intensive activity in the sphere of contemporary international art has characterized the Museum almost since its inception. Exhibitions such as the 400 flowerpots installed by Jean-Pierre Raynaud in the Museum's entrance plaza (1971), or exhibitions by Boltanski (1973) and Rauschenberg (1974), have made the Museum part of the small family of museums which attempt to deal with contemporary art, and offer an image of a young and innovative museum which takes risks as well as providing a home for established cultural values.

Soldiers visiting the exhibition 'Antipathos – Black Humor, Irony and Cynicism in Contemporary Israeli Art,' 1993.

The contemporary art exhibitions of the 1970s, as befitted the decade of Conceptualism and Minimalism, were low-budget shows generally of the kind where the curator could bring most of the works in a suitcase. During the 1980s this orientation changed, with the creation of a separate department for contemporary art and the establishment of a foundation which enabled artists from abroad to come to Israel as artists-in-residence in order to create works to be shown in the Museum. Dennis Oppenheim (1979), James Turrell (1982), Mario Merz (1983), Jonathan Borofsky (1984), Kiki Smith (1994) are among the artists who have exhibited at the museum in this context.

The resources gathered for contemporary art increased and made possible ambitious projects such as the one-man exhibition of Anselm Kiefer (1984), 'New York Now' (1987) — an exhibition of new trends in American art, Julian Schnabel (1988), 'Post-Human' — a comprehensive exhibition of contemporary international art (1993), and 'Life Size: A Sense of the Real in Recent Art' (1990) — a huge exhibition which included works in the spheres of painting, sculpture and installation by the best of important international and Israeli artists, and which marked the inauguration of the museum's new Twentieth-century Art Building.

The Billy Rose Art Garden

One of the Museum's great attractions is the Billy Rose Art Garden, designed by the Japanese-American sculptor Isamu Noguchi, and extending over five acres. It is characterized by terraces built from agricultural heaps of boulders which recall the terraces that are so widespread in the hills around Jerusalem, and the archaeological structures which may be found in the landscapes of the Judaean Hills. The surface of the Garden is covered with a layer of small stones that recall Zen gardens in Japanese monasteries. The vegetation of the Garden is the natural vegetation of the area: rosemary bushes, olive and fig trees. Water flows from a spring in a fountain-sculpture erected by Noguchi. This is an integration of Oriental-Israeli hill landscapes with archaeological allusions and a garden from the Far East. Inside this dry garden the sculptures grow like the rock-islands in the Zen gardens in Japan. This is a unique and original conception for a sculpture garden, which Noguchi himself thought of as one of his two most important works.

Cypress and olive trees grace the semi-circular terraces forming the Billy Rose Art Garden.

Pablo Picasso, *Profiles*, 1967, concrete, executed by Carl Nesjar.

In essence, the Billy Rose Art Garden offers a walkway through the history of twentieth-century sculpture. Works by Rodin, Bourdelle and Maillol represent the beginnings of modern sculpture. A sculpture by David Smith and a monumental masterpiece and other works by Henry Moore reflect the next important stages in the history of sculpture. A large Richard Serra, a brick structure by the conceptualist Sol LeWitt, and an impressive installation by the American sculptor James Turrell which allows one to gaze at the sky through an opening in the ceiling — these and others represent important contemporary offerings in the medium. The Garden continues to grow and develop, regularly absorbing new sculptures. It lives and changes like the Museum's interiors. To a large extent it proffers the art outwards, pouring it towards the city and towards nature.

Department of Design and Architecture

The Design Department was founded in 1973, on the initiative of Willem Sandberg, who himself was a talented, well-known and influential designer. From its inception it became a vibrant and influential center of activity.. The Department's exhibitions have been noteworthy not only for content, but also for the innovative way the exhibitions are designed. To this day, the Department is the only exhibition space in the country which regularly exhibits design from abroad alongside Israeli design. It was mounting exhibitions before there was real awareness in Israel of the subject of design. Exhibitions range in subject matter from Scandinavian design (1974), to important graphic and industrial designers including Ettore Sottsass (1978) and Bruno Munari (1988), textile artists like Sheila Hicks (1980), and important design studios such as Danese (1976), Superstudio of Florence (1982), Pentagram (1983), Memphis (1983) and Grapus (a poster design team from France, 1988).

The Department is also committed to the subject of architecture, and has held exhibitions of Israeli architects (Al Mansfeld – who designed the Israel Museum, Zvi Hecker, Munio Gitai), international architects such as Alvar Aalto (1987) and others, and important architectonic projects (the interesting proposal by Daniel Liebeskind for the Jewish Museum of Berlin, and the project for the Supreme Court building in Jerusalem).

The Department is designed for large and unusual exhibitions, such as a show devoted to the theme of Recycling which transformed the exhibition space into a recycling plant: the 'Lego' show – an interactive exhibition where the public created works with the aid of half-a-million 'Lego' blocks; the 'Patents' exhibition, which displayed the creativity which leads to the inventions of hundreds of different objects; and an exhibition which displayed one of the design stages of the Ford Sierra automobile.

About one hundred design exhibitions have been held at the Museum so far and many of the Department's exhibitions have been shown at art centers in Europe, the USA, and Japan. The Department has also succeeded in creating an important collection of international and Israeli design, which is often displayed in the Design Gallery and which serves as a resource center for scores of students in the Design Departments of institutions throughout the country.

Department of East Asian Art

In 1965, its first year of existence, the Israel Museum mounted an exhibition of art from the Far East. Other exhibitions followed, but the East Asian Art pavilion was inaugurated only in 1985. Donors and collectors have enriched the Department's collections, and it appears today that there is room to expand the Department's exhibition hall and storerooms.

Exhibitions of Asian art at the Museum attract a large audience, whether they are small, like the specialist displays on the Japanese sword, or major events such as '3,500 Years of Chinese Art from the Collection of the Arthur Sackler Foundation' (1987), and the 'Jacob Pins Collection of Japanese Art' (1994).

***Guanyin, Goddess of Mercy, in the form of
Yulan, the fishermaiden***
China, Southern Song Dynasty, 1127–1279
Wood with traces of gilding
H 17 cm (6 ¾ in)
Bequest of Dr Emmy Rosenbacher, Jerusalem

The Southern Song dynasty, established after the Mongols
captured the northern part of China, was an epoch of exquisite refinement. Painting, poetry and ceramics reached unsur-
passed heights. The ripeness of Buddhist sculpture of the preceding Tang period approached over-refinement. Most sculptures remaining from that period are large and wooden, originally used for worship in temples. The Buddhist divinity *bodhisattva Avalokitesvara*, the Compassionate One, was
transformed during the Song dynasty into a feminine form,
Guanyin, Goddess of Mercy.

This small sculpture was probably created for the home
altar of a wealthy, discriminating patron. The goddess holds a
fish basket containing a large fish, identifying her as *Yulan,*
a maiden who sold fish and is the patron saint of mariners.
The delicate figurine with her subtly smiling round face, her
dress with natural folds gathered in her hand, a carelessly
draped shawl around her sloping shoulders, is a sculptural
masterpiece, illustrating the exceptional quality for which the
Song period is known.

Department of the Arts of Africa, Oceania,
and the Americas

The Pavilion of Pre-Columbian Art, inaugurated in 1979, contains the
important collection of Pre-Columbian art which was donated to the
Museum in 1978, and the Galleries of Oceanian, African and North
American Art, which were inaugurated a year later. The Pre-Columbian col-
lection covers archaeological findings from the Mesoamerican (Mexico and
Central America) and Andean (South America, with special emphasis on
Peru) civilizations, prior to the arrival of Columbus and, later, Cortes and
Pizzaro. The collection covers many of the artistic developments in these
very diverse groups over a considerable time span (these civilizations date

roughly from 1500 BCE until shortly after 1500 CE, i.e. some thirty centuries). It is particularly strong in the pottery of Western Mexico. The lively human figures involved in various aspects of daily life, and the enchanting animals, especially the large-bellied dogs who were part of the household, have particular charm because of the range of emotions they so spontaneously express. The collection is also strong in the archaeology of Vera Cruz, and boasts a splendid seated male figure in the Las Remojadas style with a jaguar's head springing from its stomach, and two disturbing figures of Xipe Totec, a god symbolizing the renewal of life who was emulated by worshippers wearing the skins of freshly-killed human sacrificial victims.

The special design of the permanent exhibit, which has earned many compliments, makes use of stages covered with wooden tiles that constitute an organic base on which the terracotta sculptures rest naturally. This design principle has also been used in the impressive display of Oceanian and African art, and Indian art from North America where, too, because of the nature of the exhibits, it was important to preserve the free and natural effect. The display contains rare and impressive exhibits: masks of great importance and sculptures of the highest standard. With the aid of guides from the Youth Wing, many children learn here about these distant civilizations and satisfy their curiosity about how the boomerang works and about the symbolic meaning of the African mask.

An addition in this field will come with the exhibition of the art collection of the sculptor Jacques Lipchitz which includes pieces of major importance from African, Indian, Pre-Columbian and Eskimo art. This will allow students and visitors to learn more about the affinity of modern artists with that art which not so long ago was still called 'primitive.'

The Arts Wing is fulfilling the museum's mandate to serve as an avenue of communication by fostering cultural consciousness while at the same time conducting its activities on the borderline between education and experience, picking its way carefully between activities designed for large audiences and projects more élitist in nature.

Section of totem pole, wood, Kwakiutl people (?), British Columbia, Canada.

Fernand Léger, *Nature Morte* (Still-Life), 1919. Sam and Ayala Zacks Collection.

Lucas Cranach the Elder, Workshop
German, 1472–1553
Lucretia, c. 1535–7
Oil on panel, 63.2 × 50 cm (25 × 19 ¾ in)
Purchased with the assistance of the Association of German Friends of the Israel Museum, an anonymous donor, Dr Martin Pomp, New York, and Dr Luba Gurdus in memory of her husband Jacob

Lucas Cranach the Elder served as court artist to the Electors of Saxony in Wittenberg. He received the right not to reside at court which enabled him to run a successful workshop, where his son, Lucas Cranach the younger, joined him in 1537. Both father and son used the winged serpent as their signature, which adds to the difficulty of establishing correct attributions.

Cranach was a friend of Luther, a supporter of the Reformation and a Humanist. Though the story of Lucretia was popular with other German painters of the time, it must have been a special favorite of Cranach's patrons, as we know of 37 versions of the subject painted by both Cranach the Elder and the Younger in their workshop.

Lucretia, wife of Tarquin Collatinus, was raped by Sextus, son of the King of Rome, Tarquinus the Proud. Admitting her disgrace to her husband and father, Lucretia took her own life, sparking the revolt of Junius Brutus (509 BCE) which led to the establishment of the Roman Republic.

Lucretia's story provided the artist with an excuse for portraying a partially nude figure while treating the subject of morality.

Cranach's portrayal of the female body departs from Italian classical ideals, following more closely medieval depictions of women. Her dress, hair style, hat and trinkets are typical of those worn by Saxon princesses of the time.

Bartolomeo Bettera
Italian, 1639 – after 1688
Still-life with Musical Instruments and Books
Oil on canvas, 70 × 82.5 cm (27 ½ × 32 ½ in)
Gift of Lila and Herman Shickman, New York, to American
Friends of the Israel Museum

Bartolomeo Bettera was the most talented student and follower of the Bergamese artist, Evaristus Baschenis, originator of
the 'musical' still-life. Achieving success with this type of
painting, Baschenis opened and supervised a workshop where
many versions of this theme were treated.

In this work, music is only a memory. The atmosphere is
mute and remote. Signs of disuse and neglect are evident
everywhere; dust covers the lute in the foreground in a magnificent *trompe l'oeil,* deceiving onlookers who have to be
stopped from attempting to wipe it off. The violin strings are
broken. The painting symbolizes the idea of 'Vanitas' – human
pleasure; life itself is but a short-lived illusion while the dust
echoes '. . . All are of the dust, and all turn to dust again.
(Ecclesiastes 3:20)

The artist sometimes signed with the initials B.B divided
by a cross, which appears here on a bookmark stuck into a
thick volume.

Jacob Gerritsz Cuyp and Aelbert Cuyp
Dutch, 1594–1650 and 1620–1692
Portrait of a Family in a Landscape, 1641
Oil on canvas, 155 × 245 cm (61 × 96 ½ in)
Gift of Mr and Mrs Joseph Nash, Paris

A collaborative work of father and son, Jacob Gerritsz and
Aelbert Cuyp of Dordrecht, the composition is both a family
portrait of the hunting genre and a landscape painting.
Hunting, a privilege granted to the upper classes, had just
become fashionable when this painting was commissioned.

The figures by Jacob are rather rigid and stiff. Their faces
reveal a family resemblance and their ages are inscribed on
the ground beneath them. The maid on the extreme right is
holding bellows and has a chicken in her basket to be
prepared for the family outing. The son, accompanied by a
servant, at left, is handing his trophy – the dead fowl – to his
youngest sister, thus enlivening the composition.

The young girl, second from right, is holding a bunch of
grapes. Grapes held in this manner by a young woman
symbolized virginity and chastity, and, by implication, the
righteousness, virtue and morality of the whole family.

The vast landscape, bathed in golden hues reminiscent of
the style of Jan van Goyen, was painted by Aelbert, then a
youth of twenty-one. Cows graze and are being milked and
people are at work in the field. All that the viewer sees is the
family's property – additional evidence of God's blessing
bestowed on this affluent family.

Jan Victors
Dutch, 1619/20 – 1676
The Expulsion of Hagar, 1650
Oil on canvas 143.5 × 178.7 cm (56 ½ × 70 ¼ in)
Gift of Emile E. Wolf, New York, to American Friends of the
Israel Museum

Jan Victors, a student of Rembrandt before 1640, often painted biblical scenes and, since he was an orthodox Calvinist, restricted himself to subjects from the Old Testament. For this reason, much of his work had appeal for members of the Amsterdam Jewish Community.

The expulsion of Hagar was popular with Rembrandt and his pupils and Victors alone was responsible for several versions on this theme. By arranging his figures along the width of the canvas and by cutting them off at knee length, Victors was able to bring the scene nearer to the viewer, thus heightening the impact of the psychological drama.

Abraham, dressed as an Oriental dignitary, appears indecisive. His hand hovers above the head of his son, Ishmael, and a glowing light creates a halo symbolizing God's blessing. Conflict is emphasized by contrasting Sara, old and shrivelled, pointing the way out, with the beautiful, young Hagar, turning for a last glance at the house she is leaving, while wringing her hands in despair. Heightened feelings are evident as is the sense of color and texture, especially in Hagar's satin dress.

18th-Century English Dining Room
Presented by David Berg in memory of his mother, Ida Berg

A separate room, furnished for the sole purpose of serving meals, was a new fashion in the mid-eighteenth century. The fine pine panelling dates from c.1740 and represents the Baroque style of the time. The large table in the center is set for twelve with matching plates and glassware. The silverware is the work of outstanding craftsmen of the period such as Paul de Lamerie and Paul Storr, and many pieces are engraved with the armorials of prominent English families.

A console (side table) and the mirror above it, and the mantlepiece mirror, decorated in shell and floral motifs, are typical of Rococo taste between 1754 and 1765.

Chinese art was highly valued and esteemed at this time and here it features as the small pagoda carved in the center of the mantlepiece mirror and in the decoration of the mirror with small Chinese porcelain objects. The mahogany breakfast side table was designed in the manner of Robert Adam, the greatest exponent of Neo-Classicism and the antique revival, who was pre-eminent in the last three decades of the century.

The magnificent furnishings and objects, a mixture of tastes and styles, illustrate the look of a country home of a well-to-do gentleman in late eighteenth-century England.

William Adolphe Bouguereau
French, 1825 – 1905
Girl Holding Lemons, 1899
Oil on canvas, 65.9 × 49.8 cm (26 × 19 ½ in)
Bequest of Sam Weisbord, Los Angeles, to American Friends of the Israel Museum in memory of Goldie Weisbord

'There is only one kind of painting. It is the painting that presents the eye with perfection.' These words of the artist best express his artistic credo, which he followed throughout his long career.

William Adolphe Bouguereau was trained in the Neo-Classical academic tradition and remained faithful to classical ideals. As winner of the much coveted 'Prix de Rome', he traveled to Rome in 1850, where he was very much influenced by High Renaissance art.

Striving to create a modern version of the art of the 'living antique,' a great part of his work was devoted to peasant themes, especially Italian. Here the model, clad in white, *à la Greque,* is holding a bunch of freshly-picked lemons symbolizing a modern goddess of fertility.

The painting is an example of the artist's later style when his technique became freer, his colors more harmonious, and his drapery folds softer. The landscape of a lake and distant hills acquires an almost Impressionistic character.

The Rothschild Room
An 18th-century French Salon
Gift of Baron and Baroness Edmond de Rothschild

Children visiting the Museum react with awe before this room, feeling that it is a king's palace from a fairy tale. Their reactions are correct since the room is an attempt to represent Parisian elegance of the eighteenth century. The decor, furnishings and *objets d'art* are meant to capture the elegance and splendor of Versailles. This is a grand salon of a 'Hotel Particulier' belonging to a second-generation member of the new aristocracy, the Count de Courbet. His house was located at 46 Rue de Bac and was designed by the architect François Debias-Aubry between 1741 and 1745.

The room's panelling was removed when Baron Haussman widened the streets of Paris and demolished expendable homes. In 1880 the panels were installed in the study of Baron Edmond de Rothschild, the 'benefactor,' grandfather of the present Baron. The panels were put into storage when the house was sold. After World War II they remained in storage until 1969 when they were installed at the Israel Museum.

Over the doors, in the four corners, are the paintings of the then known four continents, while two Gobelin tapestries depicting mythological subjects flank the marble mantel. The tapestries, depicting 'Love of the Gods,' were from a series made for Louis XV. Between the tall windows are portraits of Baronesse de Vanne before her dressing table, by Aved, and Nattier's portrait of a lady as Diana. A marble sculpture by Coustou shows a follower of Diana with her hunting-horn.

Three large mirrors reflect the candlelight from the crystal chandeliers and appear to enlarge the room, adding to the atmosphere of opulence and splendor.

Claude Gellée (called Claude Lorrain), French, 1600–1682
Wooded Landscape, c. 1660–1665
Brown ink and wash on paper, 17.5 × 24.9 cm (6 ¾ × 9 ¾ in)
Gift of Mr and Mrs Eugene Victor Thaw, New York, to
American Friends of the Israel Museum

Apart from his stature as one of the pivotal figures in the history of landscape painting, Claude Lorrain has captured the hearts of lovers of drawing for several centuries. Born in Lorraine, Claude moved to Italy as an adolescent, and with the exception of two early trips to Nancy and Naples, spent his adult life in Rome and its surroundings.

This drawing comes from an album bound in parchment and first mentioned in the death inventory of Don Livio Odescalchi (1713). At that time the album contained 81 sheets by the artist. The album was then lost and only re-emerged in 1960, with 60 drawings still intact. These drawings are almost all of outstanding quality and in fresh condition, comprising, as a group, the most comprehensive anthology of Claude's work.

Joseph Mallord William Turner, British, 1775–1851
North-West View of Jerusalem, c. 1832–34
Watercolor over pencil and ink on paper, 12.1 × 20.3 cm
(4 ¾ × 8 in)
On permanent loan from the Jerusalem Foundation

Over the centuries, the city of Jerusalem has captured the
hearts and minds of many poets and painters. The Israel
Museum possesses excellent examples of the inspired visions
of the city by both major and minor artists.

Surprisingly, perhaps, Turner never visited Jerusalem and
the Holy Land but his imagination was strongly attracted to
its topography because of his knowledge of the Bible and his
familiarity with paintings and prints of the region made by
nineteenth-century Romantic artists who had traveled to the
Near East.

This view shows the city from the north, with the
Damascus Gate on the left. The Dome of the Rock is slightly
left of center and the Mount of Olives rises behind it. On the
right is the Dome of the Holy Sepulchre. In the foreground, on
the right, a group of women and children rest under the trees.
They are presumably pilgrims, dressed in what seems like a
European interpretation of oriental clothing. The entire
ensemble of landscape and figures echoes Psalm CXXII; 2-3:
'Our feet shall stand within thy gates, O Jerusalem. Jerusalem
is built as a city which is bound firmly together.'

Pablo Picasso, Spanish, 1881–1973
Portrait of an Adolescent, 1905
Wash and watercolor on paper mounted on cardboard,
37.4 × 26.7 cm (14 ¾ × 10 ½ in)
Gift of Alain Coblence, New York, in memory of Jean Davray,
to American Friends of the Israel Museum

With his move to Paris in 1904, Picasso's color scale gradually
lightened, and depictions of figures from the world of the
traveling theater and the circus, full of the joy of life, replaced
the melancholy themes of the Blue Period (1900–1904). This
drawing belongs to this new phase. Many of the drawings of
those years were made using a combined technique – ink and
wash or wash and watercolor – and were usually preliminary
sketches for details of oil paintings.

Perhaps a sketch for the left-hand figure of *Les saltim-
banques* (National Gallery, Washington, DC), this drawing
was done in the same year as the painting, and both show the
head in profile. In both, too, the expression is serious and the
gaze concentrated, lost in thought. On the other hand, a number of details which differ between the two, such as the unruly
hair, and the almost exaggeratedly long bare neck in the
drawing, as opposed to the scarf tied around the neck in the
painting, may discount this connection.

Paul Gauguin, French 1848–1903
Page from the Carnet Huyghe, 1888–1901
Graphite and charcoal on lined ledger paper, 17 × 10.5 cm
(6 ¾ × 4 ¼ in)
Gift of Sam Salz, New York, to the America-Israel Cultural
Foundation

In this 228-page notebook, one of only six which have survived, we are privileged to explore Gauguin's creative process
during his period of activity in Arles. In addition to doodles,
sketches and finished studies for paintings, the notebook contains accounts and lists which give us a precious and richly
varied insight into Gauguin's work, character and lifestyle.

The drawings on the right-hand page are some of the
studies in the notebook for the well-known painting *Old
Women of Arles* (Art Institute of Chicago).

Jules Pascin (Julius Mordecai Pincas), b. Bulgaria, active
France, 1885–1930
A Lady and Hunchback in a Cafe,
c. 1908–9
Graphite and watercolor on paper, 34.5 × 26.5 cm
(14 ¾ × 10 ½ in)
Gift of the artist's brother, Joseph Pincas, Paris

The Israel Museum is exceptionally well-endowed with works
by Jules Pascin, possessing approximately one hundred oil
paintings, watercolors and drawings, which represent nearly
every period and medium.

Pascin's figures appear to acknowledge the spectator,
usually inviting the viewer to enter into the canvas. In addition, his works are characterized by a powerful observation of
mood. Executed in Paris, the artist's home from 1905 until his
death in 1930, this drawing is charged with *fin-de-siècle*
satire and decadence so characteristic of Pascin's years of association with the satirical periodical *Simplicissimus*. The
artist has juxtaposed a mean-looking hunchback and an
attractive, if aging, woman of the *demi-monde*. Jugendstil's
flowing line and broad disregard of detail, a sensuous severity
and a decorative and nostalgic mood are combined with an
almost geometric minimalism.

Marc Chagall, Russian, active Russia, France and the USA, 1887–1985

The Promenade, 1919

Pencil, watercolor and gouache

31.8 × 22.5 (12 ½ × 8 ¾ in)

During the winter after the Russian October Revolution, Chagall produced four major paintings on the subject of his happy family life. One, *The Promenade,* presents the artist happily holding hands with his wife, who hovers in midair beside him.

Superficially, this same theme recurs in this drawing, with the couple posed in front of the town of Vitebsk. According to Chagall's former son- in-law and biographer,

Franz Meyer, however, it is a sketch for a banner celebrating a Red Army victory in early 1919 and is far removed from the subject of love!

This drawing, despite the self-portrait of Chagall with Bella, was meant to be military propaganda. It is not only a rare work from his Russian period, but also a striking example of Chagall's topsy-turvy world in which fantasy and reality are blended in ever new ways.

It is squared up for transfer to a larger scale, thus linking it to a group of sketches which were produced the previous fall. As the newly appointed Commissar of Arts in Vitebsk, Chagall had prepared sketches that were to be enlarged into large-scale banners, which Vitebsk used to celebrate the first anniversary of the 1917 October Revolution.

Max Ernst, German, 1891 – 1976
Gai reveil du geyser dans lequel une delicieuse jeune femme vetue d'une très legère chemise, 1921
Collage, gouache, india ink and pencil on cardboard,
24 × 17.5 cm (9 ½ × 6 ¾ in)
Gift of Marc Engelhard, Paris, with the help of Les Amis du
Musée d'Israel a Jerusalem, 1987

Max Ernst was one of the founders of the Cologne branch of
the Dada movement which originated in Zurich in the wake
of World War I. His collages of the period are witty, imaginative, and provocatively erotic. This collage was produced a
year before Ernst moved to France. His penchant for French
culture is revealed by the French titles he began using in 1920.
Ernst also discovered de Chirico's Pittura Metafisica which was
to lead him to more recognizable imagery, without becoming
descriptive.

    The title and imagery of this collage form an inextricable
unit, complementing each other poetically, and conveying a
mischievous mood. Its esoteric theme and title epitomize
Ernst's clever iconoclastic Dada wit.

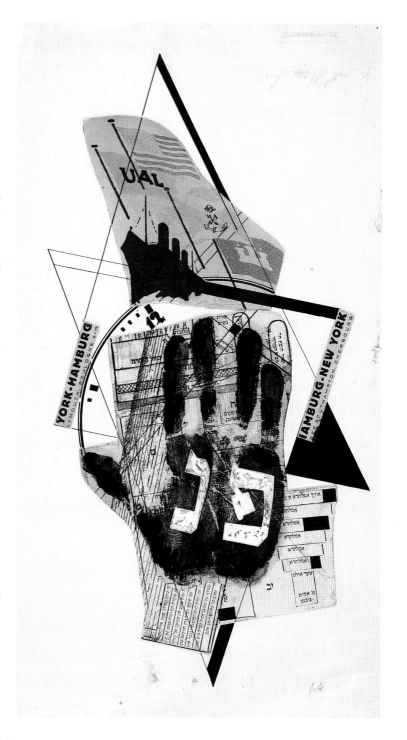

El Lissitzky, Russian, 1890–1941
Illustration for 'Shifs Karta' (Boat Ticket), in Ilya Ehrenburg's Six Stories with Easy Endings, 1922
Collage and india ink, 43.5 × 24.1 cm (17 × 9 ½ in)
The Boris and Lisa Aronson Collection at the Israel Museum
Purchased through a bequest from Dvora Cohen, Afeka, Israel

El Lissitzky, one of the leading Russian avant-garde artists,
started his artistic career promoting the revival of a Jewish
national art in Russia. Within a few years, however, he abandoned Jewish themes in favour of a universal, abstract language. This collage represents his last visual expression with a
Jewish content.

    It is unusual in its combination of dramatic visual
quality, enigmatic content, and usage of Jewish symbols. The
complex imagery includes: the imprint of a black hand, the
Hebrew letters *pei* and *nun* which are ancient Jewish symbols from gravestones meaning 'here lies buried,' examples of
Hebrew script, and a return ticket: 'Hamburg–New York.'
These are all arranged within a skewed Star of David and defy
a single interpretation.

    In addition to being an illustration to Ehrenburg's story,
the collage is most commonly interpreted as Lissitzky's affir-
mation of the new world of the Revolution and universalism
and rejection of the old.

Yossef Zaritsky, Israeli, 1891–1985
View of the Tower of David, c. 1925
Verso: Houses and Trees, c. 1925
Watercolor over pencil, 35 × 33.6 cm (13 ¾ × 13 ¼ in)
Purchase, Riklis Fund, 1969

In 1914 Zaritsky graduated from the Kiev Academy of Art. Among his fellow students were the painters Mintchine and Ryback. In 1923 Zaritsky emigrated to Eretz Israel and settled in Jerusalem.

Until 1927 he restricted himself to working in watercolor.

His work reflected the influence of the Russian painter Vrubel in the pencil drawing which formed the underlying structure for the color and in the brush technique that created a mosaic of colored planes. He worked primarily in Jerusalem and Safed, and occasionally in Tiberias and Haifa.

The recto and verso of this sheet are of entirely different character. 'View of the Tower of David' is divided into dark 'abstract' areas of soft transparent color, juxtaposed with light 'descriptive' areas containing a wealth of detail. The verso – probably earlier – drawing still betrays the influence of Vrubel in the abbreviated brush strokes.

André Masson, French, 1896–1987
Illustration for C'est les bottes de 7 lieues Cette phrase 'je me vois'
by Robert Desnos
32.9 × 24.5 cm (13 × 9 ¾ in)
Paris: Editions de Galerie Simon, 1926
Gift of Arturo Schwarz, Milan

Upon receiving the gift in 1992 of over 2000 illustrated twentieth-century artists' books, periodicals, leaflets, autographs and documents pertaining to Dada and Surrealism, the Israel Museum has become a major study center in this field.

Among the Surrealists' principal themes were love and eroticism. André Masson is represented in the collection by a large number of books illustrated with original etchings or lithographs, many of which portray womanhood and erotic themes. This etching, opposite the title page, dates from Masson's early period and stresses the body and its erogenous parts. It may stand as an example of the richness and depth of this collection as well as an example of a major interest among the Surrealists.

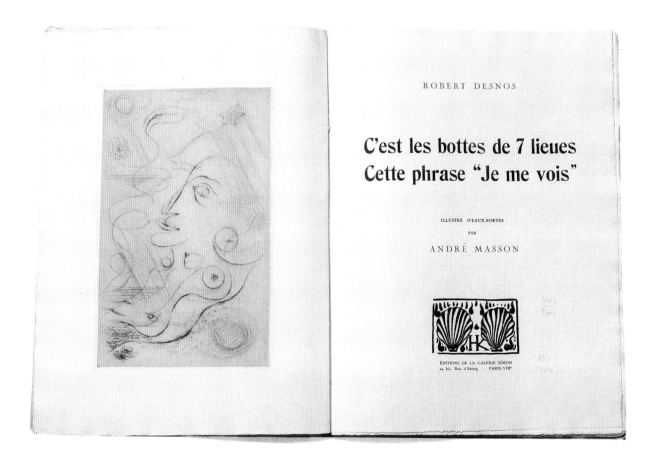

Paul Cézanne, French, 1839–1906
Country House by the Water, c. 1890
Oil on canvas, 81 × 65 cm (32 × 25 ½ in)
Gift of Yad Hanadiv, Jerusalem, from the collection of Miriam
Alexandrine de Rothschild, daughter of the late Baron
Edmond de Rothschild (1845–1934)

By the time *Country House by the Water* was painted,
c. 1890, Paul Cézanne had mastered his impetuous nature, and
had slowly evolved his own unique style. He had learned
much about color and *plein air* painting, particularly from
Pissarro's gentle prodding, but he rejected the Impressionists'
emphasis on capturing the fleeting moment. Instead, Cézanne
had arrived at a mode of expression which, while based on
nature, introduced organized, constructed forms, and a new
way of presenting depth and volume.

In this work, the centrally-placed house is composed of
simplified, geometric forms. Even its reflections and the surrounding water have an aspect of solidity and stability. Depth
and volume are achieved by the manipulation of color alone,
and result from the juxtaposition of darker and lighter shades
and tones. Structured color planes composed of directional
brush-strokes, particularly in the trees, further contribute to
the overall architectural order of the composition.

Childe Hassam, American, l859–1935
Isles of Shoals (Summer Sunlight), 1892
Oil on canvas, 61 × 51 cm (24 × 20 in)
Gift of Rebecca Shulman, New York to American Friends of
the Israel Museum

Around the 1850s, the Isles of Shoals, located off the coast of
New Hampshire, became a fashionable summer resort. In a
period of rapid urbanization, these islands provided an atmosphere of wild nature combined with comfortable lodgings for
writers, musicians, artists and well-off tourists. Here Childe
Hassam, America's foremost Impressionist, engaged in periodic
summer painting campaigns between 1886 and 1916.

Summer Sunlight belongs to the 'Shoals' works in
which a sense of bright light and fresh air usually prevails. It
was executed shortly after he returned from an extended stay
in Paris during a period when the artist produced some of his
finest paintings. Hassam's link to his French Impressionist
counterparts is evidenced both in this work's technique and
subject. Small touches of repeated colors, particularly lavender
and orange, serve to connect the figure to the landscape, as
well as the foreground and background.

A lone figure, face averted and veiled in shadows, is seated reading, a favored Impressionist subject, on the shelf-like
rocks overlooking the sea. The mood of isolation and contem-
plation, so well conveyed here, were among the qualities that
brought Hassam back time and again to this summer retreat.

Paul Gauguin, French, 1848–1903
The Fire Dance, 1891
Oil on canvas, 73 × 92 cm (28 ¾ × 36 ¼ in)
Gift of Yad Hanadiv, Jerusalem from the collection of Miriam
Alexandrine de Rothschild, daughter of the late Baron
Edmond de Rothschild (1845–1934)

Paul Gauguin's desire to find an unspoiled society, in which
people lived in harmony with nature, led him to journey to
Brittany, Martinique, Tahiti, and finally to the Marquesas
Islands. *Fire Dance, (Upa Upa)*, an extraordinary and
atypical work, was painted in the first months of his initial
visit to Tahiti (1891–93). Unlike the more stylized and imag-

ined works Gauguin would later create, this painting records
the Tahitian dances *(Upa Upa)* which the artist witnessed
at first hand. It reflects his confrontation with a strange world
whose meaning he was only just beginning to comprehend.
Yet in this mysterious nocturnal ambience, with its flickering
light effects, Gauguin has captured a native scene full of age-
old traditions and magic.

In the context of the artist's oeuvre, this painting looks
both backward and forward. Compositionally, it is related to
an earlier visionary painting, *Jacob and the Angel*, in
which the canvas is also divided diagonally by a large tree.
Gauguin made use of some of the figure groups seen in *Fire
Dance* in his subsequent graphic work.

Camille Pissarro, French, 1830–1903
Morning, Sunlight Effect, Eragny, 1899
Oil on canvas, 65 × 81 cm (24 × 32 in)
Bequest of Mrs Neville Blond, London, to the British Friends of
the Art Museums of Israel

During the last twenty years of his life, Camille Pissarro made
his home in the small village of Eragny. Though this period
was interspered with soujourns in various cities where he executed numerous series featuring urban motifs, his base
remained in the country. It was there that he completed over
350 paintings of his immediate rural surroundings.

In the summer of 1899, Pissarro was principally engaged
in a series of Eragny paintings in which figures were integrated into landscapes. Referring to these works, he wrote to his
son Lucien on 28th July, 'I have begun some motifs in the
field, some with figures. I have reason, I think, to congratulate
myself on these things.' *Morning, Sunlight Effect, Eragny,*
is from this group of about ten works in which figures appear
to melt into and become an organic part of the intimate
glades and meadows that they inhabit. The 69-year-old artist's
technical virtuousity finds expression here in the joyous, mas-
terfully and rapidly applied, strokes of multicolored paint.

Paul Signac, French, 1863–1935
The Tugboat, Canal at Samois, 1901
Oil on canvas, 66 × 82 cm (26 × 32 ¼ in)
Gift of Sara Mayer in memory of her husband, Moshe Mayer

Paul Signac was 'converted' to Neo-Impressionism
(Pointillism) in 1884 after meeting Georges Seurat, the movement's foremost practitioner and theoretician. By the early
1890s, however, a slow evolution in Signac's style is dis-
cernible. His color tones become stronger, and gradually his
brushstrokes broaden. Each stroke is slightly separated from
the others by a small area of primed white canvas which
shows through from beneath and lends a luminosity to his
paintings. This technique is already in evidence in *The
Tugboat, Canal at Samois,* which also contains both the
sharp contrast of juxtaposed colors and the unifying color
harmonies typical of his work at this time. Despite the vibrat-
ing surface produced by the individual dabs of color, the overall impression is one of calm and balance. This is achieved
through the classical symmetry of the composition, which in
turn is mitigated by the repeated, rhythmic curves of the
smoke, mountains, trees, and shoreline, all adding a decorative
elegance. *The Tugboat* also reflects Signac's fondness for the
then new, smoke-spewing steamboats. A veteran sailor, he
enjoyed combining this aspect of industrial modernism with
the more familiar elements of his work: water, sky, and the
play of light.

Claude Monet, French, 1840–1926
Pond with Water Lilies, 1907
Oil on canvas, 101.5 × 72 cm (40 × 28 ¼ in)
Gift of the Sam Spiegel Estate

During the 1890s, Monet renovated the garden at his home in Giverny, introducing improvements which allowed him to cultivate water lilies in a pond on his property. Around this time he embarked on a cycle of tranquil and contemplative waterscapes to which he would devote himself for the last twenty-five years of his life. The first series of these paintings, which had the pond as its main motif and included the Japanese footbridge that spanned it, was exhibited in 1899. By 1903, however, Monet was concentrating almost exclusively on the pond and its reflections, focusing more and more on the water surface alone. *Pond with Water Lilies* presents a section of the pond, omitting the surrounding landscape completely. The water extends to all four sides of the canvas, leaving only the foreshortened lily pads to orient the viewer. On the calm surface of the water, reflections of clouds, sky, and trees provide reference points beyond the pond. True to the Impressionist credo of an unadulterated presentation of the visual, Monet makes no distinction between the illusive reflections and reality.

Amedeo Modigliani, Italian, active France, 1884–1920
Jeanne Hebuterne, Seated, 1918
Oil on canvas, 55 × 38 cm (21 ¾ × 15 in)
Gift of Stella Fischbach in memory of Harry Fischbach to
American Friends of the Israel Museum

In July 1917, Amedeo Modigliani met Jeanne Hebuterne, a
gifted art student with long auburn hair and a swan neck. By
the time he painted this portrait of his mistress, Modigliani's
health was already precarious, and his consumption of alcohol
had reached suicidal proportions. Hebuterne was totally devoted to Modigliani during the last desperate years of his life. Less
than two years later, in January 1920, Modigliani died at the
age of 36. The day after his death, Jeanne Hebuterne, nine
months pregnant with their second child, committed suicide.

    Jeanne Hebuterne was probably painted in the south
of France in the summer-fall of 1918, during the sitter's first
pregnancy. The characteristic elongated forms and elegant
curves which are part of Modigliani's idealizing style are very
much in evidence. An harmonious bond between background
and foreground is forged by the repetition of color: blue, in the
sitter's bodice, her eyes and in the bedspread, and beige-browns
in the skin tones, sparse furnishings, and walls.

Pierre Bonnard, French, 1867–1947
The Dining Room, 1923
Oil on canvas, 77 × 75.5 cm (30 ¼ × 29 ¾ in)
Gift of the Sam Spiegel Estate

Bonnard preferred subjects culled from his intimate surroundings, and often painted similar scenes albeit with different
accents. Many of his recurrent themes are present in *The
Dining Room*. He frequently drew and painted his wife
Marthe seated at a table or with their dachshund, using still-
lifes in isolation or as part of a room setting. In this painting,
Marthe's face is turned away from the viewer, shown in profile and covered by a shadow that suggests a pensive mood. A
figure on the far right is cut off, perhaps to suggest mystery.
Only the little dog peers, with curiosity, at the viewer. All the
protagonists exist in a flattened, shallow space. In front of
them is a large table, tilted upward in Cézannesque fashion. In
contrast to the figures' relative flatness, the fruit on the table, a
grand example of Bonnard's talent as a still-life painter, is
fully modeled through a careful manipulation of color alone.
In fact, it is color that is this work's most outstanding feature.
The entire painting glows with a golden light, resulting from
the free and arbitrary combination of color harmonies and
contrasts, achieved through short strokes, varying tones, and
multiple, overlapping layers.

Henri Matisse, French, 1869–1954
Two Girls in Nice, 1921
Oil on canvas, 65 × 50 cm (25 ½ × 19 ¾ in)
Gift of the Sam Spiegel Estate

Two Girls in Nice, like most of the works that Matisse created during his Nice period, is set in the intimacy of the artist's
home. In this case the interior is that of 1, Place Charles-Felix,
where he lived from 1921 to 1938. A woman sits in a tranquil
pose, lost in thought, while her companion, relaxed, is reading.
The room is replete with patterned objects: fabric hangings, a
rug, wallpaper, window casements, and the sitters' dresses.
Though the angles of the walls lend the painting a certain
depth, the repetitious motifs of the patterned objects tend to
flatten the space and bring it to the picture's surface. The two
young women appear to float over the floor, and the design of
the rug further adds to the tilted effect. This combination of
two- and three-dimensional space, the abstract-decorative and
the real, is typical of the synthesis Matisse sought to create.
Though a certain return to realism is evident in the Nice
works, this does not constitute a regression but rather an
attempt to achieve an innovative integration of old and new
concepts.

Egon Schiele, Austrian, 1890–1918
Krumau Town Crescent I, 1915
Oil on canvas, 109.7 × 140 cm (43 ¼ × 55 in)
Received through JRSO

Austrian Expressionist Egon Schiele's relationship with the town of Krumau was ambivalent yet obsessive. During his short, intense life (he died of influenza at the age of twenty-eight), Schiele returned to visit the town many times, despite the traumatic associations it held for him. His father had attempted suicide while there and Schiele was later evicted from his apartment in the town on grounds of moral impropriety. Nevertheless, its gabled houses and topography were the source of many of his townscapes throughout his career.

In fall 1914, under the shadow cast by World War I and his fear of conscription, Schiele made one of his regular visits to Krumau, which he referred to as 'the dead city.' Shortly thereafter, in the early part of the following year, he painted *Krumau Town Crescent I,* one of his most claustrophobic urban images. Seen from on high, the compressed buildings cover almost the entire canvas. Linear patterns and painted outlines provide the compositional structure, but they are softened here by a new painterliness which pervades Schiele's work of this period. The subdued palette of warm browns and golden tones is enlivened by bright color accents in the laundry, window-frames, gables and overhangs. Like most of Schiele's townscapes, this work is unpopulated, a fact which reinforces the barren, surreal effect.

Georges Braque, French, 1882–1963
Pitcher, Guitar and Fruit, 1925
Oil on canvas, 146 x77 cm (57 ½ × 30 ¼ in)
Bequest of Elise S. Haas, San Francisco, to the America-Israel
Cultural Foundation

When Georges Braque returned to painting, after having been
seriously wounded in World War I, a certain relaxation of the
former austerity found in his Analytical and Synthetic Cubist
works was evident. His preferred subject remained the still-life,
but his color schemes were more varied, and an emphasis on
tactile values came to the fore. By the 1920s his still-lifes were
replete with painterly inventions that enlivened his canvases.

One of the themes he focused on during this period,
which is exemplified by *Pitcher, Guitar and Fruit,* was a
massive table with still-life, placed in the confined space of a
narrow, vertical format. In these monumental works, the horizontal plane of the table top is tipped forward, exposing a
clear view of the objects on it, which paradoxically are seen as
if viewed from above. This use of multiple points of view, and
such devices as the vertical division of objects into fields of
contrasting color, are among the vestiges of Cubist elements
Braque continued to employ. His palette now, however, included yellow and light and dark green in addition to the more
somber shades used before. Variegated brushwork is combined
with textural effects such as lattice pattern and simulated
woodgrain. Thus Braque, through a gradual but ongoing
elaboration of complex pictorial structures, succeeded in
introducing new ideas within a very limited range of subject
matter.

Marc Chagall, born Russia, active Russia, France and USA, 1887–1985

The Rabbi, 1912–13

Oil on canvas, 40 × 31 cm (15 ¾ × 12 ¼ in)

Received through JRSO

Upon arriving in Paris from his native Russia in 1910, Marc Chagall lost no time in acquainting himself with avant-garde painting styles. It was in Paris that he absorbed elements of Fauve color and Cubism, albeit adapting them to and combining them with the innovative Jewish and Russian folk motifs he had developed in the country of his birth. Though non-Jewish Russian peasants were frequently the subjects of his paintings during this first Paris period, around 1912 he also began a series of works on Jewish religious life. These works,

the first in his oeuvre to depict religious rather than folk motifs, were Chagall's declaration and demonstration of what he considered to be Modern Jewish Art. *Praying Jew* belongs to this group.

Shown in profile, the praying figure is executed in a modified Cubist style. Circular forms in the head, cheek, back and sleeve are balanced by sharp angular facets in trousers, shirt, nose and phylacteries box. The figure's back is elongated to accommodate the exaggerated bend of the head. Behind and above him, two Stars of David, one on the covering of a partially visible *Torah* scroll and the other free-floating, appear to press in and down on the figure. The sense of enclosed isolation is further enhanced by the darkness of the room, lightened only by a tiny window.

Naum Gabo, born Russia, active Norway, England and USA,
1890–1977
Constructed Head No. 2, 1953–7
Phosphor bronze, 44.4 × 43.5 × 43.5 cm
(17 ½ × 17 ¼ × 17 ¼ in)
Bequest of Miriam Gabo, London

With the outbreak of World War I, Naum Gabo (born Naum
Borisovich Pevsner, the son of Russian-Jewish parents) moved
to Oslo, Norway. There he created a number of spatial con-
structions so conceptually advanced that they have become
icons of modern art. *Constructed Head No. 2* is among
these early landmark works. The first version of the sculpture
(now lost and presumed destroyed) was a cardboard model
made in Oslo in early fall 1916. Gabo subsequently enlarged
the work in more durable materials. In 1923-24 he made
another version in ivory rhodoid. The Museum's version in
bronze was created between 1953 and 1957. In these construc-
tions the artist renounces the traditional notions of mass,
solidity, density and volume which had formerly governed
sculpture. Here, interlocking planes open the work up to the
penetration of light and space. Intricate flat and curved
planes, joined in a honeycomb structure, allow the viewer to
see the inside and outside of the sculpture simultaneously, and
provide constantly changing perceptions from different angles.
Gabo has successfully merged technology and art in an image
that appropriately reflects the modern world in flux.

189

René Magritte, Belgian, 1898–1967
Le Château des Pyrénées
(The Castle of the Pyrenees), 1959
Oil on canvas, 200 × 145 cm (78 ¾ × 57 in)
Gift of Harry Torczyner, New York, to American Friends of the
Israel Museum

Belgian Surrealist René Magritte's masterpiece, *The Castle of
the Pyrenees,* was commissioned by the artist's long-time
friend, international lawyer, poet, and author Harry
Torczyner. The unfolding of the commission and the evolution of the painting are documented in letters between the two
men, which were published by the Israel Museum in 1991.
Though Magritte had total freedom, the correspondence
reveals that his patron was encouraged to express his opinions
as regards the choice of subject. From a number of drawings
proposed by Magritte, Torczyner selected one of a large rock
surmounted by a castle. Intimately acquainted with the artist's
repertoire of preferred images, Torczyner added the suggestion
of a sky on a clear day and a rough darkish sea 'because over
the dark sea or ocean there rises the rock of hope, topped by a
fortress, a castle.' As Magritte worked on the painting, refining
it, he decided to exclude other proposed additions in order that
it retain the 'vigor' and 'harshness' he envisioned.

The jointly selected subject of *The Castle of the
Pyrenees* has become one of Magritte's best-known and
most-reproduced images. It embodies the disturbing juxtaposi-
tions of familiar objects typical of the artist, combined with
the poetry and mystery that captivate his viewers.

Francis Bacon, British, 1910–1992
Study for the Portrait of Lucian Freud, 1964
Oil on canvas, 196 × 146 cm (77 × 57 ½ in)
Gift of the Marlborough Gallery, London

Francis Bacon channeled his personal perception of human
nature's dark side, exacerbated by his troubled childhood in an
Ireland ravaged by civil war and the experience of World War
II, into some of the most powerful images of the late twentieth
century. The nightmarish, macabre bodily distortions in his
paintings are reflections of the violence and desolation Bacon
saw as endemic to the human condition. Though links with
Surrealism and Expressionism can be found in his work, he
viewed himself as a realist, reasoning that, 'You can't be more
horrific than life itself.'

Bacon's earliest named portrait, executed in 1951, was of
his friend and fellow-artist Lucian Freud. During the following
decade he painted Freud on many occasions; in triptych format, together with his other intimate companions of the
1960s, or alone, as is the case with this portrait, which is set in
a stark, austere interior. The figure sits uneasily on the edge of
a hard bench, illuminated by an exposed light bulb. An otherwise naturalistic rendering is subverted, however, by the swirls
of paint around the head that contort and obliterate the face.
This cruelly tortured visage is in strong contrast to the rich,
varied, and elegantly masterful application of the paint.

David Smith, American, 1906–1965
Cubi VI, 1963
Stainless steel, 285 × 73.5 × 54.5 cm (112 ¼ × 29 × 21 ½ in)
Gift of Mr and Mrs Meshulam Riklis (Judith Stern-Riklis), New
York, to American Friends of the Israel Museum

By the 1950s, David Smith, the foremost sculptor of the
Abstract Expressionist generation, had assimilated the French
modernism of his early works into a style which was both personal and reflected his American roots. From this time
onward, his iconography was limited to a small number of
themes, most prominent among them that of the heroically
isolated individual alone in his confrontation with nature.
Smith further developed this theme, starting in the early
1960s, into a magnificent series of stainless steel sculptures
which he titled *Cubi*, followed by consecutive roman numer-
als. He succeeded in making almost thirty of these monumental *Cubi* masterpieces before his tragic death in a car crash in
1965.

Like many of the *Cubis*, *Cubi VI* is intentionally
anthropomorphic. The × shape of the lower part suggests a
cross-legged stance, and the square chest is connected to a tall
vertical rectangle reaching upward like an arm. A second,
higher-placed vertical rectangle can be interpreted as the
head. The upper and lower sections are joined by a precarious-
ly-balanced diamond shape, which together with the reflective
properties of the material, give the sculpture a weightless
quality in spite of its mass and grand scale.

Henry Moore, British, 1898–1986
Vertebrae, 1968
Bronze, 710 × 355 × 270 cm
(23 ft 4 in × 11 ft 8 in × 8 ft 10 in)
Gift of the artist and of the British Friends of the Art Museums
in Israel, London 1972

Henry Moore created his first reclining female figure in 1929. Supine women would thereafter become one of his most constant themes. A few years later he began opening up his sculptures, attaching as much importance to the inner spaces created as to the solid masses. About this time he also developed the idea of sculptures composed of separate but related sections. It was, however, only after World War II that Moore combined all these elements in large-scale works in bronze.

Offering greater freedom than the stone and wood in which he had previously worked, bronze provided a stimulus to more far-reaching transformations of the human form.

Vertebrae is one of the fortunate results of this confluence of subject matter and material. Situated between earth and sky, this monumental sculpture dominates a high terrace on the western slope of the Billy Rose Art Garden. Its semi-abstract forms, the curves of which echo the undulating hilly landscape, evoke both corporal and primeval resonances. The title suggests that Moore has here delved deep into the inner structure of one of his recumbent female figures, exposing the supporting bones. Yet, at the same time, the organic forms also relate to the outer woman, while the sculpture as a whole reverberates with references to the archetypal female and all its mythic and erotic connotations.

Eva Hesse, American, 1936–1970
Accession I, 1967
Aluminum with rubber tubing
36.5 × 36 × 23 cm (14 ¼ × 14 × 9 in)
Gift of Murry and Helen Charash, New Jersey, to American Friends of the Israel Museum

Although prototypical of the four subsequent versions of this sculpture made between 1967 and 1968, _Accession I_ (1967) is, in its own right, a work of Hesse's full artistic maturity. The basic unit is a box with no top, constructed of metal, as are the rest of the works in the series, except for _Accession III,_ which is built from fiberglass. However, unlike the others which are cubic, the box in _Accession I_ is wider than it is high. Through the myriad holes in its four sides and bottom, Hesse wove hundreds of short lengths of rubber tubing bent like elongated U's, so that their curved mid-sections face outward in bumpy tiers and their twin extremities point inward. Staring down into the interior of the hard, squared-off structure, one is so mesmerized by the vibrant congestion of these extrusions that it might be tempting to say that the box is 'alive' with their presence, but nothing could be less lifelike than these silver-gray bristles. Still, their individual pliability and collective softness contrast sharply with the rigid walls they transverse, and it is that contrast which fascinates.

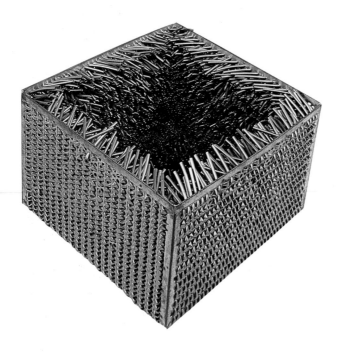

Mario Merz, Italian, born 1925
Tiger, 1983
Mixed media, canvas, rectangular metal tube structure, bales of hay
180 × 500 cm (5 ft 11 in × 16 ft 5 in)

Mario Merz is one of the most representative artists of Arte Povera, the Italian movement of the 1960s.

During three feverish weeks at the Israel Museum in 1983, within the framework of the Museum's annual Bergman Visiting Artists Program, Mario Merz created an installation comprising a number of works, using the Billy Rose Pavilion both as a studio and exhibition space. The nucleus of the installation was an igloo, surrounded by large drawings and paintings leaning on or attached to the walls.

As an antithesis to the igloo's closed domed shape, a vertical canvas, mounted on a metal construction and placed on bales of hay, leaned against the wall. A tiger, painted with vigorous brush strokes, belonging to Merz's extensive repertoire of animals and beasts, occupied its entire surface. This wild creature – a force of nature with anthropomorphic features – completed the dynamic circle of Merz's organic vision.

Anselm Kiefer, German, born 1945
Aaron, 1984
Oil, emulsion, shellac, and straw on canvas
330 × 500 cm (10 ft 10 in × 16 ft 5 in)
Gift of Norman Braman, Miami, Florida, to American Friends of the Israel Museum

During his first visit to Israel in March 1984, Kiefer was particularly attracted by the Judaean Desert's bareness and stillness, which he tried to absorb, with all its historical overtones and spirituality. Following his trip, he created _Aaron,_ which was included in his one-man exhibition held at the Israel Museum in the summer of 1984. The painting's dark and hilly landscape, with the high horizon almost touching the upper edge of the canvas and the physical materiality of the surface enriched by sand and straw, is also reminiscent of earlier landscapes derived from the artist's own country, Germany.

The choice of Aaron, who as the creator of the golden calf may be considered an artist himself, can also be interpreted as Kiefer identifying, to some extent, with Aaron's ambiguous personality. The numbered vertical stripes placed above the rod and the black hole in the lower central part of the painting, symbolize the twelve tribes of Israel.

Magdalena Abakanowicz, Polish, born 1930
Negev, 1987
Limestone from Mitzpeh Ramon
280 cm × 350 cm (9 ft × 11 ft 6 in)
Birthday gift to Rudolph B. Schulhof from Hannelore B.
Schulhof, New York

On her very first day in Jerusalem, in April 1987,
Abakanowicz, deeply moved by the powerful characteristics of
the local limestone, decided to work in stone for the first time.
The search for a suitable quarry brought her to Mitzpeh
Ramon, deep in the Negev desert, where her new and perhaps
most abstract work, named after the site, was hewn from
layers of sedimental limestone. *Negev* consists of seven
monumental ten-ton wheels, each 280 cm (9 ft) in diameter,
with a depth of 60 cm (2 ft). Their final irregular round shape
was achieved with a hammer and various pointed iron instruments usually used by the local stonemasons. At the center of
some of the wheels the artist carved a navel-like indentation,
'expressing her sense of the place: Jerusalem as the *omphalos
mundi,* the navel of the world.' The flat surface of the disks,
enriched by fossils, was left untouched.

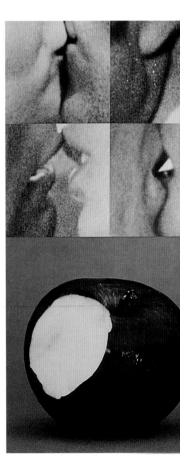

The sculpture was installed on the 'wild' western edge of
the Billy Rose Art Garden, the overall installation being 35 m
(115 ft) in length.

The location of *Negev* in Jerusalem evokes associations
with local olive crushing, with millstones, and with the prehistoric shores of the eastern Mediterranean, where, after the
Mesopotamian civilization, the wheel was in use. The seven-
wheeled sculpture also alludes symbolically to the seven
ancient gates of Jerusalem, to the seven days of Creation, to
the cult of the sun, to oneness and perfection, and even, in a
slightly more remote context, to the stone circle of
Stonehenge.

John Baldessari, American, born 1931
Buildings = Guns = People: Desire, Knowledge and Hope (with Smog)
1985 – 1990
Black and white and color photographs
397 × 946 cm (13 ft × 31 ft)
Gift of the Eli Broad Family Foundation, Los Angeles to
American Friends of the Israel Museum

To create his composite photoworks, Baldessari selects, crops,
patches, frames, rearranges and juxtaposes different components of found material such as movie stills, newspapers or
advertisements.

The work *Buildings* consists of black-and-white and
color photographs divided into five sections, with the images
symmetrically assembled within a central pyramidal
composition.

Violence is one of the Baldessari's frequent themes, balanced and neutralized by formal arrangements. Violence and
sex are equated here in the phallic gun combined with the
image of mouths kissing. The sterile building in the middle,
with its geometrical design created by the uniform window
pattern, conceals within it apartments of an identical size
inhabited by people of a similar social class. In the absence of
any hint of a specific locality, the only sign of individuality
lies in the way each window is either curtained or blinded.

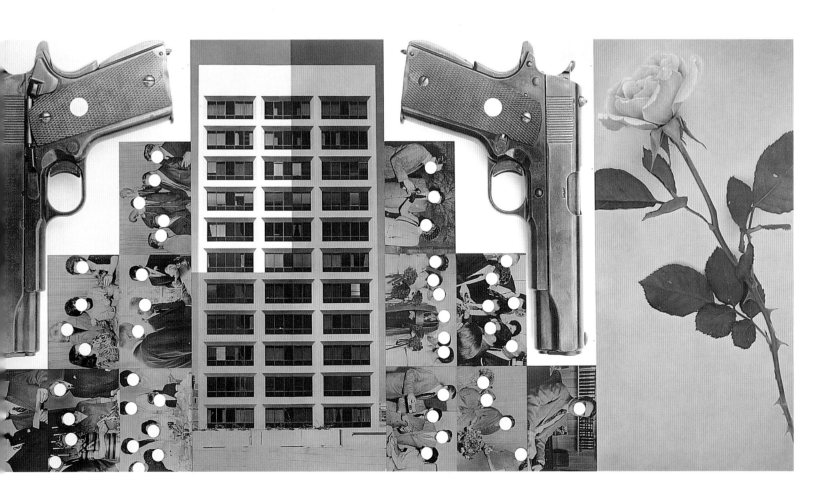

Christian Boltanski, French, born 1944
Storeroom, 1989
Used clothing, 20 lamps
Overall size: 400 × 1200 cm (13 × 39 ft)
Gift of the artist in memory of Jacques Ohayon

In 1989 Boltanski arrived in Jerusalem in order to create a new installation relating to his large body of work 'Lessons of Darkness.' For the artist, 'Lessons' evokes childhood memories of classes at school; 'Darkness' suggests evil, night and death. Death, memory and childhood can be considered as major subjects for Boltanski. 'Lessons of Darkness' consists of six works: *Storeroom, The Festival of Purim, Monument-*

Souvenir Images, Shadows, The Archives-Detective and *Altar to the Chases High School. Storeroom* is composed of used cloths which cover, in a horror vacui manner, a long wall. It inevitably conjures up associations with the piles of clothing in concentration camps, each piece bearing testimony to the fate of a single person. It is important to note, however, that Boltanski has never made direct reference to the Holocaust; 'I have never used images that came from the camps; it would be impossible for me; it would be something too shameful to use, too sacred. My work is not about the camps, it is after the camps . . . my work is not about the Holocaust; it's about death in general, about all of our deaths.'

James Turrell, American, born 1943
Space that Sees, 1992
Gray and white concrete, pink local stone and fluorescent
lights with dimmers
700 cm × 1000 cm × 1000 cm
(23 ft × 32 ft 10 in × 32 ft 10 in)
Gift of Hannelore and Ruda Schulhof, New York, to American
Friends of the Israel Museum

From his 'Jerusalem Skyspace,' Turrell chose a terrace along
the western slope of the Billy Rose Art Garden, which had
been designed by Isamu Noguchi. The entire hill was then cut
into two, so that the terrace now enfolds a 'secret' shrine–like
inner square space. A rectangular opening was cut in its
ceiling and Jerusalem stone benches with inclined backrests
were placed along the walls.

The Skyspaces involve movement over time, thus making
them, in a way, performance pieces, responding to and inter-
acting with environmental conditions and climatic fluctua-
tions. The viewer, observing the shifting hues of the sky from
inside the pristine space, undergoes an arresting experience.
Confronted by the empty space, the mind turns inward.

Space that Sees invites meditation. Twilight conditions
yield the particularly startling effect of a flat sky surface,
turning all but imperceptibly from deep blue to velvet black.
At the same time, the room itself seems to grow increasingly
brighter, so that the physical conjunction (at the roof opening)
of interior and exterior becomes a catalyst in the light's
passage from day to night. Turrell himself sees the installation
as an 'allegory of light that we generate from inside and light
that comes from outside: the emergence into space where light
comes forth as in a dream.'

Claes Oldenburg, American, born 1929
Apple Core, 1992
Stainless steel, urethane foam, resin, and urethane enamel
200 × 200 × 300 cm (6 ft 6 in × 6 ft 6 in × 9 ft 9 in)
Gift of the Morton and Barbara Mandel Fund, Mandel
Associated Foundations, Cleveland, and the artist, to American
Friends of the Israel Museum

Apple Core tilts elegantly and provocatively on its carefully
chosen site in the Billy Rose Art Garden, a self-contained
presence whose gnawed Brobdingnagian dimensions and
earth colors effect a surreal discourse with adjacent sculptures

While this work – like many of Oldenburg's larger-than-
life sculpture-objects –was created especially for its setting, the
image of a rotten apple core first figured several years earlier
in his *Haunted House* installation at the Museum Haus
Esters in Krefeld (1987). The residual apple may evoke ecological associations of the world consuming itself to extinction.
But the perishability-vulnerability of the decaying apple core
also evinces Oldenburg's consistent preoccupation with the
process of decline and death that inexorably accompanies any
life cycle like a shadow.

The existential imperative of growth and decomposition -
its poignancy once heightened by the lushness of the 'Vanitas'
pictures, with a worm or insect accentuating the moralizing
intent – is ironically underscored in *Apple Core* by both the
mock-heroic scale and the 'organic' coloring. Ultimately, these
very elements, enhanced by tongue-in-cheek sculptural-
painterly effects and hard-soft punning (the 'rotten' apple has
an actual steel core and is fashioned in stiffened urethane
foam), make *Apple Core* an endearing rather than forbidding
piece, inviting tactile exploration, and even refuge.

The apple motif itself is allusive in multiple ways.
Voluminous and sensuous, the apple graces innumerable
still-life compositions, but it is also traditionally pictured as
the forbidden fruit – an association that will not be lost on
viewers in the Jerusalemite Garden of Art.

Annette Messager, French, born 1943
The Masks, 1992–3
Taxidermic animals, black and white silver prints, mixed media and 25 metal pikes
195.58 × 553.72 × 198.12 cm
(6 ft 5 in × 18 ft 2 in × 6 ft 6 in)
Gift of Peter and Shawn Leibowitz, Great Neck, New York, to American Friends of the Israel Museum

Messager's powerful protest against cruelty and violence is expressed in the use of taxidermic animals as early as 1972 *(Pensionnaires)*. In this piece, created twenty years later, she presents thirteen stuffed animals (squirrel, chipmunk, rat, small rooster, hen, small bird, small brown rabbit, red rabbit, cat, crow, two large birds, and duck) with heads hooded by black or white cloth. Black-and-white photographs of the hooded heads, alternating with mask-like gloves, lean against the walls on top of metal pikes, fencing the animals on the floor like sinister trophies. The only creature with an unveiled head, the squirrel, its neck adorned with assorted 'amulets' is perched on two cushions like a shaman or hoodoo, surrounded by its humiliated companions.

Hooding suggests associations with the execution of condemned prisoners, and with highly-charged political situations such as the dark history of the American South, the Ku Klux Klan, or various terrorist movements. The pike holds particular significance in France, where, during the Revolution, it was the universally recognized weapon of the sovereign people and was associated with the right of citizens to bear arms. The duel role of the black gloves – as a mask and as a metonymy of human hands – hints at both the executioners and the victims.

Reuven Rubin, Israeli, 1893–1974
Self-portrait, 1923
Oil on canvas, 107 × 85.3 cm (42 × 33 ½ in)
Gift of James Rosenberg, New York, to the America-Israel
Cultural Foundation

'... Here in Jerusalem, Tel Aviv, Haifa, and Tiberias I feel
myself reborn. Only here do I feel that life and nature are mine
... All is sunshine, clear light, and happy, creative work ...'
(Reuven Rubin, 1926)

In 1923, a year after his return to Palestine from extensive travels around the world, the Romanian-born painter
Rubin decided to establish his home in the new city of Tel
Aviv. In keeping with this move, he changed his disciplined
academic painting style to a new 'naive' approach that seemed
to him more appropriate to his new lifestyle as a pioneer.

Here Rubin depicts himself as a native, bronzed by the
hot local sun, his roots running deep into the ground like
those of the cypress tree outside his window. In order to imbue
the landscape with the romantic cast of the Orient, he portrays
a caravan making its way across the dunes in the background.
The blue vase containing narcissus blossoms symbolizes the
painter's youth.

Posed with palette and brush in hand, and with the landscape that inspired him seen through the artist's window in
the background, Rubin still adhered – iconographically if not
stylistically – to the classical training he later came to eschew
in this version of the classic artist's self-portrait.

Yitzhak Danziger, Israeli, 1916–1977
Nimrod, 1939
Nubian sandstone, 95 × 33 × 33 cm (37 ½ × 13 × 13 in)
Gift of Dr David H. Orgler, Zurich and Jerusalem

'… And Cush begat Nimrod: he began to be mighty upon the earth …' (Chronicles I, 1:10)

Danziger was a graduate of the Slade School of Fine Arts in London. Upon his return to Palestine following his studies, his studio became the meeting place and workshop for a group of young artists who considered themselves 'Canaanites' and who pursued a desire to return to the country's pre-Jewish cultural roots.

As a member of this unofficial group, Danziger chose to work with red-hued sandstone brought from Petra, partly because of its earthy color and local connotations, but also because he wanted to avoid classical materials such as marble and bronze. Highly influenced by Egyptian art, he borrowed the motif of the hunting bird for his version of Nimrod, who is characterized as a fierce hunter in the Hebrew *Midrash,* from the Egyptian statue of Pharaoh-Hephren (4th Dynasty). Danziger's sandstone figure of the biblical hero Nimrod is one of the first sculptures of early modern Israeli art to depict a human figure. By omitting the figure's legs, he alludes to fragments of ancient archaeological relics, metaphorically relating it to the pagan past.

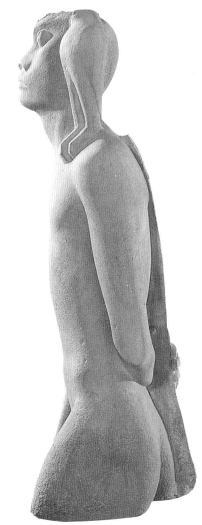

Ze'ev Raban and all Bezalel School Departments
Elijah's Chair, 1916–25
Walnut wood, leather, woolen carpet, embroidery on silk and velvet, ivory, shell, cameo, silver filigree, enamel, and brass repoussé
190 × 91 × 91 cm (74 ¾ × 35 ¾ × 35 ¾ in)
Gift of Yossi Benyaminoff, New York, to American Friends of the Israel Museum

Elijah's chair is the seat upon which the *sandak* (godfather) customarily sits holding the baby during a circumcision ceremony. According to tradition, the prophet Elijah is present at every *brit mila* ceremony to protect the baby from any harm.

This Elijah's chair was made at the Bezalel School of Arts and Crafts established in Jerusalem in 1906. Bezalel also housed workshops for the production of art objects in a variety of materials. The fledgling institution sought to create a style that would be at once 'local and Zionist.' In *Elijah's Chair* we see an amalgam of the different media taught at Bezalel, yielding an outstanding example of the motifs and iconography that characterized the school.

The chair's designer, Ze'ev Raban, was a teacher at Bezalel, widely recognized for his formative influence in the creation of the 'Bezalel style.' The artist's concept for the chair combines motifs from the Bible, the East, and Eretz Israel with a Western sense of design.

 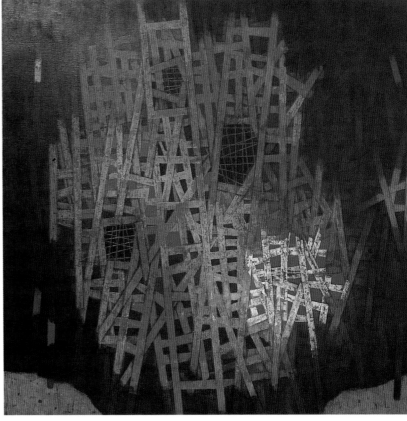

Mordechai Ardon, Israeli, 1896–1992
At the Gates of Jerusalem, triptych, 1967
Right: *Sign*
Center: *Ladders*
Left: *Rock*
Oil on canvas, 194 × 525 cm (76 ¼ × 206 ¾ in)
Gift of the artist in honor of Israel's 20th anniversary and the unification of Jerusalem

Ardon's primary motivation is his intention to meet the challenge presented by the founding of the new Jewish state through the creation of a new Israeli art, anchored in the present, but with roots firmly tied to the past.

The triptych *At the Gates of Jerusalem* was painted in 1967, the year in which the Six-Day War – and the recapturing of the Old City of Jerusalem by Israeli forces – took place.

The spiritual Jerusalem, the Jerusalem of *Sign,* is depicted through the kabbalistic images of the *sefirot* and the shattered vessels. The only clearly legible letters are the *aleph* and *bet,* harking back to the legend according to which the creation of the alphabet preceded the creation of the earth.

The 'earthly Jerusalem' is portrayed in *Rock,* featuring a section of Mount Moriah and the same piece of walled golden rock that may be seen today in the mosque built on the site of the destroyed Temple.

Interposed between the two panels are the *Ladders* of all the faiths, stretching between the earth and the heavens. Their broken parts have been repaired with delicate lines. Rays of light emanating from the darkness connect the ladders that extend from the heavenly Jerusalem to the earthly Jerusalem, auguring the redemption that will lead to the end of days.

Yossef Zaritsky, Israeli, 1891–1985
Painting, triptych, 1967
Oil on canvas, 270 × 408 cm (106 ¼ × 160 ½ in)
(three sections, each 270 × 136 cm; 106 ¼ × 53 ½ in)
Acquisition, Sandberg Prize for an Israeli Artist, 1967

Zaritsky was one of the most influential figures in Israeli art.
His dominating personality and talents as a painter gained
him the respect and admiration of the three generations of
artists who have forged the history of the artist in Israel.

It was Zaritsky's desire to advance Israeli art, instilling in
it the norms and modes of expression characteristic of the
universal language of contemporary art. His personal artistic
idiom blended the international art style with the influence of
the light and climatic conditions of Eretz Israel.

Painting belongs to a group of works, comprising quasi-
abstract treatments of the local landscape, done between 1964
and 1968. This type of painting, based on a unifying affinity
between color, material, and form, on color harmonies, and on
a firm yet amorphous structure, is a distinct expression of
Israeli 'lyrical abstraction.' The depth of the artist's expression
of the human experience through painterly rather than literary elements, as well as the quality of his work, are among the
factors that made this type of painting the leading style in
Israeli art in the 1950s and 1960s.

Arie Aroch, Israeli, 1908–1974
Agripas Street, 1964
Mixed media on wood panel, street sign
50 × 110 cm (19 ¾ × 43 ¼ in)
Gift of Walter and Marianne Griessmann, London, to the Israel
Museum, Jerusalem, and the Tel Aviv Museum of Art

For many years, this particular work by painter-diplomat Arie
Aroch was considered the icon of the local conceptual artist's
movement, '10+.' It consists of a ready-made street sign on top
of a rectangular wooden panel, upon which Aroch painted in
oil and doodled in pencil. The sign is a Jerusalem street sign
from the 1920s, a significant decade in young Aroch's life,
during which he moved from the Ukraine to Jerusalem and
enrolled in studies at the Bezalel School of Arts and Crafts. The
year 1964 was also important for Aroch; it was then that he
returned to Jerusalem after many years of serving as a diplo-
mat in various countries throughout the world.

Aroch passed Agrippas Street (in the painting this appears
as Agripas Street), a narrow, noisy thoroughfare next to the
Mahane Yehuda street market, twice a day on his way to and
from his work at the Foreign Office compound. It was
probably on one of those daily passages that he came across
the old street sign, with its sentimental associations. A devoted
admirer of Duchamp, Aroch no doubt relished the opportunity
to use a ready-made object as the crowning touch on a painting he had begun some two years earlier, but had hesitated to
finish.

Avigdor Arikha, Israeli, born 1929
Going Out, 1981
Oil on canvas, 81 × 64.8 cm (32 × 25 ½ in)
Purchased through the Ayala Zacks Abramov Fund

The painting *Going Out* portrays the artist's poetess wife Ann
from behind, her face reflected in the mirror she holds in her
hand.

Arikha defines one of his artistic motives as the creation
of a state of tension in his paintings, and indeed this work
reveals a sense of tension among its different elements, the
formal as well as the expressive.

On the one hand, the painting's composition is highly
ordered: each line relates to a parallel line, collectively forming a clear and rigid structural framework. The emphasized
flatness of the space, the neutral-abstract background, the cool
and controlled palette, the thin and chalky application of
paint, the sense of immateriality, and the fact that the figure
is rendered from behind – her coat loosened, obscuring the
shape of the body it clothes – all these create a first impression
of restraint, distance, and anonymity. On the other hand, the
work also emanates a distinctly different set of qualities: the
placement of the figure to the left of the center of the picture,
cropped by the picture frame, the wisp of hair trailing off to
the left, and the collars of her shirt and coat, pointing like
arrows to the same side, all transgress the strictly imposed
balance of the composition and instill a sense of dynamism
and tension.

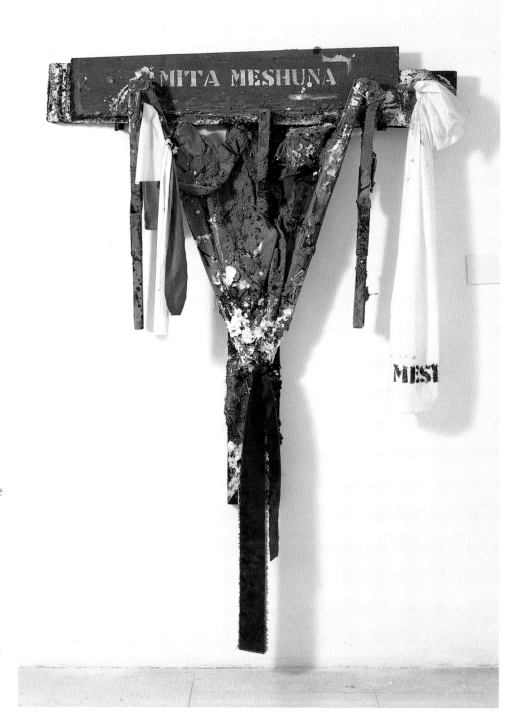

Igael Tumarkin, Israeli, born 1933
Mita Meshunah, 1984
Wood, textiles, iron, stretcher, earth, and paint
194 × 137 × 20 cm (76 ¼ × 54 × 7 ¾ in)
Purchased through a donation from the Recanati Fund for the
Acquisition of Israeli Art

Tumarkin's mixed-media sculpture was undertaken two years
after the start of the Lebanon war, a period during which
nearly every day was marked by the announcement of the
death or wounding of a soldier who had been in action on the
northern front.

This cruciform sculpture is based on the anthropomorphic shape assumed by an army stretcher, nailed and hanging
by its 'arms' to a horizontal wooden plank, upon which the
title of the work is inscribed. The first word in the title, *mita,*
constitutes a pun on the two Hebrew words (which are spelled
differently but pronounced the same) for 'death' and 'bed.'
Coupled with the word *meshunah,* the phrase means either
'unnatural death,' such as that of a soldier in battle, or 'curious
bed,' such as this field hospital stretcher.

Tumarkin used black, white, and blue strips of cloth and
tied them to the 'arms' and the lower part of the sculpture's
'body;' the black strip functions as a 'loincloth' while the other
strips suggest a torn Israeli flag.

During the years from 1982 to 1984, the artist concentrated on the themes of crucifixion and death, employing these
images to highlight worldwide cases of injustice and cruelty.

Micha Ullman, Israeli, born 1939
Day (from the 'Containers' series), 1988
Iron plates and earth, 240 × 320 × 178 cm
(94 ½ × 126 × 70 in)
Gift of Dr and Mrs Raymond Sackler, New York, to American
Friends of the Israel Museum

Day was one of three large sculptures exhibited in a solo
exhibition of Ullman's work at the Museum in 1988. The other
two sculptures in the group were entitled *Havdalah* and
Midnight. Of the three, *Day* is the most open.

The shape of the work is that of a container partially
filled with earth. Upon a second inspection, however, the
sculpture assumes the schematic form of a house turned
upside-down; the house's space is in fact negative, as if it had
been overturned, burying itself in the sand and disappearing.

This sculpture – based on the type of form that at one
moment appears stable and at the next, illusive, mutable, and
transient –is most characteristic of Micha Ullman.

Ullman expresses a world view in which doubt and
uncertainty play a central role. The significance of this work
derives from its assertion of opposites: it is at once figurative
and abstract-based on rational, geometric shapes whose content nevertheless is expressive and appeals to the emotions.

The earth used in the piece is laden with 'Israeli' - and
highly contradictory - associations: the desire to lay down
roots, the act of planting, and alongside these the need for
entrenchment, and the inevitability of interment. The earth
is an expression of permanence, but also of movement and
fluidity.

Moshe Kupferman, born 1926
Painting, 1993
Oil on canvas
130 × 195 cm (51 ¼ × 76 ¾ in)
Gift of Rita and Arturo Schwarz, Milan

This work of Moshe Kupferman offers a link between the lyrical abstraction of the recent past and modernist painting. His paintings are the result and expression of a process which is, in itself, an element of the experience and understanding of the painting. This process begins with free, uncurtailed execution, expressive to the point of bordering on personal (albeit abstract) 'confession.' The next stage involves more controlled execution, repeated again and again. Here the artist 'retracts' his 'confession,' partially obscuring it, creating pictorial relations and balances between patches of color, shapes, and concentrations of visual energy, thus distilling emotional qualities from the material and forms. The final layer reveals the traces of all previous stages, and remains as evidence of the struggle of opposites, such as expressive dramaticism versus introversion and concealment, and destruction versus construction. The modern reductionism of this work, its emphasis on the creative process, and the concentration of the painting around such basic forms as a grid, tie him to modernist painting in spite of his being 'a painter of the brush.'

The blend of monastic restraint with flickerings of expressionism and an elevated form of subtlety and sensitivity characterize Kupferman's *Painting* of 1993, making it a characteristic example and impressive summation of this artist's approach.

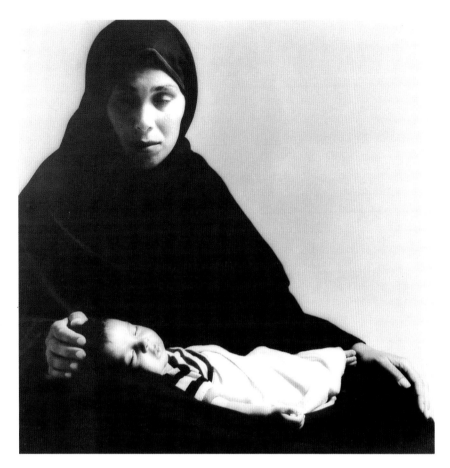

Carlo Naya, Italian, 1816–1882
Untitled, 1876
Albumen print
Gift of Gérard Lévy, Paris, in memory of his father Dr Jo Levy

Official photographer of King Vittorio Emmanuele, and well known in Italy and Europe for his carefully staged genre scenes and outdoor *tableaux vivants*, Naya was one of the prominent photographers who visited the Near East in the nineteenth century with the express purpose of producing a series of Orientalist photographs, which were in great demand on the European market.

Besides striking portrait studies he made in Cairo, his *tableaux* are incomparably lifelike and realistic and of a rare beauty. He possessed all the qualities of a master stage director as well as a profound knowledge of art history. In many of his photographic scenes, one can discern a direct influence of Renaissance composition, as though his images were sketches for murals or altarpieces.

The precision of execution and the closeness to established canons of art make Naya's Orientalist photographs stand out today, as they did in their time.

Micha Kirshner, Israeli, b. Italy 1947
Aisha el-Kord, Khan Younes Refugee Camp, 1988
Gelatin silver print, 100 × 100 cm (39 ¼ × 39 ¼ in)
Purchase, Martha Laub Fund

During the troubled years of the Intifada in the West Bank, many Israeli artists were deeply disturbed by events, especially the human rights issues involved, and devoted thought and energy to these matters of public and private concern. The resulting body of work was an attempt to confront these topics, and especially to raise public awareness.

Micha Kirshner's most controversial series of photographs were published weekly in one of the country's leading newspapers. These images are not about riots, arrests or other violent acts recorded as they happened, but rather an incisive look at the results of such actions. Using to the full the potential of the photographic vernacular, Kirshner made arrestingly 'beautiful' images of horror, thus holding a mirror to the country's conscience.

This particular image, of a blinded young woman and her baby whom she will never see again, is deeply rooted in the iconography and aesthetics of traditional art. Shown in a new and disturbing context, this tragic Madonna and child has become a classic image of these troubled times.

Man Ray, American, 1890–1976
Portrait of Marquise Casati, 1922
Gelatin silver print, 21.5 × 15.5 cm (8 ½ × 6 in)

This famous portrait of the Marquise Casati, one of the leading aristocratic figures in Paris in the 1920s, is well documented. Man Ray himself acknowledged that it was the result of a happy accident during his novice days as a photographer, shortly after his arrival in France. As he wrote in his memoirs, he 'printed up a couple [of photographs] on which there was a semblance of a face – one with three pairs of eyes. It might have passed for a surrealist version of the Medusa.' However, this print in the Israel Museum collection is unique, as the artist himself later trimmed the lower part of the photograph to the shape of Cassati's neck to emphasize its length. This unusual photograph is among the best examples of Man Ray's experiments which invariably involved creative manipulation of the work as a means of extended expression rather than a fascination with the technique itself.

Salvador Dali, Spanish, 1904–19
Horst P. Horst, American, b. Germany 1906
Costume Design for The Dream of Venus,
1939
Pen and ink on a gelatin silver print, 25.4 × 20.3 cm
(10 × 8 in)
Gift of the Gorovoy Foundation

This unique photograph, originally from the Julian Levy collection, is the fruit of a rare cooperation between a painter and a photographer. Loaded with eroticism so essential to Surrealist art, this image reflects Dali's fascination with sexuality, his fears and obsessions. The original purpose of this photograph (and a few more like it) was to serve as the basis for the design of a series of costumes for an original creation Dali was to execute in the amusement area of the New York World's Fair in 1939. The models were set up by Dali and Horst and photographed by the latter, and the final print was painted over by Dali. The final creation entitled *The Dream of Venus* was to be one of the most revolutionary realizations of the time; tridimensional, animated with living creatures wearing costumes designed by Dali himself. Crowded with aquatic ladies and sophisticated sirens, the object was to present 'a panorama of the unconscious animated by live mannequins [who would] swim and reveal to you the secrets of your dreams.' In this carefully staged photograph, Dali gives form to his fantasies and transforms his innermost visions into tangible reality.

Manuel Alvarez Bravo, Mexican, b. 1902
La Tolteca, 1931
Gelatin silver print, 24 × 19 cm (9 ½ × 7 ½ in)
Gift of the artist

This rare vintage print of an early work is typical of Bravo's
images that are infused with ideas and convey an implication
of hidden meanings. Even in this early image the flat, mini-
malist, quasi-abstract composition reflects Bravo's preoccupation with form and space. It also exhibits a certain reserve,
similar to Japanese art, especially the work of the master
printmaker Hokusai whom he admired.

Originally this photograph was entered in a contest for
an advertising image for La Tolteca cement company. Despite
the seemingly simple purpose, here too, as in most of Alvarez
Bravo's work, time and space possess certain virtues and powers rooted in a mythical past. In such a universe, images are
endowed with mystery, enchantment and magic, and trans-
port the viewer into a different dimension where one navi-
gates instinctively through the senses, rather than the intellect.
The artist's rich inner world is contrasted with the actuality of
here and now. This image seems to epitomize the artist's
claim that 'the invisible is always contained and present in a
work of art which recreates it. If the invisible cannot be seen
in it, then the work of art does not exist as such.'

Helmar Lerski, Swiss, b. Strasbourg, 1871–1956
Hands Peeling Onions, 1930s
Gelatin silver print, 6 × 6 cm (2 ¼ × 2 ¼ in)
Gift of Dan Hoffner

The Museum's holding of work by Lerski is extensive. In
addition to many prints of his portraits and 'Transformations
through Light,' it includes 152 negatives (6 × 6 cm; 2 ¼ ×
2 ¼ in) of a little-known series of photographs of human
hands. These 'hand portraits' are one of the many themes
Lerski developed during his lengthy sojourn in Israel between
1930 and 1944.

In an attempt to create idealized categories of hands at
work, which he classified by occupation, Lerski produced a
large number of carefully staged photographs of hands in
action. As a romantic socialist, Lerski saw human hands as
vessels and tools of creation, symbolic of his belief in the value
of work as an ideal and perhaps also as a reflection of man's
beauty and goodness.

Notwithstanding these beliefs, Lerski, in his hand photographs, was also defending the educational (propaganda?)
possibilities of photography against the approach of 'art for
art's sake.' For Lerski, the final image had to convey a concept, a humanist message, and, maybe, as in many of his
films, had also to propagate Zionist ideology.

Gunnar Aagaard Andersen, Danish (1919–1982)
**'Portrait of My Mother's Chesterfield
Chair' armchair,** 1965
Polyurethane foam
H 67 cm; W 107 cm; D 90 cm (H 26 ¼ in; W 42 in; D 35 ½ in)
Gift of the designer

Gunnar Aagaard Andersen was an artist and designer whose contributions are little known outside his native Denmark. Andersen loved the challenge of experimentation.

He was interested in technological advances making use of synthetic materials and was intrigued by their possibilities. In the laboratory of the Danish Polymer Industry, he personally poured liquid polyurethane foam in a single process to create chairs and sofas which respond to the body's weight like natural leather. This armchair is a unique piece but others like it are to be found in the Museum of Modern Art, New York and the Stedelijk Museum, Amsterdam. Andersen personally chose it from his own home for the Museum's collection. It was characteristic of Andersen to perceive the resemblance between this chair and the Chesterfield leather chairs so popular in the nineteenth century and to humanize an inanimate object by dubbing it a portrait. It is also referred to as 'The Chocolate Chair' because of its color and its resemblance to melting chocolate.

Lucien Bernhard, German (1883–1972)
Lloyd-Wagen
Lithograph
Unknown printer
89.5 × 118 cm (35 ¼ × 46 ½ in)
Gift of Rudolf Berman

Long before the Israel Museum actually existed, Rudolf Berman, a Viennese chemist, collected posters for his good friend, Professor Boris Schatz, the initiator of the Bezalel Art School in Jerusalem. Schatz requested that Berman purchase and send posters (a relatively new field which was achieving outstanding results at the time) so that he could expose his students to lithographic prints of high quality. From 1910 until the outbreak of war in 1914, he collected hundreds of posters designed by well-known German, Austrian, Swiss and English artists which he sent to Jerusalem. Eventually Rudolph Berman came to live in Palestine and worked as a volunteer in the Bezalel museum.

The posters are a significant part of the the holdings of the Department of Design and Architecture. They provide the foundation for a collection which now numbers thousands and includes pioneering works by twentieth-century graphic designers.

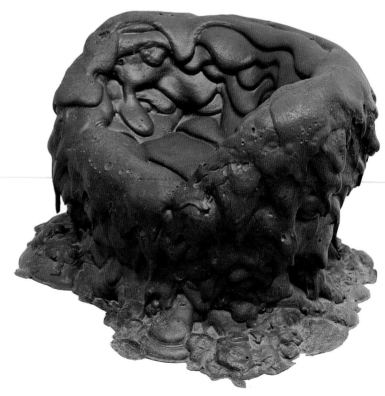

Ettore Sottsass Jr, b. Austria 1917; active in Italy
'Ananke', 'Clesitera' and 'Agelada' vessels
mid-1980s
Blown glass
Ananke H 54 cm (21 ¼ in)
Clesitera H 49 cm (19 ¼ in)
Agelada H 43 cm (17 in)
Produced by Tosi Vetri d'Arte, Murano for Memphis, Milano
Gift of Max Palevsky, Los Angeles

Ettore Sottsass Jr is an architect and designer whose work suggested new directions to be taken in the design world during the last quarter of the twentieth century. He first entered the international arena in 1981 as guru of the Memphis group based in Milan, a group which extended the frontiers of the design of furniture and furnishing accessories. As a result of the enormous attention he has received during the past decade, many of his visionary architectural projects and designs are now being realized.

Sottsass was the subject of a solo exhibition as early as 1978, and the Museum's holdings of his work is one of the largest in any public institution, comprising many dozens of objects in glass and ceramic, as well as wood and metal products, and furniture with laminated plastic patterns or made of marble.

In 1990 the department mounted a second exhibition devoted to the work of Sottsass, based exclusively on its own impressive collection, ranging from office-machines and furniture Sottsass had designed for Olivetti, to designs for Alchimia, Memphis, Alessi, and Knoll International. Also included were the unique ritual lights conceived for the 'Ceremonial Lights' exhibition at the Israel Museum in 1985.

Gerrit Thomas Rietveld, Dutch (1888–1964)
Red-Blue armchair, 1918
Painted beech wood, painted plywood
H 87 cm; W 66 cm; D 83.5 cm (H 34 ¼ in; W 26 in; D 33 in)
Gift of Dr Willem Sandberg

The first art advisor to the Israel Museum, from 1964 to 1968, was Dr Willem Sandberg, former director of the Stedelijk Museum in Amsterdam. It was Sandberg who generously donated the 'Red-Blue' chair to the collection, a piece Rietveld had presented to Sandberg as a gift.

Like the Dutch De Stijl painters, Rietveld tried to reduce the object to the smallest number of geometric components and restrict himself to the use of primary colors only. His groundbreaking work in the field of design during the 1920s contributed to the revolution in furniture which corresponded to similar streamlining movements in art and architecture.

During research for a De Stijl exhibition in 1977, Sandberg introduced Rietveld's widow, Mrs Rietveld-Schröder, to the Museum. She gave the Museum design plans and the rights to recreate a few pieces of Rietveld's furniture for the collection. This furniture was reproduced and exhibited in the 1977 show and on many occasions thereafter.

Unlike the other curatorial departments in the Museum, the Department of Design and Architecture does not have a permanent display of works from its collection. A primary purpose of the Department is to keep the public informed of important local and international trends and innovations in the field through the presentation of temporary exhibitions.

Temporary exhibitions/Architecture
Munio Gitai Weinraub – Building for a Working Society

During the summer and fall of 1994, a retrospective exhibition was on view of the work of an Israeli architect, Munio Gitai Weinraub (1909–1970), spanning his architectural activity from his student days at the Dessau Bauhaus in the early 1930s to four decades of his innovative adaptation of contemporary European architecture to the needs of a rapidly growing population and the Middle Eastern climate. The exhibition included drawings, plans, reconstructed models, furniture and photographs.

Temporary exhibitions/Design
Ceremonial Lights – Nerot Mitzvah
(1985–86)

The Design Department initiated an international project to influence the contemporary Judaica market. Jewish and non-Jewish architects and designers were invited to propose new and contemporary solutions for all seven ceremonial lights – Sabbath, Havdalah (Separation ceremony), Hanukkah, B'dikat Hametz (Search for leaven), Wedding, Memorial and Eternal – taking into account purely formal considerations while not violating halachic regulations.

In order to help the participants tackle a subject foreign to a number of them, the Design Department prepared a research paper defining the existing traditional formal restrictions and giving an historical survey of oil and light fixtures used in Jewish ritual. After two years of close contact and guidance, the result was an original group exhibition which immediately became a milestone in the evolution of modern Judaica objects. First shown in the Israel Museum in 1985–86, the show traveled to Jewish museums in Denver, San Francisco, Amsterdam and Frankfurt, and to the Yeshiva University Museum, New York City. At each venue, local designers were asked to contribute new ideas and forms, thus adding surprises to the original show and literally throwing new light on an ancient subject.

Achille Castiglioni, Italian, born 1918
Menorah (prototype), 1985
Vacuum-formed plastic, metal, rubber
Produced in collaboration with Alessi S.p.A., Crusinallo, Italy
H 40.5 cm W 40 cm (H 16 in W 15 ¾ in)

Leo Lionni, Italian, born 1910, active USA
Hanukkah lamp (prototype), 1985
Glass, fabric ribbons
Made by Gino Cenedese e Figlio, Murano (Venice), Italy
H 24 cm W 28 cm D 10 cm (H 9 ½ in W 11 in D 4 in)

Jorgen Møller, Danish
Israel Museum multipurpose oil lamp (prototype), 1987–90
Silver, brushed aluminum
Produced by Georg Jensen, Frederiksberg, Denmark
Gift of the producer
H 5.5 cm D 5.5 cm (H 2 ¼ in D 2 ¼ in)

Richard Meier, American, born 1935
Candle- and/or flower holders, 1985
Jerusalem stone
H 15 cm W 5 cm D 5 cm (H 6 in W 2 in D 2 in)

provides an accurate idea of the architecture of northern China of the period.

Originally it would have stood within a walled compound. The upper floors have openwork balconies and the roofs, supported by brackets, terminate in rounded roof-tile ends. The figures peeking through the windows add to the lively naturalism that characterizes much Han period tomb art.

Mirror with decoration of birds and floral scrolls

China, Tang Dynasty 618 – 906 CE
Mother-of-pearl inlaid in black lacquer on bronze
Diameter 17.5 cm (6 ¾ in)
Bequest of Wolf Ladejinsky, Washington DC

Throughout history mirrors, apart from their practical use, have been imbued with magical significance. A reflecting surface was thought to ward off evil spirits. The bride on the way to her marriage carried a mirror. A person who had seen a demon could cure himself by looking in a mirror. Cosmic symbols often formed the decorations on the backs of mirrors.

During the Tang dynasty, court ladies carried their small mirrors suspended from their belts. Large mirrors on stands were used for grooming, as seen in paintings of the period. Decoration on the mirrors often shows the influence of Sassanian art, such as the grape or lion motif, very much in vogue in eighth-century cosmopolitan China. This mirror, with a raised edge and mother-of-pearl inlay in lacquer, is very rare. A few mirrors of this type are preserved in the Shoso-in Treasure House of the Todaji Temple in Nara, Japan, where they have been kept since their arrival during the Tang dynasty.

Watchtower in four sections

China, probably Honan province,
Eastern Han Dynasty 25–220 CE
Red pottery with green glaze
H 129 cm (50 ¾ in)
Acquisition, with the help of the Ladejinsky Fund, bequest of Mr and Mrs J. van Witsen van der Steen, Amsterdam and Robert H. Siegel, New York

The Chinese had a firm belief in an afterlife and felt that their earthly possessions could serve them in the hereafter.

During the Han dynasty, detailed pottery models of houses, barns, servants, and animals were placed in the tombs of the upper class. This four-storied watchtower, of exceptional size and preservation, is a replica of a wooden sentry post and

Pair of famille rose covered vases (Soldier Vases)

China, Qienlong period, 1736–1795
Porcelain overglaze, enamel decoration
H 130 cm (51 ¼ in)
Promised Gift of Mr and Mrs Gerson Leiber, New York

Monumental covered vases such as these were owned only by the very wealthy as their manufacture was prohibitively expensive. Whether in the Hall of Audience of a rich Chinese family, or in the entrance of an English nobleman's hall, they proudly proclaimed, through their size and abundance of glowing enamels, their owner's ability to afford these most costly of Chinese ceramics.

Augustus II, Elector of Saxony and King of Poland, assembled the largest collection of Chinese porcelain in Europe and is said to have traded a regiment of his tallest soldiers with the King of Prussia for a collection of such vases. Hence the term 'soldier vases.'

The vases were made in three parts, skillfully joined together. They are covered in a lustrous white glaze, enameled with a variety of flowers such as magnolias, peonies and hawthorn, and painted in delicate hues. The central scene is dominated by a pair of long-tailed phoenixes on a rockery, their plumage in brilliant colors. The opulent design on the shoulders is repeated on the dome-shaped cover, which is topped by a lotus-bud finial.

The careful modeling and the masterful painting of these vases attest to the virtuosity of the Chinese potters of Jingdezhen and the enamelers of Canton in the eighteenth century.

The Goddess Tara

Nepal, c. 14th century
Gilt bronze with inlay of semiprecious stones
H 13 cm (5 in)
Bequest of Alan Flacks, Monaco

Tara is one of the benevolent deities in the Buddhist pantheon, the female counterpart of the *bodhisattva Avalokitesvara*. This popular Goddess of Mercy is a more personal deity, always present on the altar of the layman or monk, to be at the disposal of the devotee needing assistance and on hand to receive thanks for benefits granted. From early beginnings in India, her cult spread to the Himalayan regions of Nepal and Tibet where she developed a large following.

Here she is depicted as a princess, her lithe, rounded body accentuated by jewelry inlaid with semiprecious stones. *Tara*, originally meant to be supported by a lotus base which is now missing, sits in the position of royal ease, her patterned skirt ending in a pleated sash. Her right hand makes the gesture of charity and her left hand holds the stem of an open lotus. The Nepali artist has depicted the humanity of this goddess with great charm.

Page from a Ragamala series Todi Ragini

Rajasthan, Bundi, 17th century
Gouache on paper, decorated with gold leaf
Length of page: 21 cm (8 ¼ in)
Bequest of Wolf Ladejinsky, Washington DC

Rajput painting is a term describing an indigenous Indian painting tradition and is applied to works made for a particular group of Hindus, the Rajputs, a group comparable to the feudal lords of medieval Europe.

Many Rajput courts supported a school of painters who recorded activities of the nobility: amorous exploits, hunting expeditions, festivals, and legends from Hindu mythology. The paintings were used to illustrate luxurious books, which in time were taken apart and their pages dispersed. A *Ragamala* series (literally translated, a garland of melodies), is a set of paintings which are visual interpretations of Indian musical modes. Each musical mode expresses a certain mood and emotion.

Todi Ragini depicts a lady with henna on her hands and feet, holding an Indian lute and walking in a forest glade of flowering trees. This *ragini*'s mood is loneliness. Her plaintive music has attracted deer and birds, mostly in pairs. The artists of the Bundi school were particularly adept at depicting lush vegetation and using landscape to convey drama and emotion. The original silver color of the quatrefoil frame containing deer and various birds has become gray through oxidation.

Funerary Mask

Chimu, Northern Peru
900–1460 CE
Gold, copper, cinnabar
H 35 cm (13 ¾ in)
Gift of Mr and Mrs Arnold Maremont, Chicago to American
Friends of the Israel Museum

The Chimu culture of Northern Peru, a rich and extensive
empire, flourished until the destruction of its capital Chan
Chan by the Incas in 1476. Though adversaries, the Incas were
so impressed by the quality of the metalwork seized, that large
quantities of gold and silver vessels and jewelry, as well as the
top craftsmen responsible for the pieces, were saved from the
mass destruction, being brought back to the Inca capital as
booty.

As in many Peruvian cultures, mortuary rites played an
important role in the religious life of the Chimu civilisation.
Tombs of important people were filled with numerous gold
and silver objects, vessels, masks and personal adornments; the
richer the cache, the higher status they would achieve in the
afterlife. A high-quality mask such as this would have confirmed the exalted position which its owner had occupied
during his lifetime.

This example is a rich blend of metals, shapes and colors,
which create contrasts; between the red of the cinnabar and
the gold and green of the copper; and the dichotomy of the
three-dimensional geometrical shapes of the dangles that
stand out from the flat human form of the face.

Poster for the Wright Symposium on Primitive and pre-Columbian Art, 'Art as a Means of Communication'

Israel Museum, December 1984

This poster displays an array of masks from African, Oceanic,
pre-Columbian and North American cultures. The forms and
functions of the masks are as varied as the cultures from
which they came. To select just a few...

The white mask with the orange crest on the right-hand
side of the poster is a 'Tatanua' mask used in funerary rites in
New Ireland in Melanesia. The black mask is from New
Caledonia, also part of Melanesia. This is a water-spirit mask
and also symbolizes fertility.

Between these is a 'false-face' mask from the Iroquois
peoples of Northeastern America. Such a mask would be used
by a secret society of healers. If not looked after correctly, the
mask would lose its power to heal.

Crested Helmet Mask (Tatanua)

New Ireland, Melanesia
Wood, barkcloth, fiber, lime plaster, paint, operculum shell
H 38 cm (15 in)
Gift of Faith-dorian and Martin Wright, New York, to
American Friends of the Israel Museum, in memory of
Abraham Janoff

Water Spirit Mask

Northern Area, New Caledonia
Wood, fiber, feathers, human hair
H 113 cm (44 ½ in)
Gift of Faith-dorian and Martin Wright, New York, to
American Friends of the Israel Museum, in memory of
Abraham Janoff

False-Face Mask

Iroquois, Woodlands area, Northeastern America
Wood, horsehair, metal
H 25 cm (9 ¾ in)
Gift of Faith-dorian and Martin Wright, New York, to
American Friends of the Israel Museum, in memory of
Abraham Janoff

Fantastic Ceramic Figure

Esmeraldes, Northwest Ecuador
La Tolita Culture, 1–500 CE
Unslipped grey clay
H 59 cm (23 ¼ in)
Gift of Mr and Mrs Arnold Maremont, Chicago to American
Friends of the Israel Museum

This figure is the surviving lid top of an urn. The shape of the
body and the clover-leaf ring that surrounds the face are
common features of figures from the La Tolita style.

Although it has not been possible to identify the figure, it
is thought to be a representation of a 'god-impersonator,' such
as the Xipe-Totec figures from Mexico. There was much
contact between the cultures of Mexico and Ecuador, so it is
possible that this piece was influenced by Ecuador's northern
neighbors.

Xipe-Totec figures show priests dressed in the flayed skin
of the human sacrifice, part of the spring ceremonies that
were symbolic of the renewal of the earth. This second, flayed
skin that the priests wore is shown as being scaly, not unlike
the spikes of this figure.

Frontlet

19th – 20th centuries
Tlingit, Northwest Coast, North America
Wood, paint, abalone shell
H 21 cm (8 ¼ in)
Gift of Faith dorian and Martin Wright, New York, to
American Friends of the Israel Museum in memory of
Abraham Janoff

A 'frontlet' is part of a ceremonial headdress worn by the chief
and his family in many of the Northwest Coast cultures of
North America. It is a plaque which is tied with cords to the
front of the headdress, hence the name. The frontlet often
shows the chief's totem, or mythological being that has a
bearing on his life.

This example shows a raven with three smaller ravens
above it. The raven is distinguished from other birds in the
pantheon of totemic animals by its hooked beak. Eyes, teeth
and eyebrows are highlighted by abalone shell, producing an
iridescent quality similar to mother-of-pearl. The raven is a
powerful totem which gives much prestige to its owner.

The raven plays an important part in the mythology of
the peoples of the Northwest Coast, having a number of
names, amongst them the 'transformer' and the 'trickster.' In
the form of the 'Big Man' he is believed to have created the
world.

There are many legends and stories about the raven, who
reputedly had an insatiable greed. He would use his power to
cheat and trick in order to get whatever he desired, but his
antics often led to the tables being turned and his tricks would
backfire on him.

Seated Male Figure

Las Remojadas style, Veracruz, Mexico
Late Classic Period, 600 – 900 CE
Terracotta
H 64 cm (25 ¼ in)
Gift of Mr and Mrs Arnold Maremont, Chicago to American
Friends of the Israel Museum

The jaguar was the most powerful creature known to the peoples of pre-Columbian America, believed by many cultures to be a divine ancestor. The ruling class in particular considered themselves direct descendants of the jaguar. As a result, many images of the jaguar were created, made by various techniques and in numerous styles.

This figure demonstrates the symbolic relationship between the human race and the jaguar, between the earthly and the mythological.

This dichotomy is clearly shown in the stylistic differences used to portray the man and the jaguar: the naturalistic representation of the former, seated in serene meditation, contrasted with the fantastic and unworldly jaguar who explodes from his stomach.

The combination of these two figures and the different way in which they have been treated help us understand how the jaguar was perceived in pre-Columbian society. It is used here as an emblem, as a symbol of the divine kinship that existed between the ruling class and the jaguar. By placing the jaguar within the body of the man, the terracotta symbolizes the essence of rulership, rather than being intended as a representation of any particular person.

African Art Sculpture group

Depicted here are various examples of human representation in African art. They are drawn from many areas of sub-Saharan Africa: on the right, with the top hat, is a figure from Guinea Bissau on the West Coast, and next to it, a small piece from the Ndebele people of Southern Africa.

Though from disparate places and peoples, these sculptures exhibit some similar characteristics. All (discounting the equestrian figure) face the front, standing with slightly bent knees, arms on the top of the legs, or resting on the stomach. Importance is given to the navel, the connection between mother and child and the lifeline from generation to generation.

Reality is not the primary consideration. Instead, different aspects are emphasized, those considered important by the specific culture. The head of the Hemba piece is much larger than the body; on the Mende sculpture, the belly and buttocks are accentuated.

The equestrian figure, from the Dogon people of Mali, represents 'Hogon', the primordial ancestor of the tribe, and symbolic representation of the head of the 'Lebe' cult, an important religious and secular leader. He is depicted as fighter and protector, sitting regally and assured on his horse, with knife attached to his arm and quiver full of arrows at his back.

Equestrian Figure
Dogon, Mali
Wood
H 60 cm (23 ½ in)
Gift of Mr and Mrs Paul Gersh, Los Angeles to American Friends of the Israel Museum

Ancestor Figure
Hemba, Zaire
Wood
H 67 cm (26 ¼ in)
Gift of Mr and Mrs Robert Kuhn, Los Angeles to American Friends of the Israel Museum

Female Figure (minsereh)
Mende, Sierra Leone
Wood
H 81cm (31 ¾ in)
Gift of Mr and Mrs David Gerofsky, New York to American Friends of the Israel Museum

Female Figure
Igbo, Nigeria
Wood, paint, leather, fibre
H 167 cm (65 ¾ in)
Gift of Mr Armand Pierre Arman, New York to American Friends of the Israel Museum

Figure
Mumuye, Nigeria
Wood, pigment
H 105 cm (41 ¼ in)
Gift of Gaston de Havenon, New York to American Friends of the Israel Museum

Male Figure
Ndbele, Southern Africa
Stained wood
H 52 cm (20 ½ in)
Gift of Mrs Dorothy Robbins, New York to American Friends of the Israel Museum

Male Figure with Top Hat
Nalu, Guinea-Bissau
Stained wood
H 148 cm (58 ¼ in)
Gift of Mr and Mrs Robert Kuhn, Los Angeles to American Friends of the Israel Museum

Ancestor Figure
Oron, Ibibio, Nigeria
Wood
H 76 cm (30 in)
Gift of Faith-dorian and Martin Wright, New York to American Friends of the Israel Museum in memory of Abraham Janoff

Figure
Suku, Zaire
Wood, paint, cloth, string
H 45 cm (17 ¾ in)
Gift of an anonymous donor

Male Figure
Bassi-Kassingo, Zaire
Wood
H 56 cm (22 in)
Gift of Faith-dorian and Martin Wright, New York to American Friends of the Israel Museum in memory of Abraham Janoff

The Youth Wing

Nurit Shilo-Cohen

The success and popularity of the Israel Museum's Youth Wing can be evidenced by the familiar daily scene which finds eager youngsters beseeching their parents to allow them to remain a little bit longer after having spent hours visiting the wing. Does this mean that the Youth Wing has succeeded in educating future generations of museum visitors — one of the Museum's prime goals? Or does it simply show that an imaginative and fun learning environment has been created in which the child feels stimulated and at ease? But then again, isn't this precisely the kind of experience that fosters tomorrow's museum audience?

These and other fundamental questions constantly preoccupy the large and dynamic Youth Wing staff, who are busy exploring and inventing new forms of museum education. But before talking about the present, let us see how it all began, more than thirty years ago.

The Youth Wing originated on the roof of the old Bezalel Museum, back in the early 1960s. It developed from scratch, with neither budget, staff nor facilities and materials — all compensated for by the fund of enthu-

The sculptor Jacques Lipchitz working with a Youth Wing class during his visit to the Israel Museum, 1971.

siasm, idealism, vision, faith in the true way, and pioneering spirit of one person: Ayala Gordon. Perhaps it is not a coincidence that her dream took shape in the very same location where, more than fifty years earlier, Professor Boris Schatz — another artist-dreamer, driven by a child's faith — had founded his legendary school of arts and crafts and museum.

Jerusalem of the early 1960s was a small and divided city with a population of new immigrants from various ethnic and cultural backgrounds. This was before television came to Israel, before people began to travel abroad — and before the era of Teddy Kollek. There were still no community centers, and art was virtually absent from the school curriculum. In other words, this was fertile ground indeed for pioneering work in the field of art education, and although the Youth Wing started out on a modest scale, it was motivated by a strong belief in the educational potential of the museum in a young and beleaguered country beset by social problems but pinning its hopes on the young generation.

The aims of the Youth Wing in those early years were formulated by Ayala Gordon: 'To contribute towards the advancement of creativity in children, and, through works of art, to introduce them to the experience of art and world civilizations for the expansion of their cultural horizons.' In order to achieve these goals, the Youth Wing developed its unique and versatile programs, always combining theory and practice: active observation of works of art, and art-making and experimentation, using diverse materials. This particular combination is one of the aspects that distinguish the Museum's Youth Wing from similar institutions in other parts of the world. It is special not only by virtue of its size and the scope of its activities, but also in being an integral part of the larger Museum context, having grown and developed along with it from the very beginning.

The Youth Wing continued to function on the roof of Bezalel until the opening of the Israel Museum in 1965; the following year it was transferred to the heart of the Museum, where its facilities included an exhibition space, an auditorium, a play yard, and four studios. The educational programs that were developed at that time concentrated on three main areas, which are all continued today: guided tours for school-children, art classes for young children, adolescents, and adults, and educational exhibitions.

'Musi and Musa,' the Youth Wing's own adaptation of the Israel Museum logo, greet visitors to the Youth Wing.

In the 1960s, the concept of active, 'hands on' exhibitions evolved simultaneously at the Children's Museum in Boston (headed by Michael Spock), at the Exploratorium in San Francisco (headed by Frank Oppenheimer), and at the Israel Museum's Youth Wing. In later years, throughout the United States, several children's and science museums, based on the Boston and San Francisco prototypes, sprang up. One of the outstanding features of the Youth Wing exhibitions, however, is the fact that they are not geared strictly to children or adolescents, but to the entire family. Their essential aim is to create an alternative learning environment, inspiring a total experience by means of the special structure of the display environments, which integrate art and archaeology with games, simple texts, and creative activities. They are structured so as to foster learning through fun and enjoyment. The exhibitions thus combine seriousness with playfulness, spontaneous experience, surprise, and active participation. This learning process enriches the museum visit through a diversity of tactile and emotional stimuli.

The exhibitions mounted over the years have dealt with a wide range of topics, which can be divided into a number of categories: art issues, such as 'How to Look at a Painting' or 'Illusion and Reality;' world cultures, such as 'Wondrous India' or 'The Art of Mexico;' art materials, such as 'The Wonderful World of Paper' or 'Plasticine;' crafts, such as 'Let's Embroider' or 'Make Your Own Puppet Show;' the child's world, such as 'Land of Dolls' or 'The Joys of Toys;' and concepts, such as 'Big and Small' or 'Touching.'

This last exhibition provides a good illustration of the Youth Wing's methods. Entering the exhibition, visitors were confronted by hundreds of gloves filled with different materials. After being blindfolded visitors could shake hands with the gloves to experience a variety of sensations. They then entered a tunnel where they could touch sculptures, which they were later asked to identify by means of photographs. Other tactile experiences included trying to write in Braille characters and feeling their way through a room full of soft ribbons, inflated plastic balloons, or cotton wool. Requiring mental and physical visitor participation, the exhibition was both informative and great fun.

Since the Youth Wing's exhibitions are geared to the whole family, the interaction between different generations that takes place during the visit is an inseparable part of the experience. In the exhibition 'When Grandma and Grandpa were Children,' featuring cultural memorabilia of Eretz Israel from the 1930s and 1940s (presented through children's drawings, artwork,

Activity during the exhibition 'How to Look at a Painting' (1983). Children dressed as figures from a painting by Van Eyck.

posters, games, books, and everyday accessories), specific items often elicited a grandparent's reminiscences which in turn prompted questions from grandchildren. In the most recent exhibition, 'Heroes — Past and Present,' children introduced their parents to their heroes, whether culture heroes like Elvis or Michael Jackson, or protagonists from television series, such as the Ninja Turtles or the World Wrestling Federation. All these were featured in the exhibition alongside classic heroes such as Hercules, Prometheus, and Samson.

Since 1978 the Youth Wing has been housed in a large building attached to the Museum complex. In the same year

From the workshop, *Portrait of 'Mom'*.

Youngsters experiencing the exhibition, 'Big and Small' (1986).

Actor in Youth Wing's 'Journeys into History' program portrays King Sennacherib of Assyria relating his victorious seige of Lachish in front of a relief depicting the story in the Israelite Period Gallery.

another center was opened in East Jerusalem offering a similar program to Arab youth. One of the recent exhibitions held there dealt with the influence of folk art on Palestinian artists, showing contemporary works alongside traditional embroideries and pottery.

The Youth Wing presently occupies about ten per cent of the Museum premises, accounts for ten per cent of its budget and twenty-five per cent of its staff — and attracts more than thirty per cent of the total number of Museum visitors. It is the largest institution of its kind in the world.

The move to new quarters enabled a broadening of the scope and areas of activity. The guided tours for schools presently involve some 75,000 children and adolescents annually. They include exciting treasure hunts in the Shrine of the Book; 'Journeys into History' of biblical characters who talk to the children near the archaeological finds from their respective periods; and adventures for the very young, who, for example, are told to follow a 'witch' in order to find an African mask, or a 'princess' who will take them to the French eighteenth-century salon. Besides more conventional gallery tours, devoted to various themes, the Youth Wing also offer tours for groups with special needs or disabilities, such as the deaf, mute or blind.

Some 1000 students of all ages participate in the weekly art classes. The Youth Wing also includes a much-frequented library of illustrated children's books, which, every two years, awards a medal to an Israeli illustrator; a recycling room where visitors can work with a variety of scrap materials; a training center for teachers from all over the country; a department for traveling exhibitions; and a multimedia education unit. The Youth Wing publishes two widely circulated quarterlies: *Mishkafayim* (Specs),

Ethiopian immigrant child recreating his flight to Israel in 1991.

Young boy dons headdress created from scrap material in the Youth Wing's recycling room.

geared towards adolescents, and *Einayim* (Eyes), catering to younger readers.

The Youth Wing has always been an effervescent place, attuned to ongoing developments and sensitive to the changing needs of the community. Its success depends on its highly motivated staff, presently made up of some 100 art historians, curators, teachers, and artists. The dynamics of the Youth Wing make it an ideal laboratory for the exploration of and experimentation with fresh and diversified methods in art and museum education, which have influenced other museums throughout the country and abroad.

These very characteristics have indeed enabled the Youth Wing to respond to the special requirements of a country which frequently has to cope with sudden, dramatic events. A case in point was the Gulf War in the winter of 1991; although the schools were closed, the Museum, while putting its art treasures in storage, kept its doors open, and the Youth Wing staff adjusted immediately to the needs of the hour. Hundreds of children visited the Youth Wing in those weeks, creating monumental group paintings that depicted the traumas of that surrealistic 'long-distance' war — the Scud missiles, the gas masks, and hours spent huddling in the 'sealed room.' These paintings were installed in the empty Impressionist galleries, with great impact on Museum visitors.

Another instance occurred as a result of the overnight arrival of thousands of immigrants from Ethiopia, when a team of Youth Wing artists was promptly stationed in the hotels accommodating the newcomers; equipped with paper, paints, and plasticine, they helped the children to cope with the difficult first period of adjustment by use of non-verbal means of expression. Several of the children were later to return to the Youth Wing and participate in the regular art classes.

Today, as hopes for a new era of peace in this region are becoming more tangible, the Youth Wing's activities over the years among the Arab population take on added significance. Perhaps even the meetings held alternately at the Youth Wing and its East Jerusalem counterpart, the Paley Center, with a group of Jewish and Arab children who, throughout the year, plan and build a model of a shared neighborhood, constitute a small step towards mutual understanding and personal friendships.

Being intrinsically people- rather than object-oriented, the Youth Wing has, in the past few years, also endeavored to bring the Museum closer to the diverse communities visiting it and make it increasingly 'user friendly,' enabling everyone to feel more at home. This approach takes a variety of forms, including orientation maps, leaflets for visitors to exhibitions, gallery talks, and guidance from the security guards (who recently received special training on serving the public with a smile).

After more than thirty years of educational activity, the Youth Wing still adheres to many of the concepts developed in the early years, while others have been adapted to today's conditions. The present generation of children was born into an age of videos, computers, fax machines, MTV, and other new modes of communication. Distances have dwindled; the parents' working week has been shortened, and there is a constantly increasing range of leisure activities. All this only challenges the Museum to keep up its dynamic pace and to persist in its search for new and original programs and approaches.

While never resting on its laurels, the Youth Wing derives much pleasure from its achievements over the years. It is especially proud to count a number of renowned artists among the Youth Wing's former students, as well as several senior members of the Museum staff who studied or worked at the Youth Wing in its early years. It is equally satisfying to meet erstwhile students from the roof of the old Bezalel, now teachers themselves who bring their classes to the Museum, or parents who come with their children, thus sharing in the task of educating the next generation of museum-goers.

Children at play in the Youth Wing entrance courtyard.

235

Credits

Index